contents

Introduction

Through creative combinations of wonderful fresh produce, people are rediscovering the magical taste of fruits and vegetables. The Western diet has veered off in the direction of processed foods laden with fats and carbohydrates and the consumption of fresh fruits and vegetables has declined. The recent growth in popularity of juices and fresh fruit smoothies is largely in response to this sad state of affairs. It is no longer considered a chore to consume the five vegetables and fruits a day recommended by dieticians; it is a joy.

This book is packed full of fantastic combinations of fruits and vegetables for all occasions. Most are healthy, but a few are indulgent treats. The drinks are arranged in sections to help you choose the perfect drink for the occasion, be it a breakfast substitute, a revitalising drink after a workout, the children's lunch or a mocktail with friends on a summer evening.

Healthy Habit

A good balanced diet rich in fruits and vegetables is the best way to ensure bodily health and maintain a high level of energy and a balanced mind. It is vital to keep the body well hydrated, so a daily fresh green drink, fruit juice or smoothie is the perfect way to supplement the diet. This book does not preach therapeutic juicing, but instead offers a wide range of taste combinations to help you broaden the range of vegetables and fruits within your diet. Be aware that fruit juices, in particular, are high in fructose, so they can add significant calories to the diet.

BE CREATIVE

The drinks in this book should be considered a starting point. If you don't have a particular ingredient, then substitute one you do have that you think will work well. Similarly, don't feel tied to the proportions of the ingredients in these recipes. Almost all flavours and amounts here are adjustable to taste. Above all, be creative. If you are not sure that you really fancy combining asparagus with apple juice, then juice them separately and add a little at a time to see if it works for you.

Juices vs. Smoothies

Juices are fibre-free while smoothies are blended drinks that retain the pulp and fibre from the fruit. Fibre is essential for a healthy digestive and cardiovascular system and for ensuring balanced blood sugar levels. Drinking juices does not replace eating fruit in the diet, whereas consuming fruit in smoothies does. However, dieticians advise that only one juice drink per day can count toward your daily intake of fruits and vegetables.

Equipment

In order to be a successful juicer or smoothie maker, you need to invest in a few items of equipment. There are three main pieces of equipment you need: a juice extractor for the harder produce such as apples and carrots; a blender for the softer fruits such as peaches and avocados; and, optionally, a citrus press for perfect orange juice.

JUICE EXTRACTORS

The question you have to resolve here is whether to choose a centrifugal or masticating juicer.

CENTRIFUGAL JUICERS

A centrifugal juicer is the most common and the least expensive type of juicer and probably the best choice if you are a juicing novice or don't intend to juice on a grand scale. These electric juicers work by fine-shredding the produce and then spinning out the juices at a high speed. Most come with a jug, which collects the juice, and a tub, which collects the pulp and fibrous residue.

MASTICATING JUICERS

A masticating juicer comes in both manual and electric forms and tends to be more expensive than a centrifugal juicer. Masticating juicers pulverise the produce, then press the resulting pulp through a fine mesh. They are more efficient than the centrifugal juicer, producing more liquid. Juice extracted by this method also contains more nutrients and a higher level of enzymes.

TIPS FOR CHOOSING A JUICER

Will it be easy to clean? Look for hidden corners and difficult to disassemble parts. Is it dishwasher safe?

Will it be easy to feed in the fruits and vegetables? Look for a wide feeding tube.

Check the capacity of the pulp collector. Is the pulp continuously fed into the collection tub or is it collected in the spinner basket?

Can you see what is happening while you work?

How powerful is the machine? Some juicers have a higher wattage than others, while some have more than one power setting and a useful pulse action.

BLENDERS

These are plastic or glass jugs containing small blades set on a small motor unit. They are the classic machine for making smoothies or milkshakes. They blend soft fruits extremely effectively when combined with a little liquid. Some units have powerful motors that enable them to crush ice. If buying a blender specifically for making smoothies, it is worth paying a little more for one with a powerful motor.

FOOD PROCESSORS

These machines are multifunctional and often have a blender attachment. Some also have centrifugal juicing, citrus pressing and ice-crushing attachments. Generally, they are not as effective as a blender is for making smoothies, but they are still capable of making good smoothies and, with the correct attachment, juices.

IMMERSION BLENDERS

Also known as stick blenders, these can make good smoothies, but their motors are relatively small and can only handle small quantities of soft fruits. If you plan to make smoothies regularly, it is better to invest in a stand-alone blender.

CITRUS PRESSES

These come in four forms: an electric citrus press; a manual lever press, which squeezes the juice down into a jug; a handheld citrus press, made in three sizes for oranges, lemons and limes; and a hand-operated squeeze action press, which collects the strained juice in a container.

CLEANING YOUR EQUIPMENT

There is no getting away from the fact that cleaning juicers and blenders is a bothersome task. It is also true that doing so immediately after use is by far the best option since fruit pulp that has dried onto the shredders and blades is much harder to clean off.

Take your juicer or blender apart and use a small flexible spatula to remove most of the residual pulp (this makes excellent compost). Rinse all the non-electrical parts under a running faucet to remove most of the remaining bits, then leave to soak briefly in warm water. Following this, either hand wash with a dish brush or put in the dishwasher (if dishwasher safe). Wipe down the motorised unit and other fixed parts of the machine with a damp cloth.

OTHER EQUIPMENT

In addition to the big pieces of equipment, many other kitchen gadgets will come in handy.

CHOPPING BOARDS

It is useful to have a large one and a small one on hand. Plastic boards are easier to clean than wooden ones especially when using strong-flavoured ingredients such as ginger, fruits and vegetables that stain, such as beetroot and berries. To remove most stains soak in a solution of two parts water to one part white vinegar.

KNIVES

A large cook's knife is useful for chopping the skin off pineapples and melons, while a small fruit knife is better for cutting peaches and pears. For some jobs, a serrated knife comes in handy. Remember, a sharp knife is safer to use than a blunt one.

MEASURING CUPS AND SPOONS

A large 1-litre (1 ¾-pt) measuring jug, a set of measuring cups, preferably with pouring lips and a set of measuring spoons will be useful when following the recipes in this book.

SIEVES

These are useful to remove the seeds from berries and the processed skins from fruits such as apricots and tomatoes. Avoid using metallic sieves as these can react with the acids in fruits to tarnish the flavour and sometimes can turn fruits, such as plums, black.

OTHER TOOLS

Grater – A fine Microplane zester/grater is perfect for removing the zest from citrus fruits.
Zester – A small handheld zester shaves the zest from the fruit using a row of holes at the top of the zester. The resulting long strips are useful for garnishing. Some have a secondary blade for thicker strips.
Rubber spatula – This flexible spatula is perfect for scraping the last of the smoothie from the jug and for cleaning equipment.
Vegetable peeler – This is easier to use than a knife when peeling fruit such as apples and carrots.
Vegetable brush – When juicing fruits and vegetables there is no need to peel the fruit, but it must be scrupulously clean and free of wax, so scrubbing with a brush is essential.
Ice-cream scoop – A firm steel scoop is best when scooping hard ice cream and sorbets to use in making shakes and iced drinks.
Apple corer – Makes short work of the task of removing apple and pear cores. This is unnecessary when juicing but is required for blended drinks.
Cherry stoner – Although this is considered specialty equipment, it greatly simplifies the task of stoning cherries and olives.
Ice-cube trays – Look for flexible trays that release ice easily.
Ice bucket – This is a useful item for keeping juices chilled, especially when entertaining.

SERVING GLASSES AND JUGS

Smoothies and juices are drinks to enjoy and share, so look for glasses and jugs in a range of shapes and colours to complement your drinks. Look not just in homeware and department stores, but also at garage sales and in charity shops. Plastic glasses are a must have for seaside outings and for garden parties where kids are on the loose.

Juicing and Blending Techniques

The following are a few tips on how to get the best out of your juice extractor or blender.

JUICE EXTRACTORS

PREPARING FRUITS AND VEGETABLES

Wash and scrub all fruit that is not going to be peeled. This removes any dirt and chemical spray residue. To remove the wax that has been applied to give the produce a longer shelf life, use a few drops of dish soap and scrub well with a brush, then rinse thoroughly.

Most fruits and vegetables do not need to be peeled and cored; however, they do need to be chopped into pieces that will fit down the feed tube. Apples, for instance, will need to be quartered, while melons will need to be sliced into wedges.

Slice stone fruits such as peaches and mangoes in half and twist gently to separate the two halves. Carefully remove the stone.

Citrus fruits should be peeled to avoid the bitter taste of the zest spoiling the more delicate flavour of the juice. The fruit should then be chopped into large pieces.

Avoid very soft fruits and vegetables that might block the machine. If the machine does clog up, pass through a harder vegetable such as a carrot or apple.

Choose fruits and vegetables that are almost ripe rather than very ripe, as they yield the maximum amount of juice and flavour.

PROCESSING FRUITS AND VEGETABLES

Always ensure that all parts of the machine are in place and the jug is positioned under the spout.

Use the plunger provided when passing ingredients through the juice extractor.

Push the fruits and vegetables through at an even rate.

Forcing them through too quickly may clog the machine.

To keep the machine flowing freely, alternate between hard and soft ingredients. Passing the ingredients through in this way helps mix the juice, too.

ENJOYING THE JUICES

To avoid juices turning brown, drink them as soon as possible after processing. If you do need to keep the juice for a while, you may also add a little lemon juice or vitamin C powder.

If juices are too intense in flavour, dilute with a little filtered or mineral water. Children should always be given diluted juices.

Fruit juices are high in fructose – the natural fruit sugar – so dilute to avoid an initial sugar high followed by a dip in energy levels. Vegetable juices are not so high in sugar so do not require dilution for this purpose.

BLENDERS

PREPARING FRUITS AND VEGETABLES

Peel inedible skins from all fruits and vegetables, such as avocados, bananas, kiwi fruit, mangoes, papaya and pineapple. Also peel edible skins from fruits such as apples and pears, peaches and plums when a silky, smooth-finish smoothie is required. Alternatively, process with the skin intact and pass through a nonmetallic sieve before serving.

Core fruits such as apples and pears. Remove the stones from stone fruit and the seeds from grapes.

Cut all fruits into pieces small enough to pass through the feeding tube in a food processor or to sit comfortably in the base of the blender.

Fruits with small seeds such as raspberries, strawberries, passion fruit, guava and kiwi fruit should be processed whole or cut in half, then the finished smoothie may be passed through a nonmetallic sieve using a spatula to help press through.

PROCESSING FRUITS AND VEGETABLES

In a blender, add the liquid with the fruit and process on low until the fruit is cut into even-sized small pieces, then process on high until smooth. Only add ice on the blender manufacturer's recommendation.

In a food processor, add all the fruits and vegetables to the bowl of the machine and process to a thick, smooth pulp. Add the liquid, then process again until evenly mixed. Ice is generally not recommended.

With an immersion blender, use only very soft fruits such as peaches, bananas and berries. Process the fruit in a deep jug or bowl, then add the liquid and process until evenly mixed. Do not add ice.

Safety First

Always switch machines off at the plug socket before dismantling or inserting utensils into the container.

ICE

Use ice cubes in the blender to cool drinks and to thicken them. To avoid dilution make fruit juice-flavoured ice cubes. Orange-juice ice cubes are always handy to have and watermelon is also a great choice, as it will blend well with most other fruit flavours.

For interesting ice cubes, add a few berries, pomegranate seeds, a small herb leaf, an edible flower or a piece of citrus zest.

If your blender does not have the capability to crush ice, you can do it by hand. Lay the ice in the centre of a clean dish towel, fold over the cloth to enclose or put in a strong plastic bag. Smash with a mallet, rolling pin or small heavy frying pan. Store in a plastic bag in the freezer until required.

Fruit Guide

CITRUS FRUITS

Citrus fruits along with apples form the backbone of the juicing repertoire. The refreshing tangy flavour of orange juice provides the traditional kick-start to the day. All citrus fruits work well in combination with other juices and can help to balance out the intense sweetness of some fruits, such as pineapple and pear.

Buy fruit that feels heavy for its size – lighter fruit tends to indicate that it is old and its juices have dried up. Avoid any fruits with damp pale patches on the skin or, in the case of limes, yellowed patches. Buy organic fruit, particularly if using for zest. Regardless, wash well to remove waxes and pesticides. Most oranges will keep for about a week in a cool, dry place. You can store fruit longer in the fridge but return to room temperature to juice.

For optimum yield when juicing citrus, cut fruit in half and process through a citrus press. If processing through a juice extractor, remove the peel but leave the pith in place to take advantage of bioflavonoids, which aid the absorption of vitamin C. Cut into pieces to fit in the feeder tube. There is no need to remove seeds, which are high in calcium, magnesium and potassium. To blend, remove peel, pith and seeds, then cut into pieces to fit in the feeder tube; small citrus fruits can be processed whole or halved.

ORANGES

Oranges fall into two categories – sweet and bitter. Most oranges are of the sweet variety and are high in fruit sugar and very high in vitamin C. Blood oranges are particularly sweet and produce a beautiful pink to red juice. Add lemon, lime, or grapefruit juice to balance the sweetness of orange juice, or drink diluted. Sour oranges, mostly Seville oranges, are not recommended for juicing – they are very bitter with thick skins.

Calories: 48 per 100 g (3 ½ oz)
For 100 ml (3 ½ fl oz) juice: 1 large

Health Benefits
Citrus is very high in vitamin C, boosting the immune system to fight off colds and flu and rich in other antioxidants that aid general health and well-being. The fibre in oranges is good for colon health.

LEMONS

Lemons contain twice as much vitamin C as oranges but have a strong sour taste and are high in acid, so the juice should always be drunk diluted. Always buy strong-coloured lemons as they become paler with age. To maximise yield, use at room temperature or heat in the microwave for 10 seconds, then roll between the palms or on the worktop before juicing.

Calories: 29 per 100 g (3 ½ oz)
For 100 ml (3 ½ fl oz) juice: 2 lemons

Health Benefits
Very high in vitamin C, lemon is also good for boosting the immune system and is good for skin and hair health. Traditionally used for liver and kidney health. Most essential minerals required by the body are found in lemons.

LIMES

Small and bright green with a pale green flesh, limes have a refreshing acidic flavour, which is often used as an accent flavour with other fruits. Common varieties include the Persian or Tahitian lime, which has a thick skin and is the most commercially grown variety, and the Key lime, which is smaller, with a thinner skin and sharper taste. They are used in a similar way to lemons but are more acidic and contain 21 mg vitamin C per 100 g (3 ½ oz) as opposed to the 53 mg found in lemons.

Calories: 30 per 100 g (3 ½ oz)
For 100 ml (3 ½ fl oz) juice: 3 limes

Health Benefits
High in vitamin C, limes are good for boosting the immune system. Limes were the original cure for scurvy.

GRAPEFRUITS

The largest of the common citrus fruit, grapefruit may be yellow, with a sharp bitter flavour, sweetening through pink to ruby red, which has a sweet/sour taste.

Calories: 42 per 100 g (3 ½ oz)
For 100 ml (3 ½ fl oz) juice: ½ grapefruit

Health Benefits
High in vitamin C, grapefruit is good for boosting the immune system. Lycopene, which causes the pink and red colouration in grapefruit, is thought to be protective of some cancers. Also thought to help lower cholesterol.

Warning: Grapefruit should be avoided with certain medications including some chemotherapies and calcium-channel blockers; if in doubt, seek medical advice.

OTHER CITRUS FRUITS

These include varieties of mandarins, clementines, satsumas and tangelos, all of which are crosses of oranges with other citrus fruits and are sweeter than oranges. Ugli fruit is a large citrus, which has a sweet, mild flavour and is great for juicing. Minneola is a sweet citrus with few seeds. Pomelos have a grapefruit-orange flavour but are drier, so less good for juicing. Kumquats are the small cousins that can be juiced or used whole in smoothies, with discretion; they are good for garnishing glasses.

ORCHARD FRUITS

Apples and pears are the most common orchard fruits and are available year round. Their mild-tasting, sweet juices form the basis of many blended drinks. They mix well with most fruits and vegetables. Both oxidise (turn brown) quickly, so drink as soon as possible or add a squeeze of lemon juice or vitamin C powder.

Buy firm unblemished fruit, organic if possible, to minimise pesticide residues. Store apples and pears in a cool, dark place.

APPLES

The most versatile of all fruits, there are hundreds of varieties of apples. Of the commercial varieties, Golden Delicious, Royal Gala, McIntosh, or Pink Lady are good choices for sweet juice and Granny Smith for a sharper juice. Cox apples have a delicious, unique flavour and produce a thicker juice that browns more quickly than other varieties.

To juice, remove stalk and cut into quarters. The seeds are edible and contain potassium, so no need to remove.
To blend, peel, core and chop to fit feeder tube.

Calories: 52 per 100 g (3 ½ oz)
For 100 ml (3 ½ fl oz) juice: 2 apples

Health Benefits
High in pectin, which lowers cholesterol and maintains good digestive health; malic acid, also good for digestion; and vitamin C, for immune system. Good for detoxing.

PEARS

Pears are sweeter than apples and their subtle taste is quickly overwhelmed by other flavours. For that reason, pears are good for balancing out strong vegetable flavours. For juicing use ripe but firm pears – soft pears quickly clog juice extractors. Juicy, ripe pears blend well. Comice, Conference and Bosc are good varieties.

To juice, remove stalk and cut into quarters. The seeds are edible so no need to remove.
To blend, peel, core and chop to fit feeder tube.

Calories: 57 per 100 g (3 ½ oz)
For 100 ml (3 ½ fl oz) juice: 2 pears

Health Benefits
Pears are high in fibre, which is good for digestive health and lowering cholesterol. The levulose sugar found in pears is better tolerated by diabetics than most fruit sugars. Contains high levels of vitamin C for boosting immune system and vitamin K for bones, blood and brain function. Good for detoxing.

STONE FRUITS

Plums, apricots and cherries are stone fruits; as such they are more seasonal than orchard fruit. They make delicious sweet juices.

Choose unblemished fruit that is firm to touch, but yields slightly when lightly pressed. The skin should be brightly coloured and with a perfumed fragrance. Soft orchard fruits are best stored in the fridge once ripe. Wash thoroughly if not peeling.

Skins of these fruits may be removed by submerging the whole fruit in boiling water for 20 seconds, then plunging into cold water; the skin should slip off.

PEACHES AND NECTARINES

These two fruits are interchangeable, although nectarines yield slightly more juice, while peaches are slightly sweeter. Both produce a higher yield in a blender than in a juice extractor. As the juice produced is quite thick, it may be diluted with water.

To juice and blend, cut in half and remove stone, cut to fit feeder tube. Peaches should be peeled before blending.

Calories: 60 (peaches), 45 (nectarines) per 100 g (3 ½ oz)
For 100 ml (3 ½ fl oz) juice: 2 fruits

Health Benefits
Peaches and nectarines are high in vitamin C, beta-carotene and other antioxidants thought to help eyesight, digestive health and prevent some diseases of ageing and possibly some cancers. These fruits are easy to digest and mildly laxative.

PLUMS

Plums can range in colour from dark purple to yellow. They are sweet and juicy when ripe although can be sharp if under-ripe. They are best used in conjunction with other fruits and if used under-ripe they can balance out sweeter fruits. Related fruits include damsons and greengages. Prunes are dried plums and can be used rehydrated.

To juice and blend, cut in half and remove stone.

Calories: 38 per 100 g (3 ½ oz)
For 100 ml (3 ½ fl oz) juice: 4 to 6 fruits

Health Benefits
Plums are high in vitamin A for eye, bone and reproductive health and high in antioxidants, for general health. They also have good laxative properties, especially if used in prune form.

CHERRIES

Available in many varieties, sweet cherries are best for juicing. Choose ripe cherries as they do not ripen further once picked. Good to use in small quantities in combination with other fruits.

To juice and blend, remove stone, preferably with a cherry stoner.

Calories: 48 per 100 g (3 ½ oz)
For 100 ml (3 ½ fl oz) juice: about 170 g (6 oz)

Health Benefits
Cherries are high in vitamin B2 for energy release; high in beta-carotene and other antioxidants for general health and disease prevention and also contain vitamins A and C. They were traditionally used as a painkiller, to treat gout. Black cherries are also good for dental health.

BERRIES

Berries and currants are fantastic for providing smoothies and shakes with intense, brilliant flavours. They don't need to be used in large quantities – a small handful will make all the difference.

Always take time to check prepackaged berries to ensure that they are evenly ripe and that there are no squashed or mouldy berries lurking underneath the top layer. Generally, these berries are available in summer and should be eaten as soon as possible after purchase, although if kept in the fridge, they should last for a day or two. If you buy berries that you cannot eat in that time frame, lay them out in a single layer on baking sheets and freeze, then transfer to a plastic container or resealable freezer bag. Berries freeze well and frozen berries can be used in any recipe in the book either defrosted or, for an icy effect, from frozen.

To juice, note that berries do not juice well as they clog the machine. If you need to juice berries, do so in small quantities and alternate with harder fruits. No need to remove leaves or calyx from strawberries.
To blend, remove leaves and stems, including the calyx from strawberries. All berry smoothies and shakes will contain small seeds. If these are not to your liking, pass the drinks through a nonmetallic sieve before serving, but remember this will reduce the quantity of dietary fibre in the final drink.

ACAI BERRIES

Acai is a small, dark purple fruit obtained from acai palm trees from the Amazon. It is rare to find the fresh berries for sale, but they are available frozen, most commonly in purée form. Unusually acai berries contain about 50% fat, of which 75% are omegas (the good fatty acids).

Calories: 70 per 100 g (3 ½ oz)
For 100 ml (3 ½ fl oz) juice: about 200 g (7 oz)

Health Benefits
Acai berries are very high in antioxidants and vitamin A, which is good for the eyes, growth and development as well as protecting the body's cells from a number of threats including pollutants. Acai contains useful amounts of calcium for bones and regulating blood pressure. Sometimes touted as helpful in weight reduction, acai berries are traditionally used for treating diarrhea, hemorrhages, parasites and ulcers.

BLACKBERRIES

Although available for sale in food stores, the most satisfying way to obtain blackberries is to pick them from the wild. Pick at will and freeze the bounty. Blackberries produce a dark purple juice.

Calories: 30 per 100 g (3 ½ oz)
For 100 ml (3 ½ fl oz) juice: about 200 g (7 oz)

Health Benefits
Blackberries are high in antioxidants for general health, vitamin C for the immune system and fibre (particularly if unsieved). Blackberries also have useful amounts of vitamin K and manganese, a vital trace mineral.

BLUEBERRIES

Blueberries have a unique dark blue coloured juice that will dominate any other coloured juices in the blend. They are widely available year round, although they have a short natural summer season. Excellent frozen.

Calories: 57 per 100 g (3 ½ oz)
For 100 ml (3 ½ fl oz) juice: about 200 g (7 oz)

Health Benefits
Blueberries are high in pigment antioxidants and vitamin C, vitamin K and manganese for general health. These berries are good for the nervous system, for the brain and for heart health.

CRANBERRIES

These are winter berries and are sour in taste so they need to be paired with sweet fruits or added sugar. They mix particularly well with oranges and with apples and pears.

Calories: 46 per 100 g (3 ½ oz)
For 100 ml (3 ½ fl oz) juice: about 200 g (7 oz)

Health Benefits
Cranberries are high in vitamin C for the immune system, fibre and manganese. Most famously used for treating urinary tract infections, they also have anti-inflammatory effects, benefits to the cardiovascular system and are good for parts of the digestive tract.

CURRANTS

Blackcurrants are the most common, although redcurrants and whitecurrants are also available.

Calories: 71 per 100 g (3 ½ oz)
For 100 ml (3 ½ fl oz) juice: about 150 g (5 ¼ oz)

Health Benefits
Currants are very high in vitamin C and commonly used for boosting the immune system. They are a good source of potassium and manganese and are traditionally used for coughs, colds, flu, arthritis, diarrhea and as a diuretic. The seeds contain essential fatty acids useful for women's health.

GRAPES

These come in black, red and green varieties either with or without seeds. They produce a mild, fragrant juice that mixes well with other fruits and they are particularly well suited to partner with thicker juices that need thinning and in combination with vegetables.

Calories: 69 per 100 g (3 ½ oz)
For 100 ml (3 ½ fl oz) juice: about 150 g (5 ¼ oz)

Health Benefits
Grapes are a good source of vitamin C for a healthy immune system and vitamin K for bones, blood and brain function. Resveratrol, found in red and black grape skins and seeds, is believed to have beneficial effects on the cardiovascular system.

RASPBERRIES

Raspberries are as delicious as they are colourful and make a fantastic addition to fruit drinks. They are delicate and prone to moulding, so treat them with care. Raspberries freeze particularly well or can be bought frozen.

Calories: 50 per 100 g (3 ½ oz)
For 100 ml (3 ½ fl oz) juice: about 200 g (7 oz)

Health Benefits
Raspberries are high in vitamin C for the immune system; vitamin B6 for protein and sugar and fatty acid metabolism; magnesium; and iron. They have traditionally been used to maintain the digestive system, to ease indigestion and diarrhea and for women's menstrual well-being.

STRAWBERRIES

Although available year round, fresh summer strawberries are full of intense flavour compared to the lacklustre taste of commercially forced out-of-season berries. Better to freeze summer strawberries than to use the latter. Frozen strawberries lose their texture, but this is immaterial if they are destined for the blender. Hulling strawberries is the process of removing the calyx, which should be done before blending. Their flavour is enhanced when blended with a little citrus juice and they mix well with other fruits, especially bananas and raspberries.

Calories: 33 per 100 g (3 ½ oz)
For 100 ml (3 ½ fl oz) juice: about 200 g (7 oz)

Health Benefits
Strawberries are high in pectin and ellagic acid for cleansing and detoxing, vitamin C for immune boosting and are a good source of potassium and magnesium.

TROPICAL FRUITS

There was a time when these fruits were a holiday treat, but now they are in shops all year round. Melons and pineapples are great for juicing, but most others work better blended.

AVOCADOS

Avocados are considered a sweet fruit in many of their countries of origin, but they are used as a vegetable in other areas of the world. They are unsuitable for use in a juice extractor, but can be blended with fruit juices for smoothies or with tomatoes and cucumber for green drinks. The flesh will brown quickly so it needs a little lemon or lime juice.

To blend, cut in half, twist gently to remove the stone, peel and cut into chunks.

Calories: 224 per 100 g (3 ½ oz)

Health Benefits
Very high in potassium and essential fatty acids, avocados have the highest level of protein of all fruits. Also high in folic acid, vitamins A, C, E and most of the Bs and a wide range of minerals. An excellent fruit for all-round health.

BANANAS

Bananas have become a worldwide basic, so it is often forgotten that they are a tropical fruit. Bananas are not good for juicing and clog up machines. They are great in smoothies and shakes, though, where they blend successfully and usefully bulk up thinner fruit juices, giving substance to the drink. Choose ripe, unblemished bananas for their flavour and sweetness. Bananas may be peeled and frozen, then used in smoothies without thawing. This is a good use for blackening bananas in the fruit bowl. Bananas brown quickly, so benefit from the addition of a little lemon juice unless quickly processed with other acidic fruit.

To blend, peel and break into large chunks. May be processed until smooth before adding other ingredients.

Calories: 89 per 100 g (3 ½ oz)

Health Benefits
Bananas are a very good source of vitamin B6 for protein, sugar and fatty acid metabolism; vitamin C; and high levels of dietary fibre, for healthy bowels. They are also known for having a high level of potassium required for nerve, kidney and brain function and act as a counterbalance to salt, which is helpful in lowering blood pressure.

KIWI FRUIT

These are also sometimes called the Chinese gooseberry because they first originated in China, but they are now commonly cultivated in New Zealand. When buying, the furry skin should be free from wrinkles and the skin firm to touch.

To juice and blend, peel and chop, if necessary, to fit feeder tube.

Calories: 61 per 100 g (3 ½ oz)
For 100 ml (3 ½ fl oz) juice: 3 kiwi fruit

Health Benefits

High in vitamin C for the immune system and one of the few fruits to contain vitamin E, for healthy skin and vitamin K for bones, blood and brain function. Kiwi fruit are also a good source of potassium, copper and fibre. They are often part of detox and cleansing regimes and used for good digestive health.

MANGOES

A popular fruit with a sweet, fragrant orange flesh. Mangoes come in many varieties, but the Alphonso is said by many to be the best. Select mangoes that are blemish-free, yield slightly when pressed and have a slightly flowery aroma. To prepare, slice down one side of the large flat stone, score the flesh into squares, then press from the skin side to reveal the fruit chunks. Cut the chunks from the skin and repeat with the other half.

To juice, cut in half and remove the stone, cut into pieces.
To blend, stone, chunk and peel as described above.

Calories: 60 per 100 g (3 ½ oz)
For 100 ml (3 ½ fl oz) juice: ½ a mango

Health Benefits

Mangoes are high in vitamin C for the immune system and very high in vitamin A (beta-carotene) for eyes, healthy mucus membranes and good skin. They are also high in fibre and potassium.

MELONS

These are members of the gourd family and come in many varieties: cantaloupe, Charentais, galia, honeydew, horned, Ogen, musk and watermelon to name just a few. They are ripe when they feel heavy and, when gently pressed at the stem end, they give slightly and have

a perfume. Melon juice is lovely by itself and its nutrients are most efficiently absorbed this way, but it works well with other juices, especially those with strong flavours such as orange and pineapple.

To juice, peeling is optional (the skin contains good quantities of nutrients). Cut in wedges to fit the feeder tube.
To blend, peel, remove seeds and cut in wedges to fit the feeder tube.

Calories: 36 (cantaloupe), 30 (watermelon) per 100 g (3 ½ oz)
For 100 ml (3 ½ fl oz) juice: ¼ cantaloupe, 125 g (4 ½ oz) piece watermelon flesh

PINEAPPLES

These large, distinct fruits have a sweet-sharp strong flavour that has to be mixed with other fruits with care or it will be overpowering. A ripe pineapple should have a strong smell. The colour of the skin is a less informative sign of readiness as some pineapples are ripe when green. Look instead for unwrinkled skin and green healthy leaves.

To juice, peel and chop into wedges to fit the feeder tube; do not remove core.
To blend, prepare as for juicing but remove the core.

Calories: 50 per 100 g (3 ½ oz)
For 100 ml (3 ½ fl oz) juice: ¼ pineapple

Health Benefits

Pineapple contains the enzyme bromelain, which breaks down protein and is useful for digestive complaints, cleansing the blood and breaking up blood clots. It is also a good source of vitamins C and B6, fibre, manganese and copper.

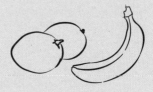

Vegetables

BEETROOT

Beetroot produces a rich, red juice with a strong, yet sweet, taste. It must be used judiciously in combination with other juices or it will dominate. Beetroot is too hard to use in a blender; however, the leaves may be juiced along with the root. Beetroot juice pairs particularly well with orange and carrot juices. Wear gloves when chopping beetroot to prevent the hands from becoming stained.

To juice, scrub thoroughly, remove the base, then chop to fit feeder tube. Not suitable for blending.

Calories: 43 per 100 g (3 ½ oz)
For 100 ml (3 ½ fl oz) juice: ½ a medium beet

Health Benefits
Beetroot has high levels of fibre, folic acid, potassium, manganese and iron and it is a good source of vitamin C. They have traditionally been used to fortify the blood, improve iron levels and for women's menstrual health. Folic acid is important for the nervous system and in the developing fetus.

PEPPERS

Ranging in colour and sweetness from green through yellow to red, peppers make excellent juice but are best used in small quantities mixed with other juices. They work particularly well with tomato and carrot juice. Although on the plant a green pepper will ripen to red, they do not continue to ripen once picked. Peppers are often waxed and need washing even when they look pristine. They are the third best source of vitamin C after chili peppers and guava.

To juice, remove green stalk then cut into pieces to fit feeder tube. There is no need to remove seeds.

Calories: 20 (green), 25 (red) per 100 g (3 ½ oz)
For 100 ml (3 ½ fl oz) juice: 3 medium peppers

Health Benefits
Peppers are high in antioxidants and vitamin C for the immune system. Red peppers have more vitamins and nutrients and contain around nine times more of the antioxidant lycopene and beta-carotene than green peppers and twice the level of vitamin C.

CARROTS

Carrots have a very sweet juice, which is one of the few vegetable juices that is drunk alone. However, they are useful as the basis of many green drinks as the sweetness works to foil the bitter taste of other vegetables. It blends well with fruits such as orange, apple, pear and pineapple. Carrots are juiced because they are too hard to be blended. Choose firm, well-coloured carrots with unwrinkled skins.

To juice, scrub thoroughly, remove the tops and tails, then chop to fit feeder tube. Not suitable for blending.

Calories: 41 per 100 g (3 ½ oz)
For 100 ml (3 ½ fl oz) juice: 2 medium carrots

Health Benefits
A single carrot contains sufficient beta-carotene to supply a day's worth of vitamin A, promoting good eyesight and skin. They contain high levels of vitamin C for the immune system, vitamin K and potassium. They also contain high levels of calcium, although to be absorbed this is best supplemented by a teaspoon flaxseed or nut oil.

CELERY

This is one of nature's lowest calorie foods. Celery stalks provide plenty of well-flavoured juice, which is best mixed with other vegetables because its taste is strong and it has a relatively high level of sodium, which is unpleasant on its own. Choose a firm bunch of celery with erect leaves and pale-coloured stalks. Fennel has similar properties to celery but with a strong aniseed-like taste.

To juice, remove leafy ends and trim the stalk end. Wash thoroughly. Can be fed whole down the feeder tube. Not suitable for blending.

Calories: 16 per 100 g (3 ½ oz)
For 100 ml (3 ½ fl oz) juice: 2 celery stalks

Health Benefits
Celery is high in vitamin C for the immune system; vitamin A for eyes, healthy mucus membranes and good skin; also vitamin K, folic acid, potassium and manganese. It is a powerful cleanser and has diuretic properties. Traditionally it has been used in association with kidney and gall bladder problems.

CUCUMBER AND COURGETTES
These vegetables both have a high water content and mild flavours, making them ideal to mix with other vegetables and fruits. Cucumber is a little sweeter than courgette. The main varieties are the garden cucumber and the longer, thinner English cucumber. Choose firm produce with bright skin. Cucumbers may be waxed to seal in their moisture, so wash with a little soap to remove and rinse well or, better still, buy organic. English cucumbers are often sold sealed in plastic to retain their moisture.

To juice, peel if desired (the skin can be a little bitter) and chop to fit the feeder tube.
To blend, peel and remove seeds, then chop to fit the tube.

Calories: 15 per 100 g (3 ½ oz)
For 100 ml (3 ½ fl oz) juice: ½ an English cucumber or 1 garden cucumber or courgette

Health Benefits
These are excellent detox ingredients with plenty of potassium to control the balance of the body's fluids and to lower blood pressure. They are high in vitamin C, for the immune system and vitamin K, for good blood clotting and healthy bones. Much of the nutritional benefit comes from the skins, so leave intact if possible.

LEAFY GREENS
These include kale, cabbage, chard, spinach and watercress. All of these should be purchased when the leaves are taut and show no signs of yellowing around the edges. Keep in a plastic bag, sprinkled with a little water in the crisper compartment of the fridge. Wash well before use. They should all be used in small quantities for their nutritional benefits or their taste will be overwhelming.

To juice, cut into strips and press through the juicer, alternating with firmer produce where possible to prevent clogging. Use outer leaves with damaged areas cut away as these leaves are higher in nutrients.

Calories: 23 per 100 g (3 ½ oz)
For 100 ml (3 ½ fl oz) juice: 20 large spinach leaves or 50 g (1 ¾ oz) baby spinach

Health Benefits
All these leafy green vegetables are high in vitamins A, C, E and K, a range of B vitamins and a wide range of minerals. Spinach is very high in potassium, which helps to regulate the body's fluid levels and promotes a healthy heart; watercress is particularly high in sulfur for efficient brain function and healthy skin and hair. The darker the leaf, the higher the levels of carotenoids, some of which turn into vitamin A and others are beneficial antioxidants.

TOMATOES
Technically a fruit, tomatoes are ideal for juicing since they contain plenty of liquid and have a bright sweet taste that combines well with other vegetables. Locally grown tomatoes in season have the best flavour, but vine-ripened and hothouse tomatoes can also be tasty. Avoid hard, pale tomatoes. Buy organic whenever possible to minimise exposure to pesticides.

To juice, cut in half or quarters to fit feeder tube.
To blend, either skin and remove seeds before use or pass through a nonmetallic sieve after processing.

Calories: 18 per 100 g (3 ½ oz)
For 100 ml (3 ½ fl oz) juice: 3 tomatoes

Health Benefits
Tomatoes are rich in vitamin C and are particularly high in the antioxidant lycopene, which is thought to protect against some degenerative diseases. Also good for vitamin A and K, for eyes, bones and blood, as well as potassium and manganese.

Additional Ingredients

SWEETENERS

AGAVE SYRUP

A very sweet syrup made from the juices of the Mexican blue agave plant. Use it as a sugar or honey substitute; 150 ml (5 fl oz) agave syrup is equal to 225 g (8 oz) sugar.

MAPLE SYRUP

Derived from the sap of the maple tree, maple syrup has a wonderful rich, tonal flavour. Do not confuse it with cheaper maple-flavoured pancake syrups. To use in place of sugar, 175 ml (6 fl oz) maple syrup is equal to 225 g (8 oz) sugar.

SUGAR

White sugar is made from both cane and beet sugar, while brown sugar may be refined or unrefined; its brown colouring is due to the presence of molasses. Demerara and muscovado are brown sugars derived from evaporated cane juice. Their rich caramelised flavours make them excellent in milk- and yoghurt-based smoothies and shakes, especially with bananas.

SUGAR REPLACEMENTS

There are many sugar replacements, but be aware that they all have different levels of sweetness. Some call for an equal amount substitution with sugar, while others require you to use only half the amount of that indicated for sugar. Some artificial sweeteners also have an aftertaste, but this can be masked with strong flavours such as coffee, pineapple or dates.

SYRUPS

There are a huge number of flavoured syrups on the market, some designed to be added to desserts, others for coffee or cocktail use. These are excellent to use in blended drinks because they easily mix with the liquid and add flavour notes.

DAIRY AND DAIRY SUBSTITUTES

MILK

Dairy milk is still the most common form of milk used and great in smoothies and shakes. For the richest flavour choose whole milk since semi and skimmed milks result in a thinner consistency and can affect the taste. Milk is a good source of calcium and protein plus a range of vitamins and minerals. Some milks are fortified with vitamin D. Whole milk is usually advised for children to promote growth and healthy bones.

ALMOND MILK

Almond milk is a slightly sweet milk that contains high levels of vitamin A, other vitamins and minerals and omega fatty acids, but it is lower in protein than soya milk. Most are not soya-free because they use soya lecithin. It is free of cholesterol and saturated fat.

COCONUT MILK AND COCONUT WATER

Coconut milk is a sweet milk naturally found in the heart of the coconut. It is particularly good combined with tropical fruits. Rarely available fresh, most varieties are made by squeezing the liquid out of coconut flesh and then adding water. It is high in saturated fats but low in calories and protein. Not to be confused with coconut water, which comes from the heart of the young coconut; this is thin, sweet and full of electrolytes, minerals and B complex.

ICE CREAM AND ALTERNATIVES

An essential component in many milkshakes, ice cream is an indulgence item that is high in fat, sugar and calories. Nondairy 'ice cream' and frozen yoghurt are generally, but not necessarily, lower in calories. Sorbet is fat-free, made as it is from just fruit, water and sugar, while sherbets contain the same ingredients plus some fat, often dairy fat, making them unsuitable for anyone with lactose intolerance.

OAT MILK

This is a cholesterol-free milk alternative made from presoaked groats, with a rich, creamy taste. It is a good source of calcium and iron and contains twice as much vitamin A as cow's milk. It is very low in fat and lactose. Note that not all brands are gluten-free.

RICE MILK

Thinner and sweeter than soya milk and higher in carbohydrates than cow's milk, rice milk is also cholesterol-free and saturated-fat-free. Rice milk is good in smoothies and dairy-free shakes. Available fortified with calcium and vitamins A and D.

SOYA MILK

Soya milk is rich and higher in fat, fibre and protein than most nondairy milks and probably the best all-around dairy milk substitute. It makes good drinks; however, its flavour is less successful in some delicate smoothies. It is cholesterol-free and saturated-fat-free, but it has a high concentration of omega-3 fatty acids. It is commonly fortified with calcium.

YOGHURT

Yoghurts are great for making creamy, thick smoothies. For the thickest yoghurt choose Greek-style yoghurts, which are also available with 0% fat. Fruit yoghurts are a good way to introduce a secondary flavour to smoothies. Yoghurt is an excellent source of calcium and probiotic yoghurt contains live cultures that aid digestion and soothe the stomach. Soya yoghurt is available plain and in a range of flavours. The brands vary in taste and texture, so test the market for your favourite.

TOFU

Tofu is a soybean curd available in several textures, but it is the silken, soft tofu with its custard-like texture and a mild, creamy flavour that is excellent in smoothies. It is a good source of non-animal protein.

FLAVOURINGS

It is surprising the difference a little extra flavouring can make in a simple juice or smoothie. Ginger, vanilla and fresh herbs are the mainstay of the drink aficionado's tricks, but creative use of other ingredients, such as a dash of chili powder, a pinch of nutmeg or star anise, can add accents that transform a drink from something simple to something quite extraordinary. Be creative and add your favourite flavours, or look at classic combinations, such as cinnamon and apple and see how that can inspire you to make your own tasty combinations.

DIETARY SUPPLEMENTS

There are a number of dietary supplements suggested in the recipes in this book, but none is an essential ingredient and may be omitted. Likewise, protein powder may be added to most smoothies, while intensely flavoured fruits and vegetables provide excellent cover for strong-tasting supplements such as aloe vera juice, spirulina and wheatgrass. Use with discretion and seek medical advice before using for serious conditions.

Breakfast Blends

Get your day off to a healthy start with one of the quick but nutritious smoothies or juices in this chapter. Even when breakfast is a rushed event, it is worth making an effort to make a fresh drink for this, the most important meal of the day. It's amazing how adding a single glass of fresh juice can enliven the body and spirit, enabling you to greet the challenges of the new day with renewed vigour. Citrus fruit is the traditional favourite to enliven the metabolism, loaded as it is with vitamin C, but other fruits such as mangoes and bananas are excellent, especially when combined with yoghurt or milk to provide much-needed protein.

1 Sunshine Citrus Blast

Wake up your metabolism with this fresh, zingy citrus fruit blend and give your body a powerful detox to blast away impurities.

INGREDIENTS

2 oranges, peeled and halved
1 pink grapefruit or pomelo, peeled and halved
1 lime, peeled and halved
1 tbsp liquid honey, optional

Squeeze the fruits using a juice extractor or citrus press. Pour into a glass and sweeten with honey to taste.

Makes 1 glass

HANDY TIP

Pomelo is sweeter and milder than a grapefruit and makes a great substitute if you want a less bitter drink without using sweeteners.

Variations

2 SUNSHINE CITRUS COLD BUST

Make the Sunshine Citrus Blast, adding a 2-cm (¾-inch) chunk of peeled ginger and 1 garlic clove to the ingredients before passing them through the juice extractor.

Handy tip: If using a citrus press to make the juice, squeeze the juice from the garlic and ginger using a garlic press.

3 SUNSHINE WAKE-UP CALL

Make the Sunshine Citrus Blast using half the quantity of fruit. Fill up the glass with sparkling mineral water.

Handy tip: This is also great with lemon-lime soda, but be sure to omit the honey.

4 SUNSHINE MELON BLAST

Make the Sunshine Citrus Blast using a juice extractor and replacing the orange with ½ a cantaloupe.

Handy tip: This variation makes a milder, less acidic drink.

5 SUNSHINE CITRUS GREENS

Make the Sunshine Citrus Blast using a juice extractor and adding 10 sprigs of watercress and 6 sprigs of parsley.

Health tip warning: Avoid parsley if pregnant.

6 ORANGE STRAWBERRY BLAST

Make the Sunshine Citrus Blast using a juice extractor, replacing the grapefruit with 75 g (2 ½ oz) strawberries.

Serving tip: Children love this drink. Make one for their lunch box.

7 SUNSHINE CITRUS SMOOTHIE

Make the Sunshine Citrus Blast, adding 125 ml (4 ¼ fl oz) plain yoghurt, 1 banana and 1 tablespoon wheat germ. Makes 2 glasses.

Nutritional tip: Wheat germ is a good source of vitamin E, B complex and protein.

8   CUPBOARD CITRUS BLAST

Make the Sunshine Citrus Blast in a blender, substituting 400 g (14 oz) tinned grapefruit and orange segments or citrus salad for the fresh oranges and grapefruit. Add the juice of 1 lime and process until smooth. Sweeten with liquid honey, if necessary.

Nutritional tip: Avoid tinned fruits in light syrup, which add unnecessary sugar; select those in natural juices.

9   SUNSHINE CITRUS SHAKE

Make the Sunshine Citrus Blast and pour into a blender with 2 scoops lemon sorbet or lemon ice cream. Process until smooth.

Serving tip: This is perfect for a summer brunch menu.

10   SUNSHINE ORANGE FLOWER BLAST

Prepare the Sunshine Citrus Blast. When you have poured the juice into a glass, add 1 teaspoon orange flower water and stir well.

Serving tip: This is an excellent nonalcoholic drink to serve with a tagine or similar North African main course.

11 Mango Lassi

This classic Indian smoothie is traditionally served alongside a fiery curry to cool down the taste buds, but it also makes a delicious breakfast smoothie that will provide time-released energy throughout the morning.

INGREDIENTS

1 mango, peeled, stoned and diced, or 330 g (11 ½ oz) mango chunks, frozen or tinned

1 to 2 tsp honey or sugar

1 tbsp lime juice

75 ml (2 ½ fl oz) plain yoghurt

Pinch fine sea salt

125 to 250 ml (4 to 8 fl oz) chilled water or low-fat milk

¼ tsp green cardamom seeds

A few green cardamom, to garnish

Put the mango flesh in the blender with the honey or sugar, lime juice, yoghurt and salt; blend thoroughly. Add sufficient water or milk to thin the lassi down to a drinking consistency. Adjust the honey or sugar to taste. Crush the cardamom seeds with a pestle and mortar and stir into the lassi. Serve very cold, garnished with a pinch of ground cardamom seeds.

Makes 2 to 3 glasses

HANDY TIP

The amount of water or milk will depend on the thickness of your chosen yoghurt. If you use full-fat or Greek-style yoghurt, be sure to dilute with water.

Variations

12 MANGO AND COCONUT LASSI

Make the Mango Lassi using low-fat coconut milk instead of water or milk and using 1 stoned date instead of sugar.
Nutritional tip: The hint of coconut and date gives this an even more exotic touch.

13 BANANA LASSI

Replace the mango in the Mango Lassi with 2 small bananas and reduce the sugar or honey to ½ to 1 teaspoon.
Serving tip: This drink is traditionally enjoyed as an energy-boosting snack in India.

14 SWEET LASSI

Make the Mango Lassi, omitting the mango, lime and salt and using plenty of water to thin the drink. Sweeten to taste as above. Flavour with 1 teaspoon rose water instead of cardamom.
Serving tip: This is a taller drink than the fruit lassi and is often served following energetic sports.

15 SALTY LASSI

Omit mango, lime and sugar when making the Mango Lassi. Dry roast ¼ teaspoon cumin in a preheated nonstick frying pan for 10 seconds and then crush with a pestle and mortar. Add to the smoothie with ¼ teaspoon salt. Serve garnished with mint leaves.
Serving tip: This drink is perfectly paired with a spicy meal.

16 SAFFRON AND PISTACHIO LASSI

Dry roast a pinch of saffron strands in a preheated nonstick pan for 10 seconds. Stir into 60 ml (2 fl oz) milk and set aside for 15 minutes to infuse and cool. Make the lassi using the infused milk and replacing the mango and cardamom with 3 tablespoons chopped pistachios.
Interesting note: Gram for gram, saffron is more expensive than gold, so serve on special occasions such as Christmas morning.

17 FROZEN MANGO AND LIME LASSI

Make the Mango Lassi, replacing the yoghurt with 2 scoops of vanilla frozen yoghurt and using the grated zest and juice of a whole lime. Thin with milk or soya milk instead of water if preferred.
Handy tip: Frozen yoghurt can be used in any of the lassi recipes given on this page.

18 QUICK MANGO LASSI

Put 125 ml (4 ¼ fl oz) each of mango juice or pulp and plain yoghurt in a blender and process until smooth. Add sufficient water to thin to taste. Stir in 1 tablespoon lime juice, a pinch of salt and ¼ teaspoon crushed cardamom seeds.
Handy tip: Mango pulp comes in tins and is great for any juicer to have stored in the cupboard.

19 Coffee Fix Shake

Forget the high-priced morning coffee that you buy on the way to work. Make your own version that is ready in moments and equally delicious. Flavour it with your favourite coffee syrup such as cinnamon, gingerbread or vanilla.

INGREDIENTS

240 ml (8 fl oz) strong coffee (instant or brewed), chilled

125 ml (4 ¼ fl oz) whole milk or single cream

1 scoop coffee ice cream

½ to 2 tsp coffee syrup, optional

Whipped cream, optional

Put the coffee, milk or cream and ice cream in a blender and process until smooth. Pour into a tall glass or travel mug and sweeten to taste with the coffee syrup. Serve with whipped cream, if desired.

Makes 1 glass

HANDY TIP

To speed things up in the morning, make the coffee the evening before and leave it in the fridge overnight.

Variations

20 SKINNY COFFEE FIX

Make the Coffee Fix Shake, replacing the whole milk with rice or almond milk and using sugar-free syrup.
Nutritional tip: Use decaffeinated coffee to keep things even healthier.

21 MOCHA FIX SHAKE

Make the Coffee Fix Shake, replacing the coffee ice cream with chocolate ice cream.
Handy tip: For extra chocolate flavour, use chocolate syrup in place of coffee syrup.

22 ESPRESSO FREDDO

Make the Coffee Fix Shake, replacing the coffee with 125 ml (4 ¼ fl oz) prepared espresso.
Serving tip: Serve with an amaretti biscuit for an authentic Italian feel.

23   SPICED COFFEE SHAKE

Make the coffee and, while still hot, add 2 allspice berries, 2 whole cloves and a 4-cm (1 ½-inch) piece of cinnamon stick. Leave to cool; drain off the spices before adding to the blender.

Serving tip: For a special dessert shake, serve with whipped cream topped with chocolate-coated coffee beans.

24   MINTY ORANGE COFFEE SHAKE

Make the coffee and, while still hot, add 2 small pieces of orange zest and 1 sprig of fresh mint. Leave to cool; remove the zest and mint before adding to the blender. If preferred, use orange-flavoured syrup.

Serving tip: Drizzle orange-flavoured chocolate over the whipped cream.

25 Date and Banana Protein Swirl

This delicious smoothie is great for anyone prone to mid-morning snacking because the combined sugars in the bananas, dates and pineapple will keep you going on warp speed for hours.

INGREDIENTS

240 ml (8 fl oz) plain yoghurt

125 ml (4 ¼ fl oz) semi-skimmed or skimmed milk

8 fresh dates, stoned and chopped

2 bananas, roughly sliced

2 slices fresh pineapple, chopped

1 scoop protein powder, optional

6 ice cubes

Put half of the yoghurt and all the remaining ingredients into a blender and process until the ice cubes are finely chopped and the other ingredients are smooth. Divide between two glasses and add the remaining yoghurt, swirling this in with a spoon to create a marbled appearance. Serve immediately.

Makes 2 glasses

FOODIE TIP

Use Medjool dates – the 'queen of dates' – praised for their sweetness, size and beautiful smooth texture.

variations

27 DATE AND BANANA TOFU PROTEIN SMOOTHIE

Make the Date and Banana Protein Swirl, replacing the yoghurt with 125 g (4 ¼ oz) silken tofu and the dairy milk with soya or rice milk. Do not swirl.

28 DATE AND BANANA PEANUT BUTTER SWIRL

Make the Date and Banana Protein Swirl, replacing the pineapple with 2 tablespoons smooth peanut butter.
Handy tip: If you like a bit of texture in your smoothie, use crunchy peanut butter.

29 BANANA BLUEBERRY PROTEIN SWIRL

Make the Date and Banana Protein Swirl, replacing the pineapple with 150 g (5 ¼ oz) blueberries.
Nutritional tip: Blueberries are great antioxidants and are best eaten raw.

30 DATE AND BANANA BUTTERSCOTCH DREAM

Make the Date and Banana Protein Swirl. When blending in the remaining yoghurt, swirl 1 tablespoon butterscotch syrup through each glass.

26 DATE AND BANANA VANILLA PROTEIN SWIRL

Make the Date and Banana Protein Swirl, but omit the pineapple. Add 1 teaspoon vanilla extract.
Handy tip: For a more intense flavour, use vanilla yoghurt.

31 DATE AND BANANA ALMOND SMOOTHIE

Omit the pineapple in the Date and Banana Protein Swirl and replace the dairy milk with almond milk. Add 2 tablespoons almond butter and 1 teaspoon vanilla extract.

32 Feeling Green Hangover Helper

One for the morning after the night before. It's full of antioxidants and hydrating fruits.

INGREDIENTS

1 tsp white tea or 1 white tea bag

175 ml (6 fl oz) very hot, not boiling, water

2 green apples, quartered

7.5-cm (3-inch) piece cucumber

50 g (1 ¾ oz) fresh spinach

15 g (½ oz) fresh mint leaves

¼ lemon

2 tbsp honey

2 sprigs mint

Put the tea leaves or bag in a teapot or heatproof jug. Steep in the hot water for 5 minutes. Drain, if using tea leaves, or remove tea bag; leave to cool.

Process all the ingredients except the honey and mint sprigs through the juice extractor. Pour into 2 glasses, sweeten with the honey and serve immediately garnished with a sprig of mint.

Makes 2 glasses

NUTRITIONAL TIP

White tea is thought to be good for hangovers because it speeds up the metabolism.

33 BALANCING HANGOVER HELPER

Make the Feeling Green Hangover Helper, replacing the white tea with coconut water and mint with basil.
Nutritional tip: Basil has an anti-inflammatory effect and helps to reduce stomach cramps.

34 KIWI WHITE TEA HANGOVER HELPER

Make the Feeling Green Hangover Helper, replacing the apples with 2 kiwis. Use 1 tablespoon feverfew flowers instead of mint, if desired.
Nutritional tip: Feverfew flowers are a traditional remedy for headaches.

35 Granola in a Glass

This is a two-in-one way to start the day: it's both a cereal and a smoothie. Plus, it's quick to prepare, making it great for mornings when time is short.

INGREDIENTS

240 ml (8 fl oz) semi-skimmed or
    skimmed milk
150 g (5 ¼ oz) mixed berries
40 g (1 ½ oz) granola
6 ice cubes

Put the milk and the berries in a blender and process until smooth. Add the granola and pulse until smooth. Add the ice and process until evenly crushed. Pour into 2 glasses and serve immediately.

Makes 2 glasses

HANDY TIP

Processing the berries and granola warms up the mixture, which is why adding the ice as a last step is essential.

Variations

36 ALMOND GRANOLA IN A GLASS

Make the Granola in a Glass using almond milk (instead of dairy milk) and selecting a granola that contains almonds. You can blend in additional almonds, if desired.
Handy tip: For a more intense almond flavour, add a few drops of almond extract.

37 FROZEN BERRY GRANOLA IN A GLASS

Make the Granola in a Glass as directed, but use frozen berries and omit ice. Blend in 125 ml (4 ¼ fl oz) plain or vanilla yoghurt.
Handy tip: Using frozen fruit in smoothies helps keep them cool and thick.

38 FLAXEN GRANOLA IN A GLASS

Add 1 tablespoon ground flaxseed to the blender when making Granola in a Glass.
Nutritional tip: Flaxseed contains vitamins, minerals and antioxidants that are essential for optimum health. It is a great addition to any of these granola smoothies.

39 GOJI AND BERRY GRANOLA IN A GLASS

Make the Granola in a Glass adding 2 to 4 tablespoons dried goji berries with the berries.
Handy tip: You can soften the goji berries first by soaking them in warm water for 20 minutes before use.

OVERNIGHT GRANOLA IN A GLASS

40

Make the Frozen Berry Granola in a Glass as directed the evening before it is required. Keep refrigerated. In the morning stir well, adding additional milk to taste. The smoothie will thicken on standing.

Handy tip: You can thin this smoothie with orange juice instead of milk.

STRAWBERRY GRANOLA IN A GLASS

41

Make the Granola in a Glass, replacing half of the milk with 125 ml (4 ¼ fl oz) strawberry yoghurt and adding 2 tablespoons orange juice. Use strawberries instead of the mixed berries.

Serving tip: This tastes good with a few extra strawberries chopped and mixed into the drink for texture.

OATMEAL BERRY SMOOTHIE

42

Omit the granola when making Granola in a Glass. In the blender, soak 20 g (¾ oz) oats in 125 ml (4 ¼ fl oz) milk for 20 minutes, then process until smooth. Add the remaining 125 ml (4 ¼ fl oz) milk and berries and blend.

Handy tip: If you like a textured smoothie, you can add the oatmeal with the other ingredients.

BLUEBERRY CHIA OATMEAL SMOOTHIE

43

Make the Oatmeal Berry Smoothie as directed above using blueberries instead of mixed berries. Soak 1 tablespoon chia seeds with the oatmeal.

PEACHY GINGERED GRANOLA IN A GLASS

44

Make Granola in a Glass, replacing the berries with 1 large stoned and skinned peach. Crumble a small ginger snap on the top of the smoothie.

45 Red Sunrise Juice

This stunning coloured drink is perfect for winter days when our immune systems are low.

INGREDIENTS

5 medium carrots, trimmed	1 apple, quartered
1 small beetroot, chopped	2 large oranges, peeled
2.5-cm (1-inch) piece ginger, peeled	½ grapefruit, peeled
	4 strawberries

Process the fruits and vegetables through a juice extractor in the order given in the ingredients list. Pour into glasses and serve immediately.

Makes 1 large or 2 small glasses

NUTRITIONAL TIP

Consume as soon as possible after juicing to gain the maximum nutritional benefits, preferably within 15 minutes.

Variations

46 FORTIFIED SUNRISE JUICE

Make the Red Sunrise Juice as directed. Whisk 1 tablespoon powdered wheatgrass or barley grass powder into the finished juice.
Nutritional tip: Wheatgrass and barley grass are high in chlorophyll, which proponents claim helps to cleanse the system and fight infections.

47 MINTED SUNRISE JUICE

Prepare the Red Sunrise Juice, omitting the ginger and putting 10 sprigs of mint through the juicer with the soft fruits.
Handy tip: Ginger is not to everyone's taste, but it is rare to find someone who does not enjoy mint, so make this variation if you are not sure of someone's preferences.

48 ORANGE SUNRISE JUICE

Replace the beetroot and the strawberries in the Red Sunrise Juice recipe with ½ a cantaloupe.
Handy tip: Children love this drink and it is a wonderful way to get even the most reluctant child to enjoy fresh fruits and vegetables.

49 DOUBLE YELLOW SUNRISE JUICE

Make the Red Sunrise Juice, replacing the beetroot and strawberries with ½ a medium cucumber and a 5-cm (2-inch) piece of peeled turmeric root.
Handy tip: If you can't find turmeric root, whisk 1 teaspoon of powdered turmeric into the finished juice.

Fortified Sunrise Juice is the perfect winter immune system booster

50 RED BOOSTER SUNRISE JUICE

Make the Red Sunrise Juice, replacing the strawberries with a red pepper.
Handy tip: If you like spicy drinks, add a red chili pepper to this drink. Juice all the other ingredients, then juice 1 or 2 chilies into a separate container. Add a little at a time to the final drink.

51 TRAFFIC SIGNAL JUICE

Make the Red Sunrise Juice, adding 4 big kale leaves before the strawberries.
Handy tip: Kale is a good ingredient to throw into a smoothie for green drink novices. It is a subtle addition to all the other wonderful flavours in this drink.

52 PINK SUNRISE JUICE

Make the Red Sunrise Juice, replacing the beetroot with 2 pink grapefruits and the oranges with ½ regular grapefruit.
Serving tip: This makes a refreshing juice to have with a sandwich at lunchtime.

53 TROPICAL SUNRISE JUICE

Make the Red Sunrise Juice, replacing the orange and grapefruit with ½ a pineapple, peeled and chopped.
Serving tip: This juice pairs well with soy sauce-marinated, grilled chicken.

54 ALOE SUNRISE JUICE

Make the Red Sunrise Juice as directed. Stir 1 to 2 capfuls of aloe vera concentrate into the finished drink, following the manufacturer's recommendations.
Nutritional tip: Breastfeeding mothers should use aloe with caution because it may cause an upset stomach in the baby.

55 Beachside Breakfast Smoothie

As the name suggests, this smoothie has a Caribbean flavour. It's sure to perk up your morning routine.

INGREDIENTS

Pulp and juice of 1 passion fruit, sieved if preferred

1 ½ mangoes, peeled, stoned and diced

240 ml (8 fl oz) pineapple juice

1 banana, peeled and quartered

2 Brazil nuts

Wedge of fresh pineapple, to garnish, optional

Put all the ingredients into a blender and blend until smooth. Pour into a glass and serve immediately. Garnish with a wedge of fresh pineapple if desired.

Makes 2 glasses

HANDY TIP

For fresh pineapple juice, pass a pineapple through the juice extractor.

Variations

56 BERRY BEACH BREAKFAST SMOOTHIE

Prepare the Beachside Breakfast Smoothie, substituting 6 medium strawberries for the passion fruit.
Handy tip: Frozen strawberries are great in this smoothie.

57 CARNIVAL BREAKFAST SMOOTHIE

Make the Beachside Breakfast Smoothie, replacing the pineapple juice with orange juice or tropical fruit juice.
Handy tip: Some people find that the acids in pineapple juice can cause mouth irritation. If this is the case, then use this variation or try using the Kona Sugarloaf variety of pineapple, which is low in acidity.

58 BREAKFAST PASSION SMOOTHIE

Make the Beachside Breakfast Smoothie, omitting the Brazil nuts and banana and adding 1 extra passion fruit.
Handy tip: As this smoothie contains 2 passion fruits, it is best to sieve them for a smoother smoothie.

59 HIGH C-BREEZE SMOOTHIE

Prepare the Beachside Breakfast Smoothie and add ¼ teaspoon camu camu powder.
Nutritional tip: Camu camu is a plant native to South America and contains very high levels of vitamin C.

60 TAKE A DATE BREAKFAST SMOOTHIE

Make the Beachside Breakfast Smoothie, replacing the passion fruit with 4 stoned and halved soft dried dates.
Handy tip: To get a really smooth texture try soaking dates in hot water for between 5 and 30 minutes, depending on the softness of the dates.

61 HAWAIIAN BEACH SMOOTHIE

Make the Beachside Breakfast Smoothie, replacing the Brazil nuts with 5 macadamia nuts.
Handy tip: Buy macadamia nuts in vacuum-packed jars or tins because they will stay fresh longer until opened.

62 TROPICAL BEACH SMOOTHIE

Prepare the Beachside Breakfast Smoothie, replacing the Brazil nuts and chopped mango with ½ a seeded and chopped papaya and a squeeze of lime juice.
Interesting note: The Mayan people of Mexico used to worship the papaya tree, calling it the 'Tree of Life' because of its medicinal benefits.

63 NUTTY FOR THE BEACH SMOOTHIE

Make the Beachside Breakfast Smoothie and add 4 walnut halves and 3 blanched almonds to the other ingredients.

64 BEACHSIDE SMOOTHIE WITH SEAWEED

Prepare the Beachside Breakfast Smoothie or any variation and add 1 teaspoon of kelp powder to the blender.
Nutritional tip: Seaweed is one of the most nutritionally complete foods, making it an excellent health supplement.

65 Three Fruit Wake-Up Juice

Three fruits add sufficiently different notes to make a really interesting taste sensation and these juices are quick and easy to prepare in the morning. The first of these is a delicious blend of strawberries, tangerine and apples.

INGREDIENTS

2 apples, peeled and quartered
8 medium strawberries
4 tangerines, peeled

Process the apples, strawberries and tangerines in a juice extractor. Pour into glasses and serve immediately.

Makes 2 glasses

HANDY TIP

Tangerines are good citruses to juice since they are small enough to be peeled and dropped whole into the juice extractor. However, you will get higher yields if you use a citrus press: 4 tangerines yield about 240 ml (8 fl oz) juice.

Variations

67 CARROT, APRICOT AND CANTALOUPE JUICE

Make the Three Fruit Wake-Up Juice using 3 carrots, 2 apricots and ½ a cantaloupe, peeled and cut into wedges.
Handy tip: You can juice cantaloupe without removing the seeds.

68 CARROT, APRICOT AND PEACH JUICE

Make the Carrot, Apricot and Cantaloupe Juice variation, replacing the cantaloupe with 3 stoned peaches.
Nutritional tip: You can leave the skin on apricots when juicing, but this is recommended only for organic fruit.

69 CARROT, APPLE AND BEETROOT JUICE

Make the Three Fruit Wake-Up Juice using 3 carrots, 2 peeled and quartered apples and 2 medium beetroot, cut into chunks.
Handy tip: You can add the washed tops of the beetroot in this juice, too.

70 CARROT, APPLE AND KIWI JUICE

Make the Carrot, Apple and Beetroot Juice variation, replacing the beetroot with 2 quartered and peeled kiwi fruit.
Handy tip: Over-ripe, over-soft kiwis don't juice well, so choose firm fruit.

66 MANGO, APPLE AND TANGERINE JUICE

Replace the strawberries in the Three Fruit Wake-Up Juice with a peeled and stoned mango.
Handy tip: Substitute 3 medium oranges for the tangerines if unavailable.

71 CARROT, APPLE AND GINGER JUICE

Make the Carrot, Apple and Beetroot Juice variation, replacing the beetroot with a 5-cm (2-inch) piece of peeled ginger.
Nutritional tip: This juice boosts your immunity.

72 CARROT, APPLE AND PEAR JUICE

Make the Carrot, Apple and Beetroot Juice variation, replacing the beetroot with 1 quartered pear.
Handy tip: Unripe pears can be quite dry, so select very ripe pears for juicing.

73 PEAR, WATERCRESS AND LEMON JUICE

Make the Three Fruit Wake-Up Juice using 4 small pears, 50 g (1 ¾ oz) watercress and ½ a lemon instead of the three original ingredients.
Serving tip: This makes a refreshing aperitif or between-course refresher.

74 APPLE, PEAR AND CRANBERRY JUICE

Make the Three Fruit Wake-Up Juice using 2 quartered apples and 1 quartered large pear instead of the original three ingredients. Divide between glasses and top with 240 ml (8 fl oz) cranberry juice.

75 APPLE, PEAR AND CUCUMBER JUICE

Make the Three Fruit Wake-Up Juice using 1 quartered apple, 1 quartered large pear and 1 small cucumber instead of the original three ingredients.

76 APPLE, PEAR AND BLUEBERRY JUICE

Make the Three Fruit Wake-Up Juice using 2 quartered apples, 1 quartered large pear and 100 g (3 ½ oz) blueberries instead of the original three ingredients.
Handy tip: Use a sharp, crisp apple like Granny Smith.

77 APPLE, PEACH AND GRAPE JUICE

Make the Three Fruit Wake-Up Juice using 3 quartered apples, 1 bunch of red seedless grapes and 1 stoned, halved peach instead of the original three ingredients.
Handy tip: Peaches and nectarines are interchangeable in most recipes.

78 Orange Almond Milk

This delicious dairy drink is the ultimate morning energy boost.

INGREDIENTS

210 g (7 ½ oz) unsalted roasted almonds

200 g (7 oz) icing sugar, divided

1 L (1 ¾ pt) mineral or filtered water

75 ml (2 ½ fl oz) orange flower water

3 L (½ gallon) milk

Put the almonds into a pan filled with boiling water and blanch for 30 seconds. Drain the almonds well, then rub in a towel to remove the skins. Put the almonds and 180 g (6 ½ oz) sugar in a blender and process until the nuts are very finely ground.

Combine the almond mixture and the water in a large bowl; cover and let stand overnight.

Drain the almond mixture through cheesecloth into a large jug. Stir in the orange flower water. Add the milk and sweeten to taste with the remaining sugar. Cover and refrigerate until well chilled. It will keep in the fridge for 2 to 3 days.

Makes 8 glasses

HANDY TIP

To roast almonds, spread on an ungreased baking sheet and bake in a 180°C (350°F) oven for 10 to 12 minutes or until they are golden brown and fragrant. Do not over brown; because of their high oil content, the almonds will continue to roast after you remove them from the oven.

Variations

79 ORANGE BRAZIL MILK

Make the Orange Almond Milk, substituting Brazil nuts for the almonds. There is no need to blanch the skin off Brazil nuts.

Nutritional tip: Since Brazil nuts are considered to be one of the superfoods, we should probably all be eating more of them.

80 VANILLA ALMOND MILK

Make the Orange Almond Milk, omitting the orange flower water. Flavour with 2 to 3 teaspoons of vanilla extract. After straining, omit icing sugar and sweeten instead with 60 to 125 ml (2 to 4 ¼ fl oz) liquid honey, to taste.

Handy tip: Vanilla extract varies in strength, so it is wise to add cautiously – using too much can result in a bitter taste.

81 DATE AND ALMOND MILK

Make the Orange Almond Milk or the Vanilla Almond Milk variation above. After straining the mix, omit icing sugar and sweeten instead with 60 to 125 ml (2 to 4 ¼ fl oz) date syrup.

Shopping tip: Date syrup is sometimes called date honey and can be bought from health food shops, specialist food shops and online. It is a great instant sweetener for juices and smoothies.

SOOTHING WARM ALMOND MILK

Make the Orange Almond Milk or the Vanilla Almond Milk variation and heat the final recipe in a saucepan or microwave until hot but not boiling.
Serving tip: Serve this drink as a nightcap.

BRAIN-BOOSTING SPICED ALMOND MILK

Prepare the Orange Almond Milk, omitting the orange flower water. Pour the milk into cups. To each cup add ½ teaspoon ground turmeric, 1 teaspoon ground cinnamon and ¼ teaspoon ground ginger. Stir well. Heat in a microwave until hot but not boiling. Garnish with a pinch of ground cardamom seeds.
Nutritional tip: These traditional Indian spices added to the almond milk calm the nerves before sleep.

SIMPLE NUT WATER

Put 150 g (5 ¼ oz) blanched almonds or Brazil nuts into a blender with 4 stoned dates, 1 teaspoon vanilla extract, 1 pinch salt and 500 ml (17 fl oz) water. Blend until smooth. Drain the nut mixture through cheesecloth into a large jug and add another 500 ml (17 fl oz) water. Cover and refrigerate.
Handy tip: If you make this often, you can buy a special nut milk bag to use instead of cheesecloth.

ORANGE AND CASHEW NUT COOLER

Put 75 g (2 ½ oz) raw, chopped cashew nuts in a blender with 500 ml (17 fl oz) water and 60 ml (2 fl oz) liquid honey and process until smooth. Drain mixture into a jug, stir in 500 ml (17 fl oz) water and 1 L (1 ¾ pt) orange juice and refrigerate until chilled.
Nutritional tip: Cashew nuts have high-energy density and fibre, both of which have been said to have beneficial effects on weight management when eaten in moderation.

86 Breakfast Orange Protein Smoothie

This recipe makes a great start to the day. Remember that the frozen yoghurt is usually quite sweet so add the honey to taste with care.

INGREDIENTS

240 ml (8 fl oz) orange juice, preferably freshly squeezed

1 tsp grated orange zest

2 scoops orange frozen yoghurt

1 egg

2 tsp wheat germ

1 tbsp liquid honey

Orange slice, to decorate

Put the orange juice, orange zest, frozen yoghurt, egg, wheat germ and honey in a blender and process until smooth. Pour into a chilled glass and serve immediately. Decorate with an orange slice, to serve.

Makes 1 large glass or 2 small glasses

HANDY TIP

For a creamier but less healthy breakfast smoothie, use orange, lemon or vanilla ice cream.

variations

87 BREAKFAST ORANGE APRICOT SMOOTHIE

Make the Breakfast Orange Protein Smoothie, replacing the orange juice with apricot nectar.
Handy tip: Apricot nectar is the thick liquid extracted from the fruit; apricot juice may contain water and sugar. You may need to thin this nectar-based drink with a little water.

88 BREAKFAST ORANGE DATE SMOOTHIE

Put the grated zest and juice of 2 oranges in a blender with 5 soft dried dates and 240 ml (8 fl oz) plain yoghurt. Process until smooth and serve in a glass.
Handy tip: Use soya yoghurt for a dairy-free version of this smoothie.

89 BREAKFAST ORANGE BANANA SMOOTHIE

Put the grated zest and juice of 2 oranges in a blender with 1 small, peeled and chopped banana and 240 ml (8 fl oz) plain yoghurt. Process until smooth and serve in a glass. Thin with a little milk if desired.
Handy tip: Banana is full of natural sugars, but if this smoothie isn't sweet enough for your taste, add ½ to 1 teaspoon liquid honey or maple syrup.

90 Maple Banana Soya Smoothie

Start the day the healthy way with this creamy soya smoothie, perfect for watching your cholesterol.

INGREDIENTS

1 banana, peeled and chopped
240 ml (8 fl oz) soya milk
1 tbsp maple syrup, plus extra for drizzling

2 tsp lemon juice
2 tsp wheat germ

Put all the ingredients in the blender and process until smooth. Pour in a glass and drizzle with extra maple syrup. Serve immediately.

Makes 1 glass

HANDY TIP

For a low-carb or sugar-free version, use unsweetened soya milk and sugar-free, maple-flavoured syrup.

91 MAPLE BANANA SMOOTHIE

Put 1 small, peeled and chopped banana, 240 ml (8 fl oz) whole milk, 2 scoops maple syrup-flavoured ice cream and 1 teaspoon lemon juice in the blender and process until smooth.
Handy tip: The riper the banana, the sweeter the flavour.

92 MAPLE BANANA ALMOND SMOOTHIE

Prepare the Maple Banana Soya Smoothie, replacing the soya milk with almond milk and garnishing with toasted, flaked almonds.
Shopping tip: While real maple syrup is expensive and utterly delicious, maple-flavoured syrup is inexpensive and makes a reasonable substitute. Sugar-free, maple-flavoured syrup is also available.

93 Eggnog Yoghurt Smoothie

Keep the festive spirit all year round with this rich and creamy smoothie. There's no alcohol in this version, so it's a great sweet treat for all the family.

INGREDIENTS

2 eggs, separated

1 ½ tbsp sugar

240 ml (8 fl oz) milk

240 ml (8 fl oz) plain yoghurt

½ tsp vanilla extract

Freshly ground nutmeg,
  to decorate

Put the egg yolks and sugar in a bowl and beat until thick and lemon-coloured. Add milk, yoghurt and vanilla and stir well. In another bowl, using clean dry beaters, beat the egg whites until stiff and fold into the yoghurt mixture. Serve at once, sprinkled with ground nutmeg.

Makes 2 large glasses

HEALTH WARNING

Raw eggs should be avoided by pregnant women and those with a compromised immune system.

Variations

94 BANANA EGGNOG SMOOTHIE

Make the Eggnog Yoghurt Smoothie, adding a well mashed or puréed banana with the yoghurt.
Handy tip: Be sure to clean the beaters after beating the egg yolks. If there is any protein from the egg yolk on the beaters, the egg white will not thicken.

95 PUMPKIN EGGNOG SMOOTHIE

Make the Eggnog Yoghurt Smoothie, adding 125 ml (4 ½ fl oz) pumpkin purée to the yoghurt. Garnish with pumpkin pie spice.
Handy tip: This is a great way to use up a bit of leftover roasted pumpkin. Just pass through a sieve to purée.

96 HOT WHEAT GERM EGGNOG

Beat the egg yolks and sugar as directed. Heat 400 ml (13 ½ fl oz) whole milk until bubbles form at the edge of the saucepan; do not boil. Beat the egg whites until stiff. Add the warm milk, 2 teaspoons wheat germ and a pinch each of ground cinnamon and ground nutmeg to the egg yolks; then process with a hand blender until smooth. Fold in the egg whites. Pour into glasses at once and serve.
Handy tip: Fresher eggs are easier to separate.

Vegan Eggnog Smoothie is a great non-dairy
alternative to this traditional festive tipple

97 VEGAN EGGNOG SMOOTHIE

Put 375 ml (12 ½ fl oz) almond milk in a blender with
½ a banana, ½ an avocado, 2 teaspoons liquid honey,
1 teaspoon pumpkin spice, ½ teaspoon ground nutmeg
and a few drops of vanilla extract. Process until smooth
and serve immediately.
Handy tip: Vanilla soya milk can be used instead of
almond milk.

98 CHOCOLATE EGGNOG SMOOTHIE

Make the Eggnog Yoghurt Smoothie, adding 60 ml
(2 fl oz) chocolate syrup with the yoghurt. Grate a
little chocolate on the top of the finished smoothie
with the nutmeg.
Handy tip: Carob syrup can be substituted for the
chocolate syrup.

99 Go Bananas Smoothie

This thick and filling smoothie is perfect to set you up for a day at school or in the office.

INGREDIENTS

1 ½ bananas, peeled and
    quartered
1 tbsp smooth peanut butter
240 ml (8 fl oz) whole milk

Combine all the ingredients in a blender and process until smooth. Pour into a glass and serve immediately.

Makes 1 glass

HANDY TIP

Use whole milk for children, but adults may prefer to use semi-skimmed milk.

Variations

100 GO WHEAT AND BANANAS SMOOTHIE

Add 1 teaspoon wheat germ to the blender along with the other ingredients when making the Go Bananas Smoothie.

Handy tip: Wheat germ contains fat so can go rancid. To increase its longevity, keep in an airtight container in the fridge.

101 GO BRAN AND BANANAS SMOOTHIE

Add 1 teaspoon of bran to the blender along with the other ingredients when making the Go Bananas Smoothie.

Nutritional tip: If using oat bran, be sure it is labelled as gluten-free if giving to someone with a gluten intolerance. Although oat bran is naturally gluten-free, some cross contamination may occur in the production of non-certified oat bran.

103 GO NUTS AND BANANAS SMOOTHIE

Add 1 tablespoon of your favourite nuts to the blender along with the other ingredients when making the Go Bananas Smoothie.

Serving tip: Serve this smoothie with a bowl of fresh fruit salad for a perfectly balanced breakfast.

102 GO SOYA BANANAS SMOOTHIE

Make the Go Bananas Smoothie, replacing the milk with the same quantity of soya milk.

Shopping tip: Some soya milk comes in aseptic packaging, which doesn't require refrigeration until opened. Keep a carton in the cupboard so you can have a breakfast smoothie even if you are out of milk.

104 GO BANANAS AND CHOCOLATE SMOOTHIE

Prepare the Go Bananas Smoothie and add 1 tablespoon chocolate spread to the blender with the other ingredients.

Family tip: Children love chocolate and by adding relatively little, you can sneak all the other good things into their breakfast, making this a good energy drink before a busy day.

105 Country Breakfast Smoothie

Using stewed fruit is a novel approach to smoothie making; it adds a mellowness of flavour that you don't get from fresh fruits.

INGREDIENTS

2 apples, peeled, cored
  and chopped
1 pear, peeled, cored and chopped
120 g (4 ¼ oz) chopped rhubarb
40 g (1 ½ oz) blackberries

2 tbsp water
1 tsp lemon juice
1 tsp honey
125 ml (4 ¼ fl oz) natural
  low-fat yoghurt

Place all of the fruits into a saucepan with the water, lemon juice and honey. Bring to the boil, then turn down to a simmer. Poach the fruit for 10 minutes or until it is tender. Remove from the heat; leave to cool.

Put the stewed fruit into a blender with the yoghurt and process until smooth. Pour into a glass and serve immediately. Drizzle a little extra honey over the smoothie if desired.

Makes 1 large or 2 small glasses

HANDY TIP

Stew fruit as it becomes available in season, then freeze in small containers for ease of use.

106 SPICED COUNTRY SMOOTHIE

Prepare the Country Breakfast Smoothie, adding 1 teaspoon apple pie spice to the stewed fruit before blending.
Foodie tip: Apple pie spice is made of 4 parts cinnamon to 2 parts nutmeg to 1 part cardamom.

variations

107 STEWED RHUBARB, APPLE AND PEAR SMOOTHIE

Omit blackberries from the Country Breakfast Smoothie.
Handy tip: This is good for people who don't like the texture of the tiny seeds in blackberries.

108 STEWED APPLE AND BLACKBERRY SMOOTHIE

Prepare the Country Breakfast Smoothie, replacing the rhubarb and pears with another apple and an additional 120 g (4 ¼ oz) blackberries.

Freezing seasonal fruit in small containers allows you to enjoy your favourite smoothies all year round

109 STEWED PEAR AND APPLE SMOOTHIE

Make the Country Breakfast Smoothie, replacing the rhubarb and blackberries with another ½ apple and ½ pear.
Family tip: This is a very gentle smoothie and would be a good meal for someone who is feeling under the weather.

110 STEWED QUINCE AND APPLE SMOOTHIE

Make the Country Breakfast Smoothie, replacing the rhubarb and blackberries with 2 small quinces.
Interesting fact: The flavour of raw quince is quite astringent so they should always be eaten cooked.

111 Quick Raspberry Smoothie

So quick and easy to make and so delightful to drink, this might well become a before-school-drop-off staple.

INGREDIENTS

120 g (4 ¼ oz) raspberries
150 ml (5 fl oz) orange juice, preferably freshly squeezed
75 ml (2 ½ fl oz) low-fat plain yoghurt

Put all the ingredients in a blender and process until smooth. Pour into a glass and serve immediately.

Makes 1 glass

HANDY TIP

Fresh or frozen raspberries can be used in this smoothie.

112 QUICK RASPBERRY LEMON SMOOTHIE

Make the Quick Raspberry Smoothie using lemon yoghurt instead of plain yoghurt.
Handy tip: Other flavoured yoghurt such as mango, coconut or cherry would work, too.

114 QUICK BLUEBERRY SMOOTHIE

Replace the raspberries with blueberries when making the Quick Raspberry Smoothie.
Serving suggestion: Making smoothies is a good way to use up blueberries that are slightly past their prime.

113 QUICK RASPBERRY PROTEIN SMOOTHIE

Make the Quick Raspberry Smoothie, adding 1 tablespoon protein powder with the other ingredients.
Serving suggestion: Place a few fresh raspberries on top of the finished smoothie.

115 QUICK BERRY SMOOTHIE

Replace the raspberries with frozen mixed berries when making the Quick Raspberry Smoothie.
Serving suggestion: Use frozen mixed berries when fresh berries are out of season.

116 Green Tea, Apple and Grape Juice

Green tea blends perfectly with fresh fruit to make unusual juices and it has considerable health benefits.

INGREDIENTS

1 pinch maccha (green tea) powder
125 ml (4 ¼ fl oz) boiling water

1 apple, quartered
150 g (5 ¼ oz) seedless green grapes

Mix the maccha powder with the boiling water. Leave to cool, then put in the fridge to chill.

Put the apple and grapes through a juice extractor. Mix the juice with the green tea and serve.

Makes 1 glass

NUTRITIONAL TIP

Green tea can help you feel mentally alert.

Variations

119 GREEN TEA AND MANGO JUICE

Replace the grapes and apples with the flesh of 1 peeled and stoned mango when making the Green Tea, Apple and Grape Juice.
Foodie note: 'Matcha' and 'maca' are less common, alternative spellings for maccha.

120 GREEN TEA AND PINEAPPLE JUICE

Make the Green Tea, Apple and Grape Juice, replacing the grapes and apples with 225 g (8 oz) chopped pineapple.
Nutritional tip: Antioxidants in green tea may help to protect against cancer.

121 GREEN TEA AND GUAVA JUICE

Replace the grapes and apples with 3 peeled guavas when preparing the Green Tea, Apple and Grape Juice.
Handy tip: Guava skin can be rough and bitter or soft and sweet so peeling before processing is optional.

117 GREEN TEA AND APPLE JUICE

Prepare the Green Tea, Apple and Grape Juice, omitting the grapes and increasing the quantity of apples to 2.
Interesting Note: Zen Buddhists developed the tea ceremony in the Chinese Song dynasty.

118 GREEN TEA AND PEACH JUICE

Make the Green Tea, Apple and Grape Juice, replacing the grapes and apples with 3 stoned peaches.
Handy tip: Mix the powder to a thick paste with drops of cold water before pouring over boiling water to prevent lumps.

122 GREEN TEA AND POMEGRANATE JUICE

Prepare the Green Tea, Apple and Grape Juice, replacing the grapes and apples with the seeds from 1 pomegranate.
Handy tip: Remove as much white membrane as possible before juicing the pomegranate.

123 GREEN TEA WITH CITRUS JUICE

Make the Green Tea, Apple and Grape Juice, omitting grapes and apple. Add 1 strip of lemon zest to the boiling water with the maccha. Press the juice from ½ a pink grapefruit and add to the chilled tea with 2 teaspoons lemon juice and honey, to taste.

124 Lemon Grape Zinger

This is a refreshing juice drink with the zing of ginger and the fizz of sparkling water that will wake you up and cleanse the body in one.

INGREDIENTS

250 g (8 ¾ oz) red seedless grapes
5-cm (2-inch) piece ginger, peeled

1 lemon, peeled and chopped
About 75 ml (2 ½ fl oz) sparking mineral water

Process the grapes, ginger and lemon in a juice extractor. Pour into a glass and top with the sparkling mineral water. Serve immediately.

Makes 1 glass

SERVING TIP

Peel a strip of lemon zest before completely peeling the lemon and use the strip to garnish the finished drink. Thread on a toothpick along with a couple of grapes and some fresh lemon balm, mint or basil.

125 LEMON BLACKBERRY ZINGER

Make the Lemon Grape Zinger, replacing the grapes with 225 g (8 oz) blackberries.
Handy tip: Make this in a blender using fresh or frozen blackberries, 1 tablespoon ginger syrup and the juice of the lemon.

126 ORANGE AND RASPBERRY ZINGER

Make the Lemon Grape Zinger, replacing the grapes and lemon with 225 g (8 oz) raspberries and 1 small orange.
Handy tip: If these zinger drinks are a little too sharp for your taste, use lemon-lime soda instead of mineral water.

Cleansing Drinks

When you're feeling sluggish, there is nothing better than a juice so enriched with goodness that you can almost feel it cleansing and detoxing your system sip by tasty sip. This chapter is full of fruit and vegetable combinations that will do just that and, if consumed regularly, will make you feel and look brighter with glossy hair, radiant skin and sparkling eyes. The simplest detox is a classic combination of apples, carrots and celery, but there is also a big selection of vegetable-based drinks in this section that are abundant in body-enhancing nutrients.

127 Detox Starter

This is a simple detox juice containing three wonderful ingredients. It tastes so good you will wonder why you haven't discovered it before.

INGREDIENTS

3 apples, quartered
2 carrots, trimmed
2 celery stalks

Process the ingredients through a juice extractor, pour into a glass and serve cold.

Makes 1 glass

NUTRITIONAL TIP

Celery is a diuretic, apple juice aids digestion and carrots are a great antioxidant.

Variations

128 MINTED DETOX

Add 1 small bunch of mint leaves and ½ a peeled lime to the extractor while making the Detox Starter.
Handy tip: Buy a potted mint plant from the shop and keep it on a sunny windowsill. Fresh mint grows well indoors, so you should be able to keep it going for a while.

129 DETOX BOOSTER

Add a 5-cm (2-inch) piece of peeled ginger and 1 teaspoon spirulina powder to the processor when making the Detox Starter.
Nutritional tip: A single teaspoon of spirulina will provide you with the daily recommended intake of B12.

130 FENNEL DETOX SPECIAL

Make the Detox Starter or the Detox Booster, replacing the celery with 1 medium fennel bulb.
Nutritional tip: Fennel contains a compound that can help relieve inflammation.

131 ZESTY DETOX

Make the Detox Starter using 3 carrots, 1 apple, 1 orange, ½ grapefruit and a small bunch of mint leaves in place of the original ingredients.
Handy tip: This variation also works well using a 5-cm (2-inch) piece of peeled ginger instead of the mint.

132 TOMMY DETOX

Make the Detox Starter, replacing the apples with 2 medium tomatoes and add ½ a peeled lemon.
Nutritional tip: Tomatoes are wonderful antioxidants and studies have shown that lycopene, which is associated with their red colour, may be beneficial to bone health.

133 DETOX REVITALISER SMOOTHIE

Put 1 peeled, cored and chopped apple in a blender with 2 chopped celery stalks and 300 ml (10 fl oz) semi-skimmed or whole milk. Process until smooth and add a pinch each of salt and sugar.
Nutritional tip: Your body depends on the right balance of electrolytes – salt and sugar are two important components that can help restore the balance.

134   DETOX BEETER

Process 1 carrot, 1 apple, 1 celery stalk and 2 small beetroot in a juice extractor.

Handy tip: This is the perfect drink to get you acquainted with drinking beetroot juice – it is sweet, light and easy to drink.

135   GENTLE DETOX BEETER

Prepare the Detox Beeter variation, replacing the apple with 1 peeled and cored pear.

Handy tip: Pears have similar attributes to apples but are less sour; the two are often interchangeable in juice drinks.

136 Green Goddess

While this may appear a strange combination at first glance, don't be fooled. The Green Goddess is a delicious and cleansing mix of fruits and vegetables that is great for digestion.

INGREDIENTS

2 celery stalks	25 g (1 oz) baby spinach,
1 apple, quartered	washed
1 kiwi fruit, peeled	½ cucumber
1 pear, quartered	Squeeze of lime juice

Put the celery, apple, kiwi fruit, pear, spinach and cucumber through a juice extractor. Pour into a glass. Top off with a squeeze of lime juice and serve immediately.

Makes 1 glass

HANDY TIP

Spinach is a natural nutrient boost to any juice or smoothie and, surprisingly, you can hardly taste it at all.

Variations

137 KIWI GREEN GODDESS

Prepare the Green Goddess, replacing the pear and cucumber with 1 additional apple and 1 extra kiwi fruit. **Handy tip:** Kiwi fruit are often hard when purchased, but will ripen quickly on a windowsill.

138 ORCHARD GREEN GODDESS

Prepare the Green Goddess, replacing the celery and cucumber with 1 additional apple and 1 extra pear. **Nutritional tip:** Apples and pears both contain large amounts of natural sugars. Juicing them concentrates the sugars so, although this juice is good for you, be aware that you are consuming large amounts of sugar.

139 CUCUMBER GREEN GODDESS

Make the Green Goddess, replacing the pear and kiwi fruit with 1 additional apple and an extra ½ a cucumber. **Handy tip:** Cucumber makes a great addition to mixed juices because it contains loads of liquid yet has a very mild flavour.

140 VEGETABLE GODDESS

Omit the apple, kiwi fruit and pear when making the Green Goddess and instead increase the spinach to 50 g (1 ¾ oz), the cucumber to 1 whole and the celery to 3 stalks. **Nutritional tip:** Nutrients in juice are absorbed faster than those in whole produce because the fibre is gone.

141 DARK GREEN GODDESS

Prepare the Green Goddess, replacing the spinach with kale.
Nutritional tip: Kale is a better source of some essential vitamins and minerals than spinach, but spinach has the edge over kale when it comes to foliate. Best to choose whichever looks freshest.

142 MEXICAN GODDESS

Prepare the Green Goddess, replacing the kiwi fruit with a small bunch of coriander.
Handy tip: If you like a spicy juice, you can add the juice of ½ to 1 red chili with the other ingredients.

143 WATERCRESS GODDESS

Make the Green Goddess, substituting 10 sprigs of watercress for the kiwi fruit.
Handy tip: Ten sprigs of watercress weighs approximately 40 g (1 ½ oz).

144 GRAPEFUL GODDESS

Make the Green Goddess, replacing the kiwi fruit with 150 g (5 ¼ oz) green grapes.
Handy tip: There is no need to remove the seeds from the grapes when juicing; in fact, the tiny seeds in grapes are crammed with nutrients.

145 GREEN GODDESS SMOOTHIE

When preparing the Green Goddess, put all the ingredients in a blender along with 175 ml (6 fl oz) almond or soya milk and blend until smooth.
Serving tip: Serve garnished with slices of cucumber cut diagonally.

146 Cucumber Agua Fresca

This water is a dieter's delight, as it contains no calories. It is simply flavoured water. You can keep adding fresh water to the vegetables and fruits for a couple of days as the water is consumed.

INGREDIENTS

1 lime, thinly sliced
½ cucumber, thinly sliced
Small bunch mint, stems removed
1 large jug, about 1.5 L (2 ½ pt) of
    cold, filtered or mineral water

Put all the ingredients in the jug of water and refrigerate. Cover and leave overnight or for at least 2 hours so that the flavour from the ingredients can infuse the water.

Makes 6 glasses

SERVING TIP

This is lovely to make for a dinner party. For a really pretty effect, serve individual glasses well laden with the fruits and vegetables.

Variations

148 GINGERED AGUA FRESCA

Make the agua fresca, replacing the lime with one sliced lemon and a 7.5-cm (3-inch) piece of ginger, peeled and sliced as thinly as possible.
Handy tip: Use the best organic lemons you can find in these infusions.

149 LEMONGRASS AND GINGER AGUA FRESCA

Make the Gingered Agua Fresca variation, adding 2 sliced stalks of lemongrass.
Serving tip: This is perfect with Thai-style curries

150 LEMONGRASS AND VANILLA AGUA FRESCA

Make agua fresca from 1 sliced stalk lemongrass, 12 basil leaves, 1 celery stalk and ¼ split vanilla bean.
Handy tip: If possible, use Thai basil for this drink. Its peppery overtones work really well with the other flavours.

151 CUCUMBER CRANBERRY AGUA FRESCA

Prepare the Cucumber Agua Fresca, replacing the lime with 1 sliced lemon and adding 40 g (1 ½ oz) cranberries.
Serving tip: Cranberries make this perfect to serve with a festive meal.

147 HERBED CUCUMBER AGUA FRESCA

Prepare the Cucumber Agua Fresca, replacing the mint with 2 sprigs of rosemary and a small bunch each of thyme and mint.
Handy tip: Wash all ingredients well to avoid muddy water!

152 LAVENDER AGUA FRESCA

Make the agua fresca from ½ a sliced cucumber, a small bunch of mint (stems discarded), plus ½ teaspoon culinary lavender.
Shopping tip: Don't eat lavender from florists as it may have been sprayed with herbicides.

Serve the Lemongrass and Ginger Aqua Fresca with Thai-style curries

153 STRAWBERRY MINT AGUA FRESCA

Make the agua fresca from 10 large strawberries, sliced thin and a small bunch of mint, stems discarded.
Serving tip: This is a nice way of introducing sugar-free liquid into a young child's diet.

155 PINEAPPLE MINT AGUA FRESCA

Make the Cucumber Agua Fresca, adding 3 slices of pineapple chopped into cubes.
Handy tip: Do not discard pineapple cores; they are full of nutrients and make an excellent glass garnish.

154 BLACKBERRY AND LEMON VERBENA AGUA FRESCA

Make the Cucumber Agua Fresca, replacing the lime and mint with 150 g (5 ¼ oz) blackberries and a small bunch of lemon verbena, stems discarded.
Handy tip: Lemon balm would also work well in this.

156 WARM LEMON WATER

Squeeze the juice from ½ a lemon into a glass of hot, not boiling, mineral or filtered water.
Nutritional tip: This traditional cleanser is a digestive aid and liver cleanser.

157 Root Juice

This juice's vibrant intense colour means that it will always impress – and so will its sweet, nutty flavour.

INGREDIENTS

2 large beetroot, trimmed
3 carrots, trimmed
2-cm (¾-inch) piece fresh
    ginger, peeled

Put all the ingredients through a juice extractor. Pour into a glass and serve immediately.

Makes 1 glass

HANDY TIP

The earthy flavour of beetroot gives this drink a substantial feel, so they make a great fill-me-up.

Variations

158 CARROT AND GINGER JUICE

Prepare the Root Juice, omitting the beetroot and increasing the quantity of carrots to 5.
Handy tip: The sweet creaminess of carrots makes this the most enjoyable of all the vegetable juices to drink on its own.

159 CARROT AND PARSLEY JUICE

Make the Root Juice, replacing the beetroot with a small bunch of parsley.
Handy tip: The chlorophyll in parsley has long been used as a breath freshener and is particularly effective in neutralising garlic odour. Do not use if pregnant.

160 BEETROOT, ORANGE AND GINGER JUICE

Prepare the Root Juice, replacing the carrots with 3 peeled oranges.
Nutritional tip: When introducing these strong juices into your diet, start slowly with one glass a day and slowly increase the amount with time.

161 BEETROOT AND CARROT JUICE

Prepare the Root Juice omitting the ginger.
Serving tip: For stunning visual effect, extract the beetroot and carrot juices separately and pour into glasses without mixing.

162 BEETROOT AND GINGER JUICE

Prepare the Root Juice, omitting the carrots and adding another large beet.
Handy tip: Don't leave your juicer to sit after use. If the residue dries on the machine it is much harder to wash.

163 BEETROOT AND ORANGE SMOOTHIE

Put 2 medium cooked and peeled beetroot in a blender with 125 ml (4 ¼ fl oz) orange juice and 75 ml (2 ½ fl oz) plain yoghurt. Blend until smooth. Thin to taste with water. Season with a pinch of salt.
Handy tip: Uncooked beetroot does not blend easily, so use cooked beetroot in a smoothie.

164 CARROT, ORANGE AND GINGER CRUSH

Replace the beetroot with 3 peeled oranges and add 6 sprigs of parsley to the juicer. Divide between glasses and top off with still or sparkling mineral water.
Handy tip: This is a good drink if you find the concentrated vegetable juice too strong.

165 CARROT, TOMATO AND GINGER CRUSH

Make the Carrot, Orange and Ginger Crush variation, omitting the oranges. Replace with 3 medium tomatoes.
Serving tip: This drink goes well with a good ham-and-cheese sandwich at lunchtime.

166 cranberry, Apple and Orange Juice

The sour flavour of cranberries is very refreshing and it makes this juice really popular with young and old alike.

INGREDIENTS

100 g (3 ½ oz) cranberries
2 apples, quartered
2 oranges, peeled and cut
    into chunks

Put all the ingredients through a juice extractor. Pour into a glass and serve immediately.

Makes 1 glass

HANDY TIP

If you are short on time you can make this from equal quantities of commercially prepared fruit juices.

variations

167 CRANBERRY AND APPLE JUICE

Make the Cranberry, Apple and Orange Juice, replacing the oranges with 2 additional apples.
Handy tip: Choose sour apples such as Granny Smith or use your favourite flavourful local apples.

168 CRANBERRY, ORANGE AND PEACH JUICE

Make the Cranberry, Apple and Orange Juice, replacing the apples with 1 peeled and stoned peach.
Handy tip: Commercial peach nectar is usually made from concentrated juice and often contains additional sugar.

169 APPLE, ORANGE AND RASPBERRY JUICE

Prepare the Cranberry, Apple and Orange Juice, replacing half of the fresh cranberries with 50 g (1 ¾ oz) raspberries.
Handy tip: If you haven't got any raspberries on hand, add a generous pour of raspberry syrup to the basic recipe.

CRANBERRY, APPLE, ORANGE AND STRAWBERRY JUICE

Make the Cranberry, Apple and Orange Juice, replacing half of the fresh cranberries with 50 g (1 ¾ oz) strawberries.

Handy tip: If making this for a family, adding the strawberries makes a sweeter drink, which some children may prefer.

CRANBERRY, APPLE, ORANGE AND MINT JUICE

Prepare the Cranberry, Apple and Orange Juice, adding 8 fresh mint leaves to the other ingredients.

Serving tip: Cranberries are a great Christmas staple and this drink is ideal to offer your guests at any Christmas celebrations.

172 Digestion Smoothie

This fibre-rich smoothie will aid your digestive system and taste wonderful while doing so.

INGREDIENTS

1 banana, peeled and quartered
5 prunes, stoned
60 ml (2 fl oz) orange juice
240 ml (8 fl oz) natural low-fat yoghurt

Put all the ingredients into a blender and blend until smooth. Pour into a glass or mug and serve immediately.

Makes 1 glass

NUTRITIONAL TIP

Sometimes the old remedies are the best. Prunes have been proven to relieve constipation; in fact, a recent study indicates that they work even better than fibre supplements. It is most effective if taken twice a day, but don't persist for more than a week without seeking medical advice.

Variations

173 DIGESTION SMOOTHIE WITH FIGS

Prepare the Digestion Smoothie, omitting the prunes and replacing them with 5 dried figs.
Nutritional tip: Figs can act as a natural laxative in some people.

174 EXOTIC FIG SMOOTHIE

Prepare the Digestion Smoothie with Figs variation and add 1 teaspoon rose water and a pinch of ground cardamom to the finished drink.
Interesting fact: Figs are not technically a fruit since they are formed by the flower and seeds of the fig plant.

175 DIGESTION SMOOTHIE WITH FLAX OIL

Prepare the Digestion Smoothie with Figs variation and add 1 tablespoon pure flax oil to the other ingredients.
Interesting fact: Flax oil is also called linseed oil, which is sold in DIY shops as a wood finish. Only eat flax oil prepared for human consumption.

176 SUPER DIGESTION SMOOTHIE

Prepare the Digestion Smoothie, adding 1 tablespoon flax oil and 2 dried figs to the other ingredients.
Serving tip: This is a good morning drink if your digestive tract is acting up. Serve with whole-wheat toast and honey.

177 VEGAN DIGESTION SMOOTHIE

Prepare the Digestion Smoothie or any of its variations substituting 175 ml (6 fl oz) low-fat coconut milk for the yoghurt.
Handy tip: Another vegan alternative is to replace the yoghurt with vanilla soya yoghurt.

178 Big Green Chiller

This wonderful concoction is a farmers' market stall in a glass!

INGREDIENTS

2 cucumbers	1 small bunch coriander
4 celery stalks	½ a lime, peeled and chopped
2 courgettes	2.5-cm (1-inch) piece ginger,
6 kale leaves	peeled
6 spinach leaves	Lime slices, to garnish

Put all the ingredients through a juice extractor. Pour into a glass and serve immediately. Garnish with a slice of lime.

Makes 1 large or 2 small glasses

HANDY TIP

The spinach used here is full-sized spinach not baby leaves. If you have baby leaves use about a handful.

179 BIG GREEN CHILLER COLD DEFIER

Prepare the Big Green Chiller, replacing the coriander with a small bunch of parsley and adding 2 peeled garlic cloves.
Nutritional tip: The garlic is used here as an immune booster and the parsley will help neutralise its odour.

180 BIG GREEN PEPPER CHILLER

Make the Big Green Chiller, replacing the courgettes with 1 green and 1 yellow pepper.
Handy tip: Mixing the green and the yellow peppers balances their sweetness.

181 BIG GREEN AND ORANGE CHILLER

Prepare the Big Green Chiller, replacing the lime with a peeled and chopped orange.
Handy tip: If the juicer gets clogged up when processing soft vegetables, push a hard carrot through the machine.

182 BIG GREEN BROCCOLI CHILLER

Replace the spinach and kale in the Big Green Chiller recipe with a small head of broccoli, broken into florets.
Nutritional tip: An ideal juice for expectant mothers, the Big Green Broccoli Chiller is full of folic acid.

183 Minty Mandarin, Lemongrass and Chili Juice

Adding chili to fruit juice might sound bizarre, but in small quantities it provides a surprisingly good flavour hit without excessive heat.

INGREDIENTS

4 mandarin oranges, peeled
    and chopped
1 lemongrass stalk, trimmed
½ a long red chili, seeded
5 fresh mint leaves

Put all the ingredients through a juice extractor. Pour into a glass and serve immediately.

Makes 1 glass

HANDY TIP

Even if you are a fan of chilies, it is advisable to remove the seeds before juicing chilies.

Variations

184 MINTY MANDARIN, LIME AND LEMONGRASS CHILI JUICE

Prepare the Minty Mandarin, Lemongrass and Chili Juice and add the juice of ½ a lime.
Nutritional tip: All types of orange are effective digestive cleansers.

185 MINTY ORANGE, LEMONGRASS AND CHILI JUICE

Make the Minty Mandarin, Lemongrass and Chili Juice, replacing the mandarin oranges with 3 peeled oranges.
Shopping tip: If you are a keen juicer, then it is economical to buy oranges in bulk given that they are the base for so many juices and smoothies.

186 MINTY MANGO, LEMONGRASS AND CHILI JUICE

Make the Minty Mandarin, Lemongrass and Chili Juice, replacing the mandarin oranges with 1 peeled and stoned mango.
Shopping tip: A ripe mango will yield slightly when gently pressed.

MINTY GRAPEFRUIT, LEMONGRASS AND CHILI JUICE

187

Prepare the Minty Mandarin, Lemongrass and Chili Juice, replacing the mandarin oranges with ½ a peeled, roughly chopped grapefruit.

Handy tip: Ruby grapefruits give the sweetest juice.

MINTY LYCHEE, LEMONGRASS, CHILI AND MINT JUICE

188

Prepare the Minty Mandarin, Lemongrass and Chili Juice, replacing the mandarin oranges with 12 peeled and stoned lychees.

Shopping tip: Lychees are expensive, so look out for cartons of lychee juice in good grocery, health or ethnic food shops and use 125 ml (4 ¼ fl oz) lychee juice instead of the 12 lychees called for in this variation.

189 Red Miracle Slushy

This is a fat-free slushy made with crushed ice and a fabulous combination of red fruits.

INGREDIENTS

320 g (11 oz) seeded and chopped watermelon

120 g (4 ¼ oz) strawberries, hulled

Juice of ½ a blood orange

10 to 12 ice cubes

Liquid honey, optional

Put the watermelon, strawberries and orange juice in a blender and begin to process. Gradually add the ice cubes and continue to process until the mixture is evenly slushy. Sweeten to taste with honey, if desired.

Makes 2 to 3 glasses

HANDY TIP

For a thicker slush, use up to 20 ice cubes.

Variations

190 WATERMELON AND CUCUMBER SLUSHY

Make the Red Miracle Slushy, replacing the strawberries and blood orange juice with 1 small cucumber and the juice of 2 limes.

Handy tip: If you think that the cucumber has been waxed, then peel before use.

191 WATERMELON AND CANTALOUPE SLUSHY

Prepare the Red Miracle Slushy, replacing the strawberries with 150 g (5 ½ oz) chopped cantaloupe and 4 mint leaves.

Handy tip: This is a great recipe for using leftover melons.

192 WATERMELON AND STRAWBERRY COOLER

Process the fruits for the Red Miracle Slushy through a juice extractor; omit the ice. Sweeten with honey, to taste.

Handy tip: You can substitute raspberries for up to half of the strawberries for a slightly less sweet drink.

193 WATERMELON AND CANTALOUPE COOLER

Take the fruits for the Watermelon and Cantaloupe Slushy variation, then process through a juice extractor; omit the ice. Sweeten with honey, to taste.

Serving tip: Serve in a hollowed-out watermelon shell.

194 FENNEL-FLAVOURED WATERMELON COOLER

Make the Watermelon and Strawberry Cooler variation, replacing the strawberries with ½ a fennel bulb.
Shopping tip: Don't buy fennel if the stalks look brown or are wilting. The outer skin should be white-green and firm.

195 SPICED WATERMELON COOLER

Make the Watermelon and Strawberry Cooler variation and stir in ¼ teaspoon ground cinnamon and a pinch of ground cardamom to the finished drink.
Serving tip: Adding a little spice adds to the sophistication of this drink, making it a great juice to serve at adult parties.

196 RED MIRACLE SMOOTHIE

Make the Red Miracle Slushy or the Watermelon and Cantaloupe Slushy, omitting the ice. Replace with 125 ml (4 ¼ fl oz) vanilla yoghurt.
Handy tip: Frozen strawberries can be used in place of fresh berries in this recipe.

197 RED ORANGE SLUSHY

Make the Red Miracle Slushy, omitting the watermelon and using the juice of 6 blood oranges.
Shopping tip: Blood oranges have a limited season: January and February in the northern hemisphere and August to October in the southern hemisphere.

198 Cleansing Juice

Try this juice to help detoxify your system when you are feeling slightly the worse for wear. Its light flavour means that you can help cleanse the body while enjoying a refreshing drink.

INGREDIENTS

2 apples
120 g (4 ¼ oz) peeled and chopped
   honeydew melon
½ small cucumber

15 sprigs watercress
1 tbsp wheatgrass powder,
   optional

Put the apples, melon, cucumber and watercress through a juice extractor. Pour into a glass, whisk in the wheatgrass powder, if desired and serve immediately.

Makes 1 serving

HANDY TIP

The high water content of cucumber makes it an excellent base vegetable in green smoothies and juices.

Variations

199 CUCUMBER AND WATERCRESS JUICE

Make the Cleansing Juice, replacing the apples and melon with an extra ½ cucumber.
Nutritional tip: Cucumber is a moderate source of vitamin A, iron and potassium.

200 APPLE AND MELON JUICE

Prepare the Cleansing Juice, replacing the cucumber and watercress with another apple and an extra 120 g (4 ¼ oz) chopped melon.

201 APPLE AND CUCUMBER JUICE

Make the Cleansing Juice, replacing the watercress and melon with an extra ½ cucumber.
Handy tip: This is one of the most basic and most cleansing juices.

202 CUCUMBER AND MINT CLEANSER

Make this cleanser by putting 1 whole cucumber, ¼ peeled lemon and a sprig of mint leaves through a juice extractor. Serve immediately.

203 PEAR CLEANSER

Prepare the Cleansing Juice, replacing the apples with 2 quartered pears.
Shopping tip: When pears are ripe, the flesh at the stem end will give slightly when gently pressed. Avoid over-ripe pears as they deteriorate quickly.

DANDELION CLEANSER

Replace the watercress in the Cleansing Juice with the roots and leaves of 2 young dandelions.
Nutritional tip: Dandelion is especially good for the liver and garden dandelions are fine when not sprayed with insecticide.

CUCUMBER AND ORANGE CLEANSER

Make the Cleansing Juice, replacing 1 apple and the watercress with 2 peeled and chopped oranges and a small bunch of mint.
Nutritional tip: You could add 2 teaspoons flaxseed oil for the benefit of its omega-3 fatty acids.

GUAVA CLEANSER

Replace 1 apple and the watercress with 2 guavas when making the Cleansing Juice recipe.
Shopping tip: If you buy guava juice or nectar, select the unsweetened varieties.

CLEANSING SMOOTHIE

Peel and core the apples and peel the cucumber; put in a blender with all the ingredients for the Cleansing Juice. Add 175 ml (6 fl oz) almond milk and a few drops of almond extract and process until smooth. Sweeten with liquid honey, if desired.

CLEANSING SMOOTHIE WITH AVOCADO

Replace the melon in the Cleansing Smoothie variation with ½ a peeled and stoned avocado.
Handy tip: Avocado is a good thickener in smoothies.

209 Grapefruit, Basil and Strawberry Crush

Three fresh foods with very different flavours – acidic, herbal and sweet – meld surprisingly well because of their shared aromatic quality.

INGREDIENTS

2 grapefruit, peeled and chopped
50 g (1 ¾ oz) strawberries
6 fresh basil leaves

Put the grapefruit and strawberries through a juice extractor. Pour into a blender with the basil and blend for 30 seconds. Pour into a glass and serve immediately.

Makes 1 glass

HEALTH WARNING

With some medications, including certain chemotherapies and calcium-channel blockers, grapefruit should be avoided. Seek medical advice if in doubt or make one of the orange-based variations.

variations

210 ORANGE, BASIL AND STRAWBERRY CRUSH

Make the Grapefruit, Basil and Strawberry Crush, replacing the grapefruit with 3 peeled and chopped oranges.
Nutritional tip: Basil is known as a soporific herb, which means that it is good at inducing a relaxed state of mind.

211 MANDARIN, BASIL AND STRAWBERRY CRUSH

Make the Grapefruit, Basil and Strawberry Crush, replacing the grapefruit with 5 peeled and chopped mandarin oranges.
Interesting fact: Crosses between mandarins and other citrus include the clementine, satsuma and tangerine.

212 APPLE, BASIL AND STRAWBERRY CRUSH

Make the Grapefruit, Basil and Strawberry Crush, replacing the grapefruit with 3 quartered apples.
Handy tip: To minimise the risk of the juicer clogging up, alternate the apple and the strawberries when juicing.

213 PINEAPPLE, BASIL AND STRAWBERRY CRUSH

Make the Grapefruit, Basil and Strawberry Crush, replacing the grapefruit with ⅓ of a pineapple, peeled and chopped.
Handy tip: Substitute 150 g (5 ¼ oz) tinned pineapple chunks in natural juices if you do not have fresh pineapple.

214 PINEAPPLE, SAGE AND STRAWBERRY CRUSH

Make the Pineapple, Basil and Strawberry Crush variation, replacing the basil with sage leaves.
Nutritional tip: Menopausal women may appreciate that sage is said to alleviate hot flashes – but breastfeeding women should avoid.

215 Tropical Defender

Great for the digestive system, the skin, the eyes and the hair, this juice will make you glow with tropical health.

INGREDIENTS

½ pineapple, peeled
½ small papaya, peeled
1 small mango, stoned and peeled
Filtered or mineral water or orange
   juice, to taste

Process all the fruit through a juice extractor and pour into a glass. This makes a thick juice, so thin to taste with water or orange juice. Serve immediately.

Makes 1 glass

HANDY TIP

There is no need to remove the seeds from the papaya before juicing.

Variations

216 PASSIONATE DEFENDER

Make the Tropical Defender, replacing the papaya with the pulp of two passion fruits.
Serving tip: The passion fruit pulp looks attractive drizzled on the top of the drink as a garnish.

217 ZINGY TROPICAL DEFENDER

Make the Tropical Defender and add 2.5-cm (1-inch) of peeled ginger with the other ingredients.
Nutritional tip: Adding a tablespoon of flaxseed oil to this recipe makes it a good juice for joint health.

218 TROPICAL COCONUT DEFENDER

Prepare the Tropical Defender and thin down the juice with coconut water instead of filtered or mineral water.
Handy tip: Alternatively, thin the juice with 2 tablespoons coconut milk mixed with water.

219 TROPICAL SALAD

Prepare the Tropical Defender, adding 320 g (11 oz) seeded and chopped watermelon and omitting the water.
Serving tip: This juice is a lovely orangey yellow colour and would look great in a multicoloured painted glass.

TANGY TROPICAL DEFENDER

220

Prepare the Tropical Defender, replacing the water with clementine juice.
Handy tip: Pomegranate is another juice that would be delicious as a thinner in this drink.

BERRY TROPICAL DEFENDER

221

Prepare the Tropical Defender, replacing the papaya with 150 g (5 ¼ oz) blueberries or raspberries. Thin with water, if desired.
Serving tip: Juice the pineapple and mango first and thin slightly with water, then juice the berries. Carefully pour the berry juice over the top, retaining the layered effect.

TROPICAL SOOTHER

222

Prepare the Tropical Defender, replacing the papaya with 150 g (5 ¼ oz) red grapes. Thin with the water, if desired.
Handy tip: Red grapes are very watery so they dilute the thick juice naturally. They also add more natural fruit sugar to this drink.

TROPICAL NECTARINE DEFENDER

223

Prepare the Tropical Defender, replacing the papaya with 1 large stoned nectarine.
Handy tip: Nectarines yield more juice than peaches, so if you substitute peaches you may have to add more liquid.

TROPICAL SMOOTHIE

224

Make the Tropical Defender in a blender, adding 75 ml (2 ½ fl oz) each of coconut yoghurt and orange juice.
Handy tip: You could also use 150 ml (5 fl oz) coconut milk in this recipe instead of the yoghurt and juice.

225 Pomegranate and Aloe Juice

Aloe vera contains a myriad of health-promoting nutrients, but most people find it is unpleasant to drink on its own. Mix it into a smoothie though and you are on to a nutritional winner.

INGREDIENTS

2 medium pomegranates

1 lime, peeled and chopped

1 to 2 tbsp aloe vera gel

Approximately 2 tsp caster sugar, to taste

To remove the seeds from the pomegranate, roll the pomegranate over the work surface with the flat of your hand applying a gentle pressure. Cut off the top and bottom, cut into wedges, then turn inside out to release the seeds. Discard the membrane sticking to the seeds. Process the seeds through a juicer with the lime. Stir in the aloe vera gel followed by the sugar, to taste.

Makes 1 large or 2 small glasses

NUTRITIONAL TIP

Begin with 1 tablespoon aloe vera gel, increasing to 2 tablespoons as the body gets used to it. See tip on page 35 on use when breastfeeding.

Variations

226 POMEGRANATE, FIG AND ALOE JUICE

Make the Pomegranate and Aloe Juice, replacing 1 pomegranate with 2 halved fresh figs.
Handy tip: One medium pomegranate should yield 75 to 115 g (2 ½ to 4 oz) of whole seeds, resulting in 125 ml (4 ¼ fl oz) juice.

227 POMEGRANATE, BLUEBERRY AND ALOE JUICE

Replace 1 pomegranate with 225 g (8 oz) blueberries or 125 ml (4 ¼ fl oz) blueberry juice when making the Pomegranate and Aloe Juice.
Shopping tip: Blueberry juice can be bought as a concentrate from health food and good supermarkets.

228 PINEAPPLE, BLUEBERRY, GINGER AND ALOE JUICE

Make the juice from ⅔ of a peeled and chopped fresh pineapple and 300 g (10 ½ oz) blueberries; alternatively use 240 ml (8 fl oz) pineapple and 125 ml (4 ¼ fl oz) blueberry juice. Stir the aloe vera gel into the combined juice.
Nutritional tip: Aloe vera is a potent anti-inflammatory, a great antioxidant, good for the digestion and promotes recovery after exercise.

229 POMEGRANATE, ACAI AND ALOE JUICE

Prepare the Pomegranate and Aloe Juice, adding 60 ml (2 fl oz) acai berry purée to the pomegranate juice with 60 ml (2 fl oz) filtered or mineral water.
Shopping tip: Acai berry purée is available in pouches from health food shops and online.

230 SIMPLY GOOD BERRY JUICE

Prepare the Pomegranate and Aloe Juice, replacing 1 pomegranate with 50 g (1 ¾ oz) each of blueberries, strawberries and raspberries. Omit the aloe vera gel.
Shopping tip: Aloe Vera is available in leaf form in some areas where it is found in health food shops or international markets.

231 Broccoli, Pear and Green Juice

The pears make this juice moderately sweet, balancing out the earthy taste of the broccoli. Don't be alarmed at the amount of broccoli here, it only yields around 2 tablespoons juice.

INGREDIENTS

100 g (3 ½ oz) broccoli florets and chopped stems

2 medium-sized apples, roughly chopped

2 medium-sized pears, roughly chopped

2 celery stalks

115 g (4 oz) crushed ice

Process the broccoli, apples, pears and celery through a juice extractor. Divide the ice between the glasses and pour over the juice. Serve immediately.

Makes 2 glasses

NUTRITIONAL TIP

If you eat only one vegetable, for your health's sake, make it broccoli. Eating it raw protects its abundance of nutrients.

Variations

232 BROCCOLI, KIWI AND GREEN CLEANSER

Make the Broccoli, Pear and Green Juice, replacing 1 pear with 2 peeled kiwi fruits.
Health tip: Kiwi fruits are good digestive aids and are effective in cleansing drinks.

233 ASPARAGUS, APPLE AND GREEN CLEANSER

Make the Broccoli, Pear and Green Juice, replacing the broccoli with 170 g (6 oz) asparagus tips.
Nutritional tip: Asparagus is unusual among vegetables for being high in vitamin A.

234 BROCCOLI, CARROT AND ORANGE CLEANSER

Prepare the Broccoli, Pear and Green Juice, replacing the pears with 3 trimmed carrots and ½ a peeled and chopped orange.
Serving tip: Broccoli has a natural affinity to orange juice. Garnish this drink with a little grated orange zest.

235 BROCCOLI, GRAPE AND GREEN CLEANSER

Prepare the Broccoli, Pear and Green Juice, replacing the pears with 300 g (10 ½ oz) red grapes.
Handy tip: Alternate putting broccoli and apple through the extractor to keep the juicer flowing smoothly.

236 High-Fibre Immune Booster

This blended drink contains a wealth of essential vitamins and minerals with a good dose of fibre, proteins and oils.

INGREDIENTS

240 ml (8 fl oz) orange juice,
    preferably freshly squeezed
1 banana, peeled and chopped
1 tbsp grated peeled fresh ginger or
    ¼ tsp ground ginger

1 tbsp lemon juice
1 garlic clove
1 tbsp flax oil
1 tbsp lecithin granules

Put all the ingredients in a blender and process until smooth. Pour into a glass and serve immediately.

Makes 1 glass

NUTRITIONAL TIP

Lecithin is a common compound found in cells of all living organisms and is vital for proper biological function. It is thought to be particularly helpful in the treatment of dementia, liver conditions and for boosting the immune system.

variations

CREAMY IMMUNE BOOSTER

Replace the banana in the High-Fibre Immune Booster with 125 ml (4 ¼ fl oz) natural strawberry or cherry yoghurt.

Handy tip: Most fruit yoghurts will work in this recipe, but don't forget that they contain sugar and add to the overall calories.

HIGH-FIBRE STRAWBERRY BOOSTER

Use only ½ a banana and add 75 g (2 ½ oz) strawberries when making the High-Fibre Immune Booster.

Handy tip: Raspberries, blueberries, or stoned cherries would be good if you want a change from strawberries.

HIGH-FIBRE CRANBERRY BOOSTER

Use only ½ a banana and add 75 g (2 ½ oz) cranberry sauce when making the High-Fibre Immune Booster.

Handy tip: Cranberries are extremely sour so using cranberry sauce adds a little sweetness to the drink.

PROTEIN FIBRE BOOSTER

Add 1 tablespoon spirulina or protein powder to the finished High-Fibre Immune Booster.

Interesting fact: Spirulina was harvested by the Aztecs who called it *tecuitlatl*. In their stories of the conquest, Cortés' soldiers mentioned cakes made from spirulina.

241 Citrus Liver Flush

The liver has a great deal to cope with given the modern lifestyle and diet. This citrus mixture is designed to give the liver an antioxidant and nutrient cleanup.

INGREDIENTS

1 grapefruit	1 tbsp flax oil
2 lemons	Generous pinch ground cumin
1 garlic clove, crushed	Pinch ground cayenne
2.5-cm (1-inch) piece ginger, peeled and grated	Liquid honey or agave syrup, optional
2 mint leaves	
150 ml (5 fl oz) filtered or mineral water	

Squeeze the juice from the grapefruit and lemons. Put in a glass. With the motor running, drop the garlic clove into the blender to fine chop, followed by the ginger, mint leaves and water. Drain this liquid through a nonmetallic sieve into the glass. Add the flax oil, cumin and cayenne and mix well. Sweeten with honey or agave syrup, if desired.

Makes 1 glass

SERVING TIP

This juice is best without the sweetener – try it first without and see if you really find it necessary.

242 White Tea and Ginseng Smoothie

White tea is the least processed tea available, so it retains the highest level of the antioxidants that fight free radicals in the body. The buds and small early leaves are picked from the tea bushes and then steamed, dried and slightly oxidised to produce a more subtly flavoured tea than green or black tea, where the leaves are rolled and left to oxidise for longer.

INGREDIENTS

1 tsp white tea leaves or 1 white tea bag

1 tsp sliced ginseng root or ginseng powder

240 ml (8 fl oz) very hot, not boiling, water

1 small wedge honeydew melon, peeled, seeded and chopped

2 slices pineapple, peeled, cored and chopped

150 ml (5 fl oz) orange juice, preferably freshly squeezed

Put the tea leaves or bag in a teapot or heatproof jug, add the ginseng and pour over the water. Steep for 2 to 3 minutes. Drain, if using tea leaves and ginseng root, or remove tea bag. Leave to cool.

Pour the cooled tea into the blender, then add the melon, pineapple and orange juice and process until smooth. Pour into glasses and serve immediately.

Makes 2 glasses

HANDY TIP

As with green tea, white tea is best brewed from very hot but not boiling water, which damages and scalds the delicate leaves.

Variations

243 WHITE TEA AND GINGER SMOOTHIE

Prepare the White Tea and Ginseng Smoothie, replacing the ginseng with 1 tablespoon grated ginger or 1 teaspoon powdered ginger.

244 WHITE TEA AND ECHINACEA SMOOTHIE

Make the tea in the White Tea and Ginseng Smoothie, replacing the ginseng with 1 teaspoon white tea, 1 teaspoon echinacea root or powder and ¼ teaspoon grated ginger.
Interesting fact: Echinacea acts as a natural antibiotic.

245 WHITE TEA, GUAVA AND GINSENG SMOOTHIE

Make the White Tea and Ginseng Smoothie, adding 1 ripe guava with the other fruit.
Nutritional tip: These tropical fruits give a huge nutrient burst when combined.

246 WHITE TEA, PASSION FRUIT AND GINSENG SMOOTHIE

Make the White Tea and Ginseng Smoothie, adding the sieved pulp of 1 passion fruit with the other fruit.
Shopping tip: The more wrinkly and the blacker the passion fruit, the more juicy it is likely to be.

247 WHITE TEA AND CHERRY SMOOTHIE

Make the White Tea and Ginseng Smoothie, replacing the pineapple with 150 g (5 ¼ oz) stoned cherries.
Handy tip: You can use frozen cherries in this smoothie.

248 WHITE TEA AND RASPBERRY SMOOTHIE

Make the White Tea and Ginseng Smoothie, replacing the pineapple with 150 g (5 ¼ oz) raspberries.

Handy tip: If you don't like raspberry seeds, drain this smoothie through a nonmetallic sieve before serving.

249 Ayurveda Detoxifying Tea

Drinking warm water helps flush toxins out of the body through the urine. This tea also contains spices used in traditional Ayurvedic healing for their digestive properties – it tastes good, too.

INGREDIENTS

1 L (1 ¾ pt) boiling water

½ tsp coriander seeds

½ tsp fennel seeds

¼ tsp cumin seeds

4 cardamom pods, lightly crushed

Pour the boiling water into a teapot or heatproof jug, add the spices and steep for 10 minutes. Drain and drink warm.

Makes 950 ml (32 fl oz)

HANDY TIP

You can keep the tea warm in a thermos flask.

Restorative Drinks

When you are feeling low in energy or spirit, getting the juicer or blender out might not be your top priority, but try it and you will discover that the results make the effort worthwhile. There are a wide selection of drinks in this chapter to help you out of the hole. If you've a cold coming on, then it's a vitamin C boost that you need or a dose of echinacea. For upset stomachs, nothing is better than ginger and, to purify the blood, beetroot juice is just the thing. There are a selection of good general tonics in this chapter as well as more specific ones that help in the battle against winter ailments, digestive upsets and stress.

250 Maxi 'C'

This drink is the ultimate pick-me-up for when you feel a cold coming on. It's packed full of vitamin C in its strongest and purest form.

INGREDIENTS

150 g (5 ¼ oz) blueberries or
  blackcurrants
150 g (5 ¼ oz) cherries or
  redcurrants
2 kiwi fruit, peeled
2 oranges, peeled and
  chopped

Put the blueberries, cherries, kiwi fruit and oranges through a juice extractor. Pour into a glass and serve immediately.

Makes 1 glass

HANDY TIP

There are a great many wild, edible berry varieties; this recipe can change with the seasons by substituting in ones you scavenge or find at a farmers' market.

Variations

251   SUPER 'C'

Replace the blueberries and cherries in the Maxi 'C' recipe with 150 g (5 ¼ oz) blackberries and 120 g (4 ¼ oz) strawberries.
Handy tip: Blackberries are abundant in autumn; pick them directly into small plastic bags and put them in the freezer. Because you'll be using them for juices, you don't have to freeze them all separately first as it doesn't matter if they all stick together.

254   KIWI FRUIT AND ORANGE JUICE

Make the Maxi 'C,' omitting the blueberries and cherries and increasing the quantity of kiwi fruit to 4 and the oranges to 3.
Handy tip: If you have a cold, it is suggested that you drink lots of fluids, including both water and juices.

252   TROPICAL 'C'

Replace the blueberries and cherries in the Maxi 'C' recipe with 210 g (7 ½ oz) chopped mango and 225 g (8 oz) chopped papaya.
Interesting fact: Papaya is also called pawpaw.

255   UGLI 'C'

Make the Maxi 'C,' replacing the oranges with 1 large peeled and chopped ugli fruit.
Interesting fact: Ugli fruit is a cross between a grapefruit, a Seville orange and a tangerine.

253   HEALTH PLUS 'C'

Make the Maxi 'C,' replacing the kiwi fruit with another orange.
Nutritional tip: Studies indicate that polyphenols in oranges protect against viral infections.

256   GREAT 'C'

Make the Maxi 'C,' replacing the oranges with 2 small grapefruit.
Nutritional tip: Grapefruit pith contains bioflavonoids, so don't remove the pith when juicing in order to retain useful antioxidants.

257 Cold Remedy

Manuka honey has antibacterial properties and is used to soothe cold symptoms and speed up your recovery.

INGREDIENTS

2 lemons, peeled and chopped
2-cm (¾-inch) piece ginger, peeled

1 tbsp manuka honey
175 ml (6 fl oz) boiling water
Sprig of fresh rosemary

Process the lemons and ginger through a juice extractor. Put into a large mug and mix with the manuka honey, boiling water and rosemary. Let steep for 5 minutes and drink while still warm.

Makes 1 mug

INTERESTING FACT

Manuka honey is tested and certified for its antibacterial properties. Honey with an AMK (Active Manuka Honey) rating of 10 or more should be chosen for medicinal purposes.

Variations

258 ORANGE COLD REMEDY

Make the Cold Remedy, replacing the lemons with 1 large peeled and chopped orange.
Family tip: Children often like this drink better than the Cold Remedy containing sharp lemon juice.

259 ORANGE AND LEMON COLD REMEDY

Prepare the Cold Remedy, replacing 1 lemon with 1 orange.
Serving tip: Double the recipe and take this soothing drink to work in a thermos.

260 GRAPEFRUIT COLD REMEDY

Make the Cold Remedy, replacing the lemons with 1 peeled, chopped grapefruit.
Handy tip: Ruby grapefruit would be delicious in this drink.

261 COUGH REMEDY

Prepare the Cold Remedy, or any of the variations, omitting rosemary and replacing it with 2 sprigs of thyme.
Handy tip: Thyme has long been known as an expectorant, which makes coughs more productive.

262 Thandai

This Indian drink is made for the Indian festival of *Holi*, a spring festival also known as the festival of love. It is renowned for its cooling and health-giving properties.

INGREDIENTS

1 L (1 ¾ pt) whole milk	½ tsp cardamom seeds
40 g (1 ½ oz) blanched almonds	20 white peppercorns
1 tbsp pumpkin seeds	60 g (2 oz) icing sugar
2 tbsp poppy seeds	A few saffron strands
2 tbsp fennel seeds	

Boil the milk and leave to cool. Meanwhile, in a small food processor bowl or coffee grinder, grind the almonds, pumpkin, poppy, fennel and cardamom seeds and the white peppercorns to a powder. Add the ground almond-spice mixture to the cooled milk and mix well. Refrigerate the mixture for at least 2 hours or overnight to infuse.

Drain the mixture through a fine sieve or cheesecloth, add the sugar and mix well. Serve chilled, garnished with a few sprigs of saffron.

Makes 6 glasses

HANDY TIP

Indian sweets and drinks are very sweet, so add the sugar to suit your taste.

Variations

263 THANDAI WITH ROSE WATER

Add 1 ½ tablespoons of rose water with the sugar when making the Thandai. Omit the saffron and instead garnish with dried rose petals.
Shopping tip: Rose petals can be purchased at health food and international food stores.

264 THANDAI WITH ORANGE FLOWER WATER

Prepare the Thandai, adding 1 ½ tablespoons of orange flower water with the sugar.
Interesting fact: In Morocco, orange flower water is given to arriving guests to use to wash their hands before a meal.

265 THANDAI WITH ANISE

Make the Thandai, replacing the fennel seed with anise seed.
Serving tip: Thandai drinks are served when the temperatures are high and are renowned for their cooling properties.

266 ALMOND WATER THANDAI

Make the Thandai, replacing the milk with filtered or mineral water. There is no need to boil the water.

267 Fat-Burner Smoothie

Strictly speaking, this smoothie doesn't burn fat. Guarana, however, is said to speed up the metabolism, so it will definitely help maximise your digestive efficiency, especially if combined with exercise.

INGREDIENTS

40 g (1 ½ oz) strawberries, hulled

40 g (1 ½ oz) raspberries

40 g (1 ½ oz) blueberries

40 g (1 ½ oz) cranberries

60 ml (2 fl oz) apple juice

1 tsp guarana powder

1 tbsp aloe vera juice

Put all the ingredients into a blender and blend for 1 minute or until smooth. Pour into a glass and serve immediately.

Makes 1 glass

HANDY TIP

Because guarana contains caffeine, it can be a good pick-me-up if you are feeling tired or lacking in energy.

Variations

268 FAT-BURNER SMOOTHIE WITH GREEN TEA

Make the Fat-Burner Smoothie, replacing the apple juice with 60 ml (2 fl oz) diluted, cooled, green tea.
Handy tip: You could use white tea in this variation.

269 BERRY APPLE SMOOTHIE

Prepare the Fat-Burner Smoothie, omitting the aloe vera juice and the guarana.
Nutritional tip: This is the version for children since it is inadvisable to give them nutritional supplements without professional advice.

270 DAIRY FAT-BURNER SMOOTHIE

Make the Fat-Burner Smoothie, replacing the apple juice with 60 ml (2 fl oz) plain yoghurt.
Serving tip: This creamy variation is delicious as a breakfast smoothie.

271 DAIRY-FREE CREAMY BERRY SMOOTHIE

Make the Fat-Burner Smoothie, replacing the apple juice with 60 g (2 oz) silken tofu.
Nutritional tip: Silken tofu is a good source of protein.

272 FAT-BURNER SMOOTHIE WITH GINGER

Make the Fat-Burner Smoothie and add 1 teaspoon peeled and grated ginger before blending.
Serving tip: As an alternative to grated ginger, use 2 teaspoons ginger syrup. Note that the resulting drink will be a little sweeter.

273 BLUEBERRY FAT-BURNER SMOOTHIE

Make the Fat-Burner Smoothie, replacing the berries with 150 g (5 ¼ oz) of blueberries.
Handy tip: Turn the blender up to full speed slowly – this allows the big chunks to break up more effectively.

274 ORANGE, BERRY FAT-BURNER SMOOTHIE

Make the Fat-Burner Smoothie, replacing the apple juice with 60 ml (2 fl oz) orange juice.
Serving tip: Garnish this drink with a twist of citrus made from a thin slice of orange slit into the centre and twisted into a figure-eight shape.

275 POMEGRANATE, BERRY FAT-BURNER SMOOTHIE

Make the Fat-Burner Smoothie, replacing the cranberries and blueberries with 75 g (2 ½ oz) pomegranate seeds.

276 Nectarine, clementine and orange Flower Water Juice

The soothing flavour of orange flower water completes a fabulous fruity trio in this drink.

INGREDIENTS

2 nectarines, halved and stoned
2 clementines, peeled
½ tsp orange flower water

Put the nectarines and clementines through a juice extractor. Pour into a glass, mix in the orange flower water and serve immediately.

Makes 1 glass

INTERESTING FACT

Orange flower water is a byproduct from the distillation of orange blossoms for neroli essential oil, which is used in the beauty industry and in traditional medicine.

Variations

277 MANGO, CLEMENTINE AND ORANGE FLOWER WATER JUICE

Prepare the Nectarine, Clementine and Orange Flower Water Juice, replacing the nectarines with 210 g (7 ½ oz) peeled and chopped mango.
Serving tip: These juices can be drizzled over vanilla ice cream. For a thicker juice use just one clementine.

278 PINEAPPLE, CLEMENTINE AND ORANGE FLOWER WATER JUICE

Prepare the Nectarine, Clementine and Orange Flower Water Juice, replacing the nectarines with 225 g (8 oz) peeled and chopped pineapple.
Interesting fact: Traditionally orange flower water is renowned for its uplifting qualities and is thought to relieve stress and anxiety.

279 PAPAYA, CLEMENTINE AND ORANGE FLOWER WATER JUICE

Prepare the Nectarine, Clementine and Orange Flower Water Juice, replacing the nectarines with 225 g (8 oz) peeled and chopped papaya.
Nutritional tip: Papain, found in papaya, is an enzyme that helps in natural digestion.

280 PEACH, CLEMENTINE AND ORANGE FLOWER WATER JUICE

Make the Nectarine, Clementine and Orange Flower Water Juice, replacing the nectarines with 2 peaches.
Handy tip: If you are using flat or doughnut peaches, use 3 peaches.

281 NECTARINE, CLEMENTINE AND ROSE WATER JUICE

Make the Nectarine, Clementine and Orange Flower Water Juice, omitting the orange flower water and mixing in ½ teaspoon rose water.
Serving tip: These drinks always feel very feminine and are perfect to serve at a baby shower.

282 LEBANESE ORANGE FLOWER WATER DRINK

Stir 2 to 3 teaspoons orange flower water into 240 ml (8 fl oz) very hot water. Sweeten with about 1 teaspoon honey, to taste. Drink while warm.
Serving tip: If you are serving this drink variation to a friend, garnish with the small leaves and the tip of a mint sprig.

283 ORANGE AND ORANGE FLOWER WATER JUICE

Stir 1 teaspoon orange flower water into 240 ml (8 fl oz) freshly squeezed orange juice.
Handy tip: This also works well with ruby or pink grapefruit juice.

284 Green Restoration Smoothie

Avocado, as well as being a delicious addition to a smoothie, contains folic acid, which can reduce cholesterol levels, and, is high in folate, which helps to keep a healthy heart.

INGREDIENTS

½ medium avocado, peeled, stoned and chopped	1 small bunch parsley
	5 tsp lemon juice
1 small cucumber, peeled, seeded and chopped	1 tsp olive oil
	240 ml (8 fl oz) crushed ice

Put the avocado, chopped cucumber, parsley, lemon juice and oil in a blender and process until smooth. Add the crushed ice and process until smooth. Drain into glasses and serve immediately.

Makes 2 glasses

HANDY TIP

Avocado goes brown quickly. To avoid this keep the avocado stone in the bowl with the chopped avocado flesh until processing.

Variations

285 GREEN RESTORATION SMOOTHIE WITH LIME AND MINT

Make the Green Restoration Smoothie, replacing the lemon with lime and the parsley with 8 large mint leaves.
Health tip: Make this when pregnant and avoiding parsley.

286 GREEN RESTORATION MEXICANA SMOOTHIE

Make the Green Restoration Smoothie with Lime and Mint variation. Add 1 teaspoon fresh, chopped jalapeño flesh – no seeds.
Handy tip: For a milder flavour add 1 to 2 teaspoons sweet chili sauce.

287 GREEN RESTORATION SMOOTHIE WITH LIME AND BASIL

Make the Green Restoration Smoothie, replacing the lemon with lime and the parsley with 6 large basil leaves.
Handy tip: Reserve some cucumber rind for a garnish.

288 ALMOND GREEN RESTORATION

Make the Green Restoration Smoothie using ⅓ of the cucumber and 8 parsley leaves and adding 175 ml (6 fl oz) almond milk.
Nutritional tip: Avocado is a good antioxidant.

289 CARIBBEAN GREEN RESTORATION SMOOTHIE

Make the Green Restoration Smoothie using ⅓ of the cucumber and omitting the parsley. Instead mix in 175 ml (6 fl oz) coconut milk.
Nutritional tip: Coconut milk is high in calories.

291 Twist in the Tail

Ginger has remarkable health benefits, so try this deliciously spicy drink to settle your stomach.

INGREDIENTS

2 large bananas

2 limes, grated zest and juice

240 ml (8 fl oz) ginger beer

1 tsp grated, peeled ginger

Maple syrup, to taste

Put the bananas, lime juice and zest, half of the ginger beer and the grated ginger in a blender. Process until smooth. Divide between two tall glasses and top up with the remaining ginger beer. Sweeten with maple syrup, to taste.

Makes 2 glasses

HANDY TIP

If making this drink following a bout of sickness, you may wish to use slightly flat ginger beer.

292 GRAPEFRUIT TWIST IN THE TAIL

Make the Twist in the Tail, replacing the limes with the juice of 1 grapefruit and ½ teaspoon grapefruit zest.
Handy tip: Few recipes call for grapefruit zest, but it imparts a delicious citrus flavour.

290 SPICED CHIA GREEN RESTORATION SMOOTHIE

Make the Green Restoration Smoothie and add 1 teaspoon grated ginger, ½ teaspoon ground turmeric, ¼ teaspoon cinnamon and 2 tablespoons chia seeds.

293 MINTED TWISTER

Make the Twist in the Tail, replacing the ginger and ginger beer with 5 mint leaves and lemon-lime soda.
Handy tip: Use a diet soda to reduce the calorie count.

294 Mango Buttermilk Smoothie

This is a deliciously creamy shake. Those with digestive problems are often advised to drink buttermilk as it is easier to digest than milk.

INGREDIENTS

170 g (6 oz) chopped mango
125 ml (4 ¼ fl oz) buttermilk
1 tsp liquid honey
½ tsp lemon juice
¼ tsp grated lemon zest
75 ml (2 ½ fl oz) crushed ice
2 strawberries, for garnish

Put the mango, buttermilk, honey, lemon juice and zest and crushed ice in a blender and process until smooth. Garnish with strawberries and serve immediately.

Makes 2 glasses

HANDY TIP

Check the labels when purchasing buttermilk as some brands are higher in fat than others.

Variations

295 STRAWBERRY, MANGO BUTTERMILK SMOOTHIE

Make the Mango Buttermilk Smoothie using 85 g (3 oz) chopped mango and 75 g (2 ½ oz) halved strawberries.
Interesting fact: Buttermilk is lower in fat than whole and semi-skimmed milk because the fat has been removed to make butter.

296 BANANA DATE SMOOTHIE

Make the Mango Buttermilk Smoothie, replacing the mango and honey with 1 small chopped banana and 4 soft dates.
Nutritional tip: Buttermilk is a good source of potassium, vitamin B12, calcium and riboflavin.

297 BANANA, VANILLA BUTTERMILK SMOOTHIE

Make the Mango Buttermilk Smoothie, replacing the mango with 1 small chopped banana and a ¼ teaspoon vanilla extract.
Handy tip: For a more extravagant touch, use the scraped seeds of ¼ vanilla bean instead of vanilla extract.

298 BLUEBERRY, MANGO BUTTERMILK SMOOTHIE

Make the Mango Buttermilk Smoothie using 85 g (3 oz) chopped mango and 75 g (2 ½ oz) blueberries.
Serving suggestion: Garnish this smoothie by threading mint leaves and blueberries (alternating) on a toothpick to swizzle in the glasses.

299 PEACH BUTTERMILK SMOOTHIE

Make the Mango Buttermilk Smoothie, replacing the mango with 1 stoned and chopped peach.
Serving suggestion: If you do not like the texture of the peach skin in the smoothie, simply drop the whole peach into boiling water for 1 minute, then dip in cold water and the skin should slip off.

300 PEACH AND BLUEBERRY BUTTERMILK SMOOTHIE

Make the Peach Buttermilk Smoothie using only ½ a peach and adding 40 g (1 ½ oz) blueberries.
Handy tip: Frozen peaches and blueberries may be used in this smoothie if fresh fruits are not on hand.

301 Taste of the East Kefir Smoothie

Kefir is a slightly sour fermented milk that originates in the Caucasus Mountains. It is similar in taste and texture to drinking yoghurt and makes delicious smoothies.

INGREDIENTS

¼ honeydew melon, seeds and rind removed

3 apricots, stoned, skinned and halved

1 small banana, peeled and chopped

2 sprigs of mint

500 ml (17 fl oz) kefir

8 ice cubes

Place all ingredients in the blender and process until smooth. Pour into glasses and serve immediately.

Makes 2 glasses

NUTRITIONAL TIP

Kefir contains about three times as many probiotics as yoghurt. Probiotics are the organisms that help stem the growth of harmful bacteria and boost the immune system.

Variations

302 TASTE OF PUMPKIN KEFIR SMOOTHIE

Make the Taste of the East Kefir Smoothie, replacing the banana, apricots and mint with 125 ml (4 ¼ fl oz) pumpkin purée and 1 teaspoon ground cinnamon or pumpkin pie spice.
Handy tip: Some pumpkin purées are quite thick, so you may need to add a little more kefir or water to thin this smoothie to taste.

303 TASTE OF CHERRIES KEFIR SMOOTHIE

Make the Taste of the East Kefir Smoothie, replacing the apricots with 75 g (2 ½ oz) stoned cherries and a generous pinch of ground cinnamon.
Handy tip: You could use drinking yoghurt in place of kefir in any of these smoothies.

304 TASTE OF PERSIMMON KEFIR SMOOTHIE

Make the Taste of the East Kefir Smoothie, replacing the apricots with 1 large persimmon, skinned and quartered.
Interesting fact: Persimmons, also known as kaki, have a uniquely fragrant flavour, described as a blend of apple, plum and date and have a thick, silky texture.

305 TASTE OF WATERMELON KEFIR SMOOTHIE

Make the Taste of the East Kefir Smoothie, replacing the banana, melon and apricots with 1 wedge of watermelon, ½ a medium orange, peeled and chopped and ½ teaspoon each of vanilla extract and orange zest.
Handy tip: This is a thinner kefir drink than the others here. To thicken it up add 1 tablespoon gelatin powder to the smoothie just before blending.

306 TASTE OF ORANGE DATE KEFIR SMOOTHIE

Make the Taste of the East Kefir Smoothie, replacing the melon and apricots with a medium orange, peeled and chopped, 4 stoned soft dates and a pinch of ground cardamom.
Handy tip: Pre-ground cardamom loses much of its flavour; it's best to grind the seeds fresh from one green cardamom pod using a mortar and pestle.

307 CLASSIC BERRY KEFIR SMOOTHIE

For one serving, put 175 ml (6 fl oz) kefir in a blender with 50 g (1 ¾ oz) each of fresh raspberries, strawberries or blackberries. Blend until smooth. Sweeten with 1 teaspoon liquid honey and a generous pinch of ground cinnamon.
Handy tip: You could use ½ a banana in place of one of the berry types in this recipe.

308 Keep-it-Moving Smoothie

This fibre-rich smoothie will aid your digestive system and, in addition to its health benefits, it tastes wonderful.

INGREDIENTS

1 banana, peeled and chopped
5 prunes, stoned
60 ml (2 fl oz) freshly squeezed
    orange juice
240 ml (8 fl oz) plain yoghurt
1 tbsp crushed flaxseed

Put all the ingredients in a blender and process until smooth. Pour into a glass and serve immediately.

Makes 1 glass

HANDY TIP

Do not substitute flaxseed oil for flaxseed; flaxseed oil is not a constipation remedy.

Variations

309 MIXED FRUIT KEEP-IT-MOVING SMOOTHIE

Prepare the Keep-it-moving Smoothie, omitting the yoghurt and increasing the prunes to 9. Add 175 ml (6 fl oz) apple juice with the other ingredients.
Handy tip: You can use water in place of apple juice if this suits you better.

310 KEEP-IT-MOVING SMOOTHIE WITH PSYLLIUM HUSK

Make the Keep-it-moving Smoothie, replacing the flaxseed with 1 tablespoon psyllium husk powder.
Nutritional tip: Psyllium husks are good for relieving constipation and for keeping things regular.

311 SPINACHY KEEP-IT-MOVING SMOOTHIE

Make the Keep-it-moving Smoothie, adding 25 g (1 oz) baby spinach leaves to the other ingredients.
Serving tip: Chill glasses in the fridge to keep these smoothies nice and cold.

312 FIGGY KEEP-IT-MOVING SMOOTHIE

Make the Keep-it-moving Smoothie, replacing the prunes with two fresh figs and increasing the orange juice to 75 ml (2 ½ fl oz).

313 Echinacea Tea Smoothie

Echinacea is great for warding off colds and the tea makes a clean, refreshing smoothie base.

INGREDIENTS

1 green tea bag
1 tsp dried echinacea root
1 tsp finely chopped ginger
300 ml (10 fl oz) very hot, but
   not boiling, water
1 tsp liquid honey

1 peach or nectarine, skinned,
   stoned and quartered
1 pear, peeled, cored and
   quartered

Put the tea bag in a teapot or heatproof jug, add the echinacea root and ginger and pour over the water. Remove tea bag after 5 minutes, steep for a further 10. Sieve, stir in honey. Leave to cool completely.

Pour the cooled tea into a blender, add the fruit, then process until smooth. Serve immediately.

Makes 2 glasses

HANDY TIP

To speed up the cooling process, add a couple of ice cubes to the tea.

315 ECHINACEA PASSION FRUIT SMOOTHIE

Replace the peach or nectarine with the pulp of two passion fruit, when making the Echinacea Tea Smoothie.

316 ASIAN PEAR ECHINACEA SMOOTHIE

Make the Echinacea Tea Smoothie, replacing the pear with 1 Asian pear.
Handy tip: Asian pears have a very high water content, so they are ideal in smoothies and juices. Their texture is crisp and grainy.

314 ECHINACEA PLUM SMOOTHIE

Replace the peach or nectarine with 3 peeled and stoned plums when making the Echinacea Tea Smoothie.
Handy tip: Plums are a natural laxative.

317 LEMON-GINGER SMOOTHIE

Make the Echinacea Tea Smoothie but omit the green tea, echinacea root and chopped ginger. Make the tea base from 1 lemon-and-ginger fruit tea bag.
Handy tip: This tea base may be used for many recipes.

318 Linden Flower Fruit Charm

Linden flower (also called lime flower) is made into a tea and is a traditional remedy for stress and anxiety. Here, it is combined with delicious fruits that each have a heady, flowery scent of their own. Just looking at this juice will make you feel restored.

INGREDIENTS

1 tsp dried linden (lime) flowers
60 ml (2 fl oz) boiling water
4 apricots, stoned
1 mango, stoned and sliced
1 orange, peeled and chopped

Put the linden flowers in a teapot or heatproof jug and pour over the water. Steep for 10 minutes. Drain and leave to cool.

Process the apricots, mango and orange in a juice extractor. Stir the cooled linden flower infusion in with the juice. Pour into a glass and serve immediately.

Makes 1 glass

HEALTH WARNING

Those with heart disease should not drink linden flower infusion.

Variations

319 LEMON BALM FRUIT CHARM

Make the Linden Flower Fruit Charm, but omit linden flowers. Make the infusion using 1 tablespoon fresh or 1 teaspoon dried lemon balm leaves.
Interesting fact: Lemon balm is good for flatulence!

320 LINDEN SWEET CHARM

Make the Linden Flower Fruit Charm, replacing the mango with 1 quartered apple.
Serving suggestion: For extra visual appeal, garnish this drink with a slice of star fruit.

321 LINDEN SUNNY CHARM

Make the Linden Flower Fruit Charm using only ½ a mango and adding 150 g (5 ½ oz) diced cantaloupe.
Interesting fact: Linden flowers come from the Tilia tree, which is more commonly referred to as a lime tree.

322 LINDEN SOFT CHARM

Make the Linden Flower Fruit Charm, replacing the orange with 150 g (5 ¼ oz) red grapes.
Interesting fact: The colour of the grape juice depends on the colour of the pigments in the grape skin.

323 LINDEN GREEN CHARM

Make the Linden Flower Fruit Charm and process 2 kale leaves with the fruit.
Nutritional tip: Among other nutrients, kale is high in vitamin A, making it good for skin and eyes.

324 Guava To Go-Go Smoothie

Guava has a natural affinity to pineapple and other tropical fruit.

INGREDIENTS

1 guava
1 banana
1 slice of pineapple, chopped
240 ml (8 fl oz) pineapple juice
1 tsp lemon juice
4 ice cubes
1 tbsp liquid honey

Cut the guava in half and scoop out the pulp. Put in the blender together with the banana, chopped pineapple, half of the pineapple juice, the lemon juice and the ice. After the ice is blended, add the honey and the remaining pineapple juice. Pour into a glass and serve immediately.

Makes 1 glass

325 CREAMY GUAVA TO GO-GO SMOOTHIE

Make the Guava to Go-Go Smoothie but reduce the pineapple juice to 125 ml (4 ¼ fl oz). When blending the fruit add 125 ml (4 ¼ fl oz) plain yoghurt. Add the lemon juice after the initial blending.

326 GUAVA AND STRAWBERRIES TO GO-GO SMOOTHIE

Use only ½ a banana and add 75 g (2 ½ oz) of strawberries.
Handy tip: Red and pink guavas make a fantastically bold juice, especially if combined with strawberries or watermelon.

327 Heart Beet Juice

The combination of the red beetroot juice, the fantastic red blood orange juice and the creamy orange from the carrot makes this one of the most stunning juice combinations.

INGREDIENTS

2 medium beetroot, trimmed
  and halved
2 blood oranges (or regular
  oranges), peeled and
  roughly chopped
4 carrots, trimmed

Process the ingredients in a juice extractor and serve immediately.

Makes 2 glasses

NUTRITIONAL TIP

Beetroot juice, which is high in iron, is regarded as a blood purifier and is said to help replenish the body's red blood cells.

Variations

328 HEART BEET BOOSTER JUICE

Prepare the Heart Beet Juice and add the green tops of the beetroot with the other ingredients.
Handy tip: For a scent of herbs, add 2 sprigs of rosemary to the finished drink.

329 HEARTY ZINGER JUICE

Make the Heart Beet Juice and add 4 large romaine lettuce leaves and a 2.5-cm (1-inch) piece of peeled ginger to the juicer.
Handy tip: Romaine is the best lettuce to use in juices because its crisp green leaves contain plenty of liquid.

330 GRAPE HEART BEET JUICE

Make the Heart Beet Juice, replacing 2 carrots with 150 g (5 ¼ oz) red grapes.
Serving tip: Some sports nutritionists advise that beetroot juice enhances physical exercise. Drink this before your next workout and see if it works for you.

331 RED HEART BEET JUICE

Make the Heart Beet Juice, replacing the carrots with two more blood oranges.
Handy tip: As a rough guide, 1 ½ medium beetroot should produce about 240 ml (8 fl oz) juice.

332 Tomato Juice

Sometimes the basics are the best. This simple juice is a real tonic.

INGREDIENTS

8 medium tomatoes
Salt, optional
Pepper, optional
Lemon juice, optional
Worcestershire sauce, optional

Process the tomatoes in a juice extractor. Pour into a glass and season to taste with salt, pepper, lemon juice and/or Worcestershire sauce. Serve immediately.

Makes 1 large or 2 small glasses

Shopping Tip

Get the very best tomatoes you can find: heirloom tomatoes from a farmers' market are often the most tasty. Firm, pale hothouse tomatoes are not worth juicing.

Variations

333 TOMATO JUICE WITH CORIANDER AND LIME

Make the Tomato Juice, replacing the lemon juice and Worcestershire sauce with lime juice and a small bunch of coriander.
Handy tip: You can replace the coriander with parsley, but this is not advised if you are pregnant.

334 TOMATO AND CELERY JUICE

Make the Tomato Juice using 6 tomatoes and 2 celery stalks.
Handy tip: There is no need to trim the leaves from celery stalks when juicing.

335 TOMATO AND PEPPER JUICE

Make the Tomato Juice using 6 tomatoes, 2 seeded red peppers and 1 celery stalk. Replace the lemon juice with lime juice and add 6 basil leaves.
Handy tip: For a more astringent juice, use green peppers.

336 TOMATO SALAD JUICE

Make the Tomato and Pepper Juice variation, replacing 1 pepper with 4 romaine lettuce leaves and 4 radishes.
Handy tip: Discard the leaves from the radishes before juicing.

337 TOMATO AND CARROT JUICE

Prepare the Tomato Juice using 6 tomatoes, 2 trimmed carrots and 1 celery stalk.
Handy tip: Pep up this variation with a few mint, coriander, or basil stalks and a little grated orange zest.

338 TOMATO AND WATERCRESS JUICE

Make the Tomato Juice using 6 tomatoes, 1 bunch of watercress and 1 celery stalk.
Nutritional tip: Both tomatoes and watercress are high in zinc, a trace element that helps make new cells and enzymes, aids digestion and assists with the healing of wounds.

339 TOMATO AND PARSNIP JUICE

Prepare the Tomato Juice using 6 tomatoes, 2 trimmed parsnips and 1 celery stalk.
Handy tip: Parsnips add a creamy texture and an earthy flavour to a vegetable juice.

340 TOMATO AND CUCUMBER JUICE

Make the Tomato Juice using 6 tomatoes, 1 small cucumber and 3 sprigs of mint.
Handy tip: If using an English cucumber rather than a garden cucumber, use only half the cucumber.

341 TOMATO AND ORANGE JUICE

Make the Tomato Juice using 5 tomatoes and 2 small peeled and chopped oranges.
Nutritional tip: This wonderful variation is a combination of two vitamin C-rich fruits!

342 Fabulous Fennel Fusion Juice

Fennel has a delicious liquorice flavour that is quite strong as a stand-alone juice but is fabulous mixed with sweeter fruits such as apples, pears and oranges.

INGREDIENTS

2 small fennel bulbs
2 celery stalks
2 pears, quartered
1 orange, peeled and chopped

Process the ingredients in a juice extractor. Pour into glasses and serve immediately.

Makes 2 glasses

NUTRITIONAL TIP

Fennel juice contains anethol, an essential oil that acts as an anti-inflammaroty and anti-spasmodic. It is therefore good for stomach, bowel and menstrual cramps.

Variations

343 FENNEL AND APPLE FUSION JUICE

Make the Fabulous Fennel Fusion Juice, replacing the pears with 2 green apples.
Interesting fact: Although fennel is described as having an aniseed flavour, the two plants have no common botanical characteristics.

344 FENNEL GINGER FUSION JUICE

Make the Fabulous Fennel Fusion Juice and add a 2.5-cm (1-inch) piece of peeled ginger with the other ingredients.
Serving tip: This is very refreshing with a wrap at lunchtime.

345 FABULOUS FENNEL AND LIME JUICE

Make the Fabulous Fennel Fusion Juice, replacing the orange with 1 lime.
Handy tip: You usually get about 2 tablespoons juice from a lime.

346 FABULOUS FENNEL AND CUCUMBER JUICE

Make the Fabulous Fennel Fusion Juice, replacing the celery with ½ a cucumber.

Handy tip: Once you get the taste for green juices, it is good to begin to reduce the amount of sugar-dense fruit juices you use and move on to the more vegetable-based juices.

347 FABULOUS FENNEL AND KALE JUICE

Make the Fabulous Fennel and Cucumber Juice variation and add 3 kale leaves. Add a 2.5-cm (1-inch) piece of peeled ginger, if desired.

Interesting fact: Cavolo Nero (Tuscan kale), the prized Italian green, is a variety of kale.

348 FABULOUS FENNEL AND CABBAGE JUICE

Make the Fabulous Fennel and Cucumber Juice and add ¼ of a red cabbage.

Nutritional tip: Red cabbage is good at cleaning up the toxins in the body. Don't knock it until you've tried it!

349 Acai-Boosted Frosted Smoothie

This is a vitamin C hit that's second to none in waking up the taste buds and giving you a new burst of life. Acai berries are one of the very best antioxidants out there and good anti-inflammatory agents, too. Because whole acai berries can be hard to find, this recipe uses the bottled juice.

INGREDIENTS

75 g (2 ½ oz) frozen blueberries
75 g (2 ½ oz) frozen strawberries
125 ml (4 ¼ fl oz) acai juice
125 ml (4 ¼ fl oz) pomegranate
   juice
240 ml (8 fl oz) raspberry
   sorbet or sherbet
10 ice cubes

Put all the ingredients in a blender and process until smooth. Pour into a glass and serve immediately with a straw.

Makes 1 glass

HANDY TIP

If you are not going to use all the acai juice within a few days, freeze the rest in muffin tins. Once frozen, store in resealable plastic bags.

Variations

351 ACAI-BOOSTED PEACH SMOOTHIE

Make the Acai-Boosted Frosted Smoothie, replacing the blueberries and strawberries with 200 g (7 oz) frozen cubed peach and the pomegranate juice with orange juice.
Handy tip: If you substitute tinned peaches for the fresh in this variation, select those in natural syrup, drain well and refrigerate before use.

352 ACAI-BOOSTED PINEAPPLE FROSTED SMOOTHIE

Make the Acai-Boosted Frosted Smoothie, replacing the blueberries with 75 g (2 ½ oz) frozen pineapple and the raspberry sorbet or sherbet with orange sorbet or sherbet.
Handy tip: Use the fruit juices straight from the fridge to keep the maximum chill.

353 ACAI-BOOSTED TROPICAL FROSTED SMOOTHIE

Make the Acai-Boosted Frosted Smoothie, replacing the blueberries with 75 g (2 ½ oz) frozen pineapple and the raspberry sorbet or sherbet with coconut sorbet or sherbet.
Handy tip: For a creamy treat, use coconut ice cream.

350 ACAI-BOOSTED, RASPBERRY FROSTED SMOOTHIE

Make the Acai-Boosted Frosted Smoothie, replacing the blueberries with frozen raspberries and the pomegranate juice with orange juice.
Handy tip: Although sherbets and sorbets are similar, sherbets can contain milk, egg whites or gelatin.

354 GOJI-BOOSTED FROSTED SMOOTHIE

Make the Acai-Boosted Frosted Smoothie, replacing the acai berry juice with goji berry juice.
Nutritional tip: Goji is a great antioxidant and is used in natural medicine to reduce cholesterol and blood glucose.

355 Chamomile Mango Soother

Chamomile tea soothes the nervous system and has been used as a relaxing nighttime drink for centuries. Here it is used as the base for a wonderful calming smoothie – just the thing after a stressful day.

INGREDIENTS

1 tsp dried chamomile flowers or 1 chamomile tea bag

60 ml (2 fl oz) very hot, not boiling, water

125 ml (4 ¼ fl oz) soya or almond milk

½ mango, skinned, stoned and quartered

1 tsp peeled and grated ginger

1 tsp liquid honey, optional

Put the dried chamomile flowers or tea bag in a teapot or heatproof jug and pour over the water. Steep for 5 minutes. Drain, if using dried flowers, or remove tea bag. Leave to cool.

Pour the cooled tea into a blender, add the soya or almond milk, mango, ginger and honey, if using, to the blender and process until smooth. Pour into a glass and serve immediately.

Makes 1 glass

HANDY TIP

If you find fresh, unsprayed flowers, use 1 tablespoon, about 10 flowers, to make the tea infusion.

variations

356 CHAMOMILE PAPAYA SOOTHER

Make the Chamomile Mango Soother, replacing the mango with ½ a papaya.
Interesting fact: Chamomile tea is also traditionally used to prevent and treat colds and to protect against bacteria-related illness.

357 CHAMOMILE CANTALOUPE SOOTHER

Make the Chamomile Mango Soother, replacing the mango with 150 g (5 ½ oz) of cantaloupe chunks and ½ a banana, peeled.
Interesting fact: Chamomile is Greek for ground apple and was used by the ancient Greeks as a medicinal staple.

358 CHAMOMILE SILKY MANGO SOOTHER

Prepare the Chamomile Mango Soother, replacing the soya or almond milk with plain or vanilla yoghurt.
Handy tip: You could use any of the herbal teas sold as nighttime soothers in this smoothie.

359 Wheatgrass Pineapple Shot

Wheatgrass is one of the superfoods of our time – with one wheatgrass shot having the same nutritional equivalence as 1 kg (2 ¼ lb) of green leafy vegetables. Wheatgrass aficionados will have a special juicer for this ingredient as it doesn't process well in a centrifugal juice extractor. Three handfuls of fresh wheatgrass will yield 60 ml (2 fl oz). The recommended daily dose is 2 tablespoons, increasing to 60 ml (2 fl oz) over time. For ease of use, this recipe calls for wheatgrass powder.

INGREDIENTS

150 g (5 ¼ oz) pineapple chunks
1 small bunch fresh mint leaves
1 tsp wheatgrass powder,
    or 1 daily dose following
    the manufacturer's
    recommendations

Put the pineapple and mint in a juice extractor and process. Whisk in the wheatgrass powder. Pour into a glass and serve immediately.

Makes 1 small glass

HEALTH WARNING

Taking more than the recommended daily dose of wheatgrass can cause nausea and diarrhea.

Variations

360 WHEATGRASS CARROT SHOT

Put 3 trimmed carrots and ½ a peeled and chopped orange through a juice extractor. Whisk in 1 teaspoon wheatgrass powder and serve immediately.
Shopping tip: You can buy fresh wheatgrass online.

361 WHEATGRASS, ORANGE AND MINT SHOT

Make the Wheatgrass Pineapple Shot, replacing the pineapple with 2 small peeled and chopped oranges.
Handy tip: Always mix wheatgrass into juice for flavour.

362 WHEATGRASS APPLE SHOT

Prepare the Wheatgrass Pineapple Shot, replacing the pineapple and mint with 2 apples and ½ teaspoon cinnamon.
Serving tip: Have your wheatgrass shot shortly before eating a meal.

363 WHEATGRASS TOMATO SHOT

Prepare the Wheatgrass Pineapple Shot, replacing the pineapple with 4 tomatoes.
Handy tip: For extra power, add a garlic clove when juicing the fruit.

364 WHEATGRASS BEETROOT SHOT

Prepare the Wheatgrass Pineapple Shot, replacing the pineapple with 1 medium beetroot and ½ a cucumber.
Shopping tip: Wheatgrass shots are also available frozen.

365 Ginger Shot

Ginger is an essential ingredient in Indian Ayurvedic medicine and has been used in China for more than 2,000 years. It has powerful digestion-aiding properties and is an anti-inflammatory. Given that poor digestion and inflammation are two of our biggest health worries, adding a shot a day may well boost your health.

INGREDIENTS

½ apple
1 lemon, peeled and chopped
5-cm (2-inch) piece ginger, peeled

Process the ingredients through a juice extractor. Pour into a glass and serve immediately.

Makes 1 glass

SERVING TIP

If you have a cold, drink this warm with a little honey.

Variations

367 FLU SHOT

Make the Apple Ginger Shot variation, adding 1 trimmed carrot and ¼ of a peeled lemon.
Nutritional tip: Carrots are high in vitamin A, which is good for the immune system and plays a part in maintaining healthy lungs.

368 CAYENNE, LEMON AND GINGER SHOT

Make the Ginger Shot and add a pinch of cayenne pepper.
Serving tip: Ginger is good for motion sickness, including seasickness, so downing a ginger shot before taking to the waves is a wise precaution.

369 ORANGE GINGER SHOT

Make the Ginger Shot, replacing the apple with 1 peeled and chopped orange.
Handy tip: A clementine or mandarin orange makes a slightly sweeter base for the ginger in this variation.

366 APPLE GINGER SHOT

Make the Ginger Shot but omit the lemon and use a whole large apple.
Handy tip: If you are using organic ginger, there is no need to peel it.

370 GINGER AND TURMERIC SHOT

Make the Ginger Shot, adding a 5-cm (2-inch) piece of turmeric root to the juicer with the other ingredients.
Nutritional tip: Turmeric is a powerful anti-inflammatory and is used to treat a wide range of conditions.

371 Garlic and Lemon Shot

Supercharge yourself with this immune-boosting shot. Garlic is particularly effective as an anti-inflammatory, antibiotic and anti-viral, making it great for a range of ailments.

INGREDIENTS

1 lemon, peeled and chopped
1 to 2 cloves of garlic
Generous pinch cayenne pepper
1 tbsp manuka or liquid honey

Process the lemon and garlic through a juice extractor. Let sit for 10 minutes. Stir in the cayenne pepper and honey. Pour into a glass and serve.

Makes 1 glass

HANDY TIP

If you prefer, press the garlic through a garlic press and mix with the squeezed juice of the lemon, let sit for 10 minutes, then sieve before adding the cayenne pepper and honey.

372 GARLIC AND LIME SHOT

Make the Garlic and Lemon Shot, replacing the lemon with a lime and add 4 sprigs of coriander.

373 ORANGE, GARLIC AND TURMERIC SHOT

Make the Garlic and Lemon Shot, replacing the lemon with an orange and adding a 2.5-cm (1-inch) piece of turmeric root.

Super Energy Boosters

If the moment strikes when you want to reach out for the chocolate bar or the cappuccino, stop! This chapter is full of super-healthy, everyday and exotic vegetable and fruit combinations that will give you an energy boost and revive low blood-sugar levels. Within moments you will feel revived and raring to go and, best of all, you will have done the right thing for your body. There are times when we all skip meals or miss out on a decent breakfast and those are the times when yoghurt- or banana-based smoothies come into their own. After a long day at work, or a challenging workout, leafy green vegetables with a high-iron content are just what we need.

374 Apple Salad Juice

The combination of the acidic sweetness of apples blends particularly well with the earthiness of vegetables. Apples are great for anyone who is feeling run down and they can have an invigorating effect on the skin. These are great starter drinks for those unsure about drinking vegetable juices.

INGREDIENTS

4 apples
15 baby spinach leaves
1 orange or yellow pepper
1 cucumber
½ lime, peeled
5-cm (2-inch) piece ginger, peeled
Pinch nutmeg
1 tsp spirulina powder, optional

Juice the fruits, vegetables and ginger. Stir in the nutmeg. Take 2 tablespoons of this juice and mix it with the spirulina until smooth, then stir into the remaining juice.

Makes 2 glasses

HANDY TIP

If serving to guests, put small pieces of chopped apple dipped in lemon juice on skewers with a few chunks of cucumber and balance them over the top of the glasses.

Variations

375 VEGETARIAN SPECIAL SALAD JUICE

Prepare the Apple Salad Juice. Mix 1 to 2 tablespoons tahini with a little of the juice to make a paste, then stir into the rest of the juice.

Handy tip: Tahini gives added protein and B vitamins to this drink.

378 ORCHARD SALAD JUICE

Make the Apple Salad Juice, using only 2 apples and adding 2 pears.

Handy tip: Pears will sweeten the overall taste of this juice.

376 APPLE SALAD HANGOVER HELPER

Add 60 ml (2 fl oz) liquid aloe vera and a generous pinch of fine sea salt to the completed Apple Salad Juice.

Nutritional tip: Not only is aloe vera high in the vitamins and minerals depleted from the body by alcoholic excesses but it also helps mitigate the harmful acetaldehydes that are made as alcohol is broken down in the body.

379 GREEN SALAD JUICE

Prepare the Apple Salad Juice, replacing the spinach with 4 broccoli florets.

Nutritional tip: Broccoli is regarded as a superfood in part because of its high vitamin and mineral content.

377 WALDORF SALAD JUICE

Make the Apple Salad Juice, replacing the pepper with 3 sticks of celery. Add 1 tablespoon flax oil.

Nutritional tip: Adding flax oil provides essential fatty acids to this drink.

380 SUMMER SALAD JUICE

Omit the spinach when making the Apple Salad Juice and replace it with 4 large romaine lettuce leaves.

Serving tip: Although drinks are best made fresh, these liquid salads may be made in the morning and taken for lunch in a thermos.

381   FRUITY SALAD JUICE

Make the Apple Salad Juice, but omit the peppers and
replace with 75 g (2 ½ oz) raspberries or cranberries.
Handy tip: This mild juice is a great introduction for
anyone who thinks that they won't like vegetable juices.

382   NIP SALAD JUICE

Prepare the Apple Salad Juice, replacing the spinach,
peppers and cucumber with 3 parsnips and a small bunch
of mint. Omit the ginger.
Handy tip: Parsnip makes a surprisingly thick, sweet juice,
which adds body to the drink.

383   JALAPEÑO SALAD JUICE

Add ½ to 1 seeded jalapeño chili with the rest of the
ingredients when preparing the Apple Salad Juice.
Handy tip: The chili works to take the edge off
the sweetness.

384 Peach and Raspberry Smoothie

This classic combination relies on the sweetness of a ripe peach – but be sure the peach is not over-ripe, or it will have an unpleasant taste.

INGREDIENTS

1 peach, peeled, stoned and quartered

75 g (2 ½ oz) raspberries

125 ml (4 ¼ fl oz) plain low-fat yoghurt

125 ml (4 ¼ fl oz) milk

Put all the ingredients in a blender. Blend for 1 minute or until smooth. Pour into a glass and serve immediately.

Makes 1 glass

HANDY TIP

Make ice cubes from coconut water to give your smoothies extra nutrients and taste. Add a couple of coconut ice cubes to each glass.

Variations

385 PEACH, RASPBERRY AND MINT SMOOTHIE

Add 6 fresh mint leaves to the blender when making the Peach and Raspberry Smoothie.
Handy tip: This is creamiest made with whole milk, but semi-skimmed or skimmed milk work well, too.

386 PEACH AND ORANGE SMOOTHIE

Make the Peach and Raspberry Smoothie, replacing the raspberries and milk with 175 ml (6 fl oz) orange juice.
Handy tip: Orange and raspberry juice would also be nice in this smoothie.

387 RASPBERRY AND ORANGE SMOOTHIE

Make the Peach and Raspberry Smoothie, omitting the peach and milk. Increase the quantity of raspberries to 150 g (5 ¼ oz) and add 125 ml (4 ¼ fl oz) orange juice to the blender.
Handy tip: You may use frozen raspberries.

388 PEACH, RASPBERRY AND ORANGE SMOOTHIE

Make the Peach and Raspberry Smoothie, replacing the milk with 60 ml (2 fl oz) orange juice.

389 PEACH AND PASSION SMOOTHIE

Prepare the Peach and Raspberry Smoothie, replacing the raspberries with the flesh of 2 passion fruit.
Handy tip: To remove the passion fruit pulp, cut the passion fruit in half and scoop out the pulp with a teaspoon.

390 PEACH, MANGO AND VANILLA SMOOTHIE

Make the Peach and Raspberry Smoothie, replacing the raspberries with ½ a stoned, peeled and chopped mango and the plain yoghurt with vanilla yoghurt.
Handy tip: Add a few drops of vanilla extract if there is no vanilla yoghurt on hand.

391 PEACH AND BLACKBERRY SMOOTHIE

Make the Peach and Raspberry Smoothie, replacing the raspberries with 75 g (2 ½ oz) blackberries.
Handy tip: Be careful when handling blackberries as they can stain the skin.

392 GREEN PEACH SMOOTHIE

Make the Peach and Blackberry Smoothie variation, replacing the raspberries with 50 g (1 ¾ oz) baby spinach leaves plus 1 teaspoon grated ginger.

393 RICH PEACH AND RASPBERRY SMOOTHIE

Make the Peach and Raspberry Smoothie, replacing the milk with full or low-fat evaporated milk.

394 Blueberry and Strawberry Smoothie

Take advantage of the fresh wild blueberries that are available in late summer if you can.

INGREDIENTS

75 g (2 ½ oz) blueberries	240 ml (8 fl oz) plain low-fat
50 g (1 ¾ oz) strawberries,	yoghurt
hulled	60 ml (2 fl oz) milk

Put all the ingredients in a blender. Blend for 1 minute or until smooth. Pour into a glass and serve immediately.

Makes 1 glass

HANDY TIP

For blender smoothies, it is not necessary to cut out the white core of the strawberry, just chop off the green bits.

Variations

396 BLUEBERRY, STRAWBERRY AND APPLE SMOOTHIE

Prepare the Blueberry and Strawberry Smoothie, omitting the milk and replacing it with the same amount of apple cider.
Shopping tip: When buying apple juice, select organic cloudy apple juice (nonalcoholic fresh apple cider).

397 BLUEBERRY, STRAWBERRY AND PINEAPPLE SMOOTHIE

Prepare the Blueberry and Strawberry Smoothie, replacing the milk with the same amount of pineapple juice.
Serving tip: Thread a few blueberries on a cocktail stick and use as a swizzle stick in any of these variations.

398 BLUEBERRY, RASPBERRY AND APPLE SMOOTHIE

Prepare the Blueberry and Strawberry Smoothie, replacing the milk with 60 ml (2 fl oz) apple juice and the strawberries with 150 g (5 ¼ oz) raspberries.
Handy tip: If not drinking your smoothies immediately, add a teaspoon of lemon juice to minimise oxidation.

395 BLUEBERRY, STRAWBERRY AND ORANGE SMOOTHIE

Prepare the Blueberry and Strawberry Smoothie but replace the milk with the same amount of orange juice.
Handy tip: For a dairy-free version, use soya yoghurt.

399 BLUEBERRY, STRAWBERRY AND ALMOND SMOOTHIE

Prepare the Blueberry and Strawberry Smoothie, replacing the milk with almond milk. For a stronger almond taste, add 1 tablespoon grated almond paste.

400 BLUEBERRY LAVENDER SMOOTHIE

Make the Blueberry, Strawberry and Almond Smoothie variation, omitting the almond paste. Add ½ teaspoon dried lavender flowers and 1 teaspoon lemon zest to the blender.
Handy tip: Lavender has a soothing effect on the mind.

401 BLUEBERRY, STRAWBERRY AND POMEGRANATE SMOOTHIE

Make the Blueberry and Strawberry Smoothie, replacing the milk with pomegranate juice.
Handy tip: Not everyone likes using pomegranate seeds in smoothies, but the juice is wonderful.

402 BLUEBERRY AND BANANA SMOOTHIE

Make the Blueberry and Strawberry Smoothie, replacing the strawberries with 1 small banana.
Nutritional tip: There is some evidence that blueberries help keep the brain in good shape.

403 BLUEBERRY AND ELDERBERRY SMOOTHIE

Prepare the Blueberry and Strawberry Smoothie, replacing the strawberries with 40 g (1 ½ oz) elderberries.
Handy tip: Elderberries are available in autumn.

404 BLUEBERRY AND POMEGRANATE SMOOTHIE

Make the Blueberry and Strawberry Smoothie, omitting the strawberries and replacing the milk with pomegranate juice.

405 PB and J Smoothie

This all-American sandwich favourite transfers beautifully to a sweet smoothie that children will love as a special treat – maybe combined with exercise!

INGREDIENTS

1 banana, peeled and quartered

1 tbsp grape jam

1 tbsp smooth peanut butter

125 ml (4 ¼ fl oz) plain low-fat yoghurt

60 ml (2 fl oz) milk

Put all the ingredients into a blender and process until smooth. Pour into a glass and serve immediately.

Makes 1 glass

NUTRITIONAL TIP

Peanut butter is an excellent source of protein.

Variations

406 PB AND ORANGE MARMALADE SMOOTHIE

Prepare the PB and J Smoothie, omitting the grape jam and replacing it with orange marmalade.
Handy tip: The bitterness of the peel in the marmalade will reduce the sweetness of this smoothie.

407 PB AND CHOCOLATE SMOOTHIE

Prepare the PB and J Smoothie, omitting the grape jam and replacing it with the same quantity of chocolate spread (such as Nutella).
Handy tip: Wash out the blender particularly thoroughly after working with peanut butter just in case the next person to use it has a nut allergy.

408 HIGH-PROTEIN PB SMOOTHIE

Make the PB and J Smoothie, omitting the grape jam and adding 1 tablespoon protein powder.
Handy tip: Protein powder should be stored in a cool, dark place.

409 PB AND GRAPE SMOOTHIE

Make the PB and J Smoothie, replacing the grape jam with 75 g (2 ½ oz) red grapes.
Nutritional tip: Resveratrol, found in the skin of red grapes, has a protective function for the heart.

410 PB AND OATMEAL SMOOTHIE

When making the PB and J Smoothie, first put 2 tablespoons rolled oats into the blender and process until powdered, then add the remaining ingredients.
Serving tip: The oatmeal increases the GI (glycemic index) of this smoothie, keeping you fuller for longer.

411 PB AND BERRY SMOOTHIE

Make the PB and J Smoothie, replacing the grape jam with 50 g (1 ¾ oz) frozen mixed berries.
Handy tip: Bottled or tinned cherries would work in place of the mixed berries in this variation.

412 PB AND GREEN BERRY SMOOTHIE

Make the PB and Berry Smoothie variation, adding 25 g (1 oz) baby spinach leaves.
Serving tip: This is a child-friendly green smoothie.

413 PB AND DATE SMOOTHIE

Prepare the PB and J Smoothie, replacing the grape jam with 4 stoned soft dates.
Handy tip: Take the tiny woody stem out of dates before processing.

414 PB AND CHOCOLATE TRAIL MIX SMOOTHIE

Add 1 tablespoon chocolate whey protein powder and 1 tablespoon raisins when making the PB and J Smoothie.
Handy tip: Dried cranberries can often be substituted for raisins in recipes.

415 Guarana Papaya Smoothie

Guarana is a great energy booster, as it contains almost twice the amount of caffeine as coffee beans. Guarana powder is bitter if drunk with just water. This smoothie is a delicious way to drink it sweetened with fruit.

INGREDIENTS

1 tsp guarana powder	1 tbsp liquid honey
240 ml (8 fl oz) plain yoghurt	2 to 4 tbsp milk
225 g (8 oz) peeled and chopped papaya	

Put the guarana powder, yoghurt, papaya and honey in a blender and process until smooth. Add the milk to thin to the consistency of your choice.

Makes 2 glasses

INTERESTING NOTE

Guarana powder is made from the seeds of the guarana bush, a relative of the maple found in the Amazon basin.

Variations

416 GUARANA BANANA SMOOTHIE

Make the Guarana Papaya Smoothie, replacing the papaya with 1 ripe banana.
Nutritional tip: Some evidence suggests that guarana suppresses the appetite by creating a sensation of fullness.

417 GUARANA, STRAWBERRY AND BANANA SMOOTHIE

Make the Guarana Papaya Smoothie, replacing the papaya with 75 g (2 ½ oz) strawberries and 1 small banana.
Serving tip: Serve garnished with a slit strawberry wedged onto the rim of the glass.

418 GUARANA ACAI SMOOTHIE

Make the Guarana Papaya Smoothie, replacing the papaya with 60 ml (2 fl oz) acai purée and 1 small banana.
Interesting note: Acai berries are hard to find but are available in purée form in health food shops.

419 COCONUT GUARANA FRUIT SMOOTHIE

Make the Guarana and Papaya Smoothie or the banana variation above, substituting coconut yoghurt for the plain yoghurt and omitting the honey.
Handy tip: Some coconut yoghurt is dairy-free.

420 CRUNCHY TOPPED GUARANA SMOOTHIE

Make the Guarana and Papaya Smoothie or any of its variations and put into glasses. Mix together 1 tablespoon each of grated coconut, toasted pumpkin seeds and toasted sunflower seeds, then use as a topping.

421 Banana and Lentil Smoothie

Lentils come in a variety of colours and they are all high in fibre and help to lower bad cholesterol.

INGREDIENTS

2 heaping tablespoons split
    red lentils
1 banana, peeled and chopped

300 ml (10 fl oz) orange juice,
    preferably freshly squeezed
150 ml (5 fl oz) almond milk

Place the lentils in a saucepan, cover with plenty of cold water and bring to the boil. Lower the heat and simmer for about 20 to 25 minutes until soft. Drain and leave to cool.

Add the cooled lentils, banana and orange juice to the blender and process until smooth. Add the milk and process to mix. Pour into glasses and serve immediately.

Makes 2 glasses

422 BANANA, PINEAPPLE AND LENTIL SMOOTHIE

Make the Banana and Lentil Smoothie, replacing the orange juice with pineapple juice.
Handy tip: Red lentils don't need presoaking.

423 BLUEBERRY AND LENTIL SMOOTHIE

Prepare the Banana and Lentil Smoothie, replacing the banana with 150 g (5 ¼ oz) blueberries.
Serving tip: The added carbs in all these drinks make them great to take out on busy days.

424 Yoghurt, Wheat Germ and Treacle Smoothie

This thick and rich smoothie is best made with Greek-style yoghurt, which imparts a wonderful creaminess. Black treacle is a healthy sweetener that contains significant amounts of vitamin B6 and healthy minerals.

INGREDIENTS

240 ml (8 fl oz) Greek-style yoghurt

1 tbsp black treacle

1 tsp wheat germ

Ice cubes

Place the yoghurt, treacle and wheat germ in a blender and process until smooth. Pour over ice cubes into glasses and serve immediately.

Makes 1 large or 2 small servings

HANDY TIP

To reduce fat intake, choose nonfat or reduced-fat Greek-style yoghurt.

Variations

425 MANGO AND WHEAT GERM SMOOTHIE

Add ½ a stoned, peeled and chopped mango to the other ingredients when making the Yoghurt, Wheat Germ and Treacle Smoothie recipe.
Handy tip: Black treacle is more of a dietary supplement than a sweetener.

426 ICED CHERRY AND WHEAT GERM SMOOTHIE

Add 75 g (2 ½ oz) stoned frozen cherries to the other ingredients when preparing the Yoghurt, Wheat Germ and Treacle Smoothie.
Handy tip: If using fresh cherries, add 2 ice cubes.

427 BLACKBERRY AND WHEAT GERM SMOOTHIE

Add 75 g (2 ½ oz) blackberries and 1 teaspoon grated orange zest to the other ingredients when preparing the Yoghurt, Wheat Germ and Treacle Smoothie.
Serving tip: Instead of incorporating the orange zest, you could put it on the top of the smoothie as a garnish.

428   RICOTTA AND WHEAT GERM SMOOTHIE

Make the Yoghurt, Wheat Germ and Treacle Smoothie using only 125 ml (4 ¼ fl oz) Greek-style yoghurt and adding 125 ml (4 ¼ fl oz) ricotta cheese. Add 1 teaspoon grated lemon or orange zest.
Handy tip: Ricotta is available in whole milk and skimmed milk varieties.

429   FROZEN YOGHURT AND WHEAT GERM SMOOTHIE

Replace the yoghurt in the Yoghurt, Wheat Germ and Treacle Smoothie with 2 scoops of vanilla or lemon frozen yoghurt.
Handy tip: The sugar in frozen yoghurt adds calories to this smoothie.

430   YOGHURT, WHEAT GERM AND MAPLE SMOOTHIE

Make the Yoghurt, Wheat Germ and Treacle Smoothie, replacing the treacle with maple syrup.
Handy tip: Store opened bottles of maple syrup in the fridge.

431 Rooibos and Berry Smoothie

Rooibos tea makes an excellent base for this high-protein smoothie made with antioxidant-rich frozen berries; it's brilliant as part of a workout routine.

INGREDIENTS

1 rooibos tea bag
125 ml (4 ¼ fl oz) very hot, not
  boiling, water
225 g (8 oz) frozen mixed berries
125 ml (4 ¼ fl oz) silken tofu

1 tbsp vanilla protein powder
1 tsp liquid honey, optional

Put the bag in a teapot or heatproof jug and pour over the water. Steep for 8 to 10 minutes, then remove the tea bag. Leave to cool.

Put the tea, berries, tofu and protein powder into a blender and process until smooth. Sweeten to taste with honey and pour into glasses. Serve immediately or transfer to a thermos.

Makes 2 glasses

INTERESTING FACT

Rooibos is grown from a small shrub that is only found near Cape Town, South Africa.

Variations

432 ROOIBOS AND PEACH SMOOTHIE

Make the Rooibos and Berry Smoothie, replacing the berries with 275 g (9 ¾ oz) frozen peach chunks.
Interesting fact: Rooibos tea is also known as red bush tea.

433 ROOIBOS, STRAWBERRY AND ORANGE SMOOTHIE

Make the Rooibos and Berry Smoothie, replacing the berries with 150 g (5 ¼ oz) frozen strawberries and ½ a peeled and chopped orange.
Nutritional tip: Rooibos tea is tannin-free and contains 9 essential trace minerals.

434 ROOIBOS NUTTY SMOOTHIE

Prepare the Rooibos and Berry Smoothie, replacing the tofu with 125 ml (4 ¼ fl oz) almond milk and 1 tablespoon smooth peanut, cashew, or almond butter.
Shopping tip: A wide range of nut butters is available in good health shops or good supermarkets.

435 FRUIT TEA SMOOTHIE

Make the Rooibos and Berry Smoothie, replacing the rooibos tea bag with a mixed red berry tea bag.
Handy tip: Don't be skeptical about using silken tofu in smoothies. It adds a lovely creamy richness.

436 Star Fruit -Scented Tropical Green Juice

Star fruit, also know as carambola, is a delicate scented fruit that gives a fragrant note to this delicious, energy-boosting tropical juice.

INGREDIENTS

2 star fruits

85 g (3 oz) mango, peeled and stoned

⅓ pineapple, sliced

1 kiwi fruit, peeled

115 g (4 oz) spinach or kale leaves

125 ml (4 ¼ fl oz) coconut milk

Process the star fruit, mango, pineapple, kiwi fruit and spinach through a juice extractor. Stir in the coconut milk, pour into glasses and serve immediately.

Makes 12 glasses

HEALTH WARNING

Star fruit should be avoided by anyone with kidney problems.

variations

 ### STAR FRUIT -SCENTED ZINGER

Make the Star Fruit-Scented Tropical Green Juice but replace the mango with ½ a cucumber and a 2.5-cm (1-inch) piece of ginger. Omit the coconut milk.
Nutritional tip: Star fruit is very low in calories at 31 calories per 100 grams (3 ½ oz).

 ### HINT OF PINK STAR FRUIT-SCENTED JUICE

Make the Star Fruit-Scented Tropical Green Juice, replacing the mango with 150 g (5 ½ oz) watermelon. Use 60 ml (2 fl oz) coconut milk.
Interesting fact: Star fruit is native to Southeast Asia and China.

 ### STAR FRUIT -SCENTED, BLUEBERRY AND PINEAPPLE JUICE

Make the Star Fruit-Scented Tropical Green Juice, replacing the mango with 150 g (5 ¼ oz) blueberries.
Serving tip: This drink is a thirst quencher and, kept chilled, is delicious to take on a hike.

440 STAR FRUIT AND ANISE TROPICAL GREEN JUICE

Prepare the Star Fruit-Scented Tropical Green Juice and stir in ¼ teaspoon ground star anise to the finished juice.

Handy tip: Star anise has a long shelf life if kept cool and dark.

441 STAR FRUIT -SCENTED GREEN SMOOTHIE

Make the Star Fruit-Scented Tropical Green Juice but reduce the spinach or kale to 60 g (2 oz). Seed the star fruit; peel and core the pineapple. Put all the ingredients in a blender and process until smooth. Pour into glasses and serve immediately.

Serving tip: Cut a couple of slices off the star fruit to use as a garnish.

442 Big Leaf Smoothie

The star of this juice is the big-leafed chard, which comes in a myriad of rainbow colours. Combined with the pineapple, it makes a refreshing smoothie that also builds up your bones and muscles.

INGREDIENTS

3 large chard leaves, central
    vein removed
150 g (5 ¼ oz) pineapple chunks
½ banana, peeled

2 soft, stoned dates
500 ml (17 fl oz) coconut,
    filtered, or mineral water
1 tsp flaxseed oil

Put all the ingredients in a blender and process until smooth. Serve immediately.

Makes 1 large or 2 small glasses

NUTRITIONAL TIP

Add 1 teaspoon sesame seed oil for a metabolism boost and extra vitamin E and sprinkle a few sesame seeds over the finished juice for a little protein.

Variations

443 BIG LEAF JUICE

Make the Big Leaf Smoothie, replacing the banana with a quartered apple and omitting the water. Process the ingredients through a juice extractor, then add the flaxseed oil to the pressed juice.
Handy tip: If making juice, there is no need to remove the central veins from the chard leaves.

444 BIG LEAF SMOOTHIE WITH APPLE

Make the Big Leaf Smoothie, replacing the pineapple with 2 cored and quartered apples.
Handy tip: If chard is not on hand, spinach or kale make excellent substitutions.

445 BIG LEAF SMOOTHIE WITH PEAR

Make the Big Leaf Smoothie, replacing the pineapple and dates with 2 cored and quartered pears.
Handy tip: Using pears in place of pineapple and dates will make this a slightly thinner smoothie.

446 BIG LEAF SMOOTHIE WITH MELON

Make the Big Leaf Smoothie, replacing the pineapple with 150 g (5 ½ oz) cantaloupe or galia melon.
Shopping tip: Check the melon is ripe before buying. It should smell strongly and be firm but not rock hard.

447 ENERGY BOOST BIG LEAF SMOOTHIE

Prepare the Big Leaf Smoothie, adding 1 teaspoon spirulina to the blender.

Nutritional tip: Spirulina (blue-green algae) is an energy-boosting supplement.

448 HIGH-ENERGY PINEAPPLE SMOOTHIE

Make the Big Leaf Smoothie, replacing the chard leaves and banana with 150 g (5 ¼ oz) papaya chunks. Use only 240 ml (8 fl oz) coconut water. Add 1 teaspoon spirulina to the smoothie.

Handy tip: For a richer taste, use coconut milk.

449 BIG LEAF AND AVOCADO SMOOTHIE

Make the Big Leaf Smoothie, replacing the banana with ½ a stoned and peeled avocado.

Nutritional tip: Avocados provide a complex range of proteins, good fats, vitamins and minerals and are excellent for vegans or others on a meat-free or dairy-free diet.

450 BIG LEAF SMOOTHIE WITH ALFALFA

Prepare the Big Leaf Smoothie, adding 50 g (1 ¾ oz) alfalfa sprouts.

Nutritional tip: Alfalfa is a legume, in the same family as peas and beans.

451 Spicy Rocket Celery Juice

Rocket has all the benefits of leafy greens plus a distinct pepper flavour. Perfect for pepping up smoothies for those who like them spicy.

INGREDIENTS

50 g (1 ¾ oz) rocket
4 celery stalks
1 pear
4 sprigs coriander
½ lime, peeled
125 ml (4 ¼ fl oz) coconut water

Process the rocket, celery, pear, coriander and lime in a juice extractor. Stir in the coconut water. Pour into a glass and serve immediately.

Makes 1 glass

NUTRITIONAL TIP

Vitamin C promotes the formation of collagen, which is necessary to maintain strong and healthy bones.

Variations

452 SPICY ROCKET, CELERY AND CUCUMBER JUICE

Add ½ a cucumber to the other ingredients when making the Spicy Rocket Celery Juice.
Serving tip: This makes a great companion for a toasted cheese sandwich.

453 SPICY ROCKET, CELERY AND ORANGE JUICE

Make the Spicy Rocket Celery Juice, replacing the pear with 1 peeled and chopped orange.
Handy tip: If you like the ingredients together in a salad, the chances are you will like them in a juice.

454 SPICY ROCKET, CELERY AND GRAPE JUICE

Prepare the Spicy Rocket Celery Juice, replacing the pear with 300 g (10 ½ oz) of green or red grapes.
Nutritional tip: Juicing allows you to consume a variety of fresh produce with a wide range of nutrients.

455 SPICY ROCKET AND TAHINI JUICE

Stir 1 teaspoon tahini into a paste with a little of the coconut water, add the remaining water; stir into the finished Spicy Rocket Celery Juice.
Handy tip: Tahini is made from sesame seeds.

456 Morello Cupboard Smoothie

Cupboard ingredients can make good smoothies. This recipe calls for a few non-refrigerated items you just might have sitting around.

INGREDIENTS

60 ml (2 fl oz) cranberry juice	75 ml (2 ½ fl oz) vanilla
170 g (6 oz) bottled, stoned	soya yoghurt
morello cherries, drained	5 ice cubes

Place all of the ingredients into a blender and process until smooth. Pour into glasses and serve immediately.

Makes 2 glasses

HANDY TIP

If the cherries are packed in natural juice, use the juice to make another fruit smoothie by combining it with mangoes and bananas.

457 MORELLO AND RASPBERRY SMOOTHIE

Make the Morello Cupboard Smoothie using only 240 ml (8 fl oz) of bottled morello cherries and add 125 ml (4 ¼ fl oz) bottled or tinned raspberries.

Variations

458 FRUIT SALAD SMOOTHIE

Make the Morello Cupboard Smoothie, replacing the cherries with tinned or bottled fruit salad.
Handy tip: Do not use the fruit salad juice as you need to balance the sweet fruit with the sour cranberry juice.

459 APRICOT COMPOTE SMOOTHIE

Make the Morello Cupboard Smoothie, replacing the cherries with 240 ml (8 fl oz) apricot compote, 2 tinned pear halves and ½ teaspoon ground cinnamon.
Handy tip: Replace yoghurt with milk for a lighter effect.

460 ALMOND MORELLO GLORY

Make the Morello Cupboard Smoothie, replacing the soya yoghurt with 125 ml (4 ¼ fl oz) almond milk.
Serving tip: Garnish the smoothie with a few toasted slivered almonds.

461 FIG AND RASPBERRY SMOOTHIE

Make the Morello Cupboard Smoothie, replacing the cherries with 4 bottled whole figs, halved, 125 ml (4 ¼ fl oz) bottled or tinned raspberries and a generous pinch of cinnamon.
Handy tip: Remove hard tips from figs before processing.

462 CHERRY PIE FILLING SMOOTHIE

Prepare the Morello Cupboard Smoothie, replacing cherries with 125 ml (4 ¼ fl oz) cherry pie filling and 1 teaspoon lemon juice. Increase cranberry juice to 125 ml (4 ¼ fl oz).
Nutritional tip: This smoothie can't be classified as healthy!

463 Rhubarb and Orange Smoothie

Stewed rhubarb makes an excellent smoothie base. This drink calls for blood orange juice, which enhances the vibrant colour.

INGREDIENTS

120 g (4 ¼ oz) chopped rhubarb
½ tsp orange zest
175 ml (6 fl oz) blood orange juice, preferably freshly squeezed
2 tbsp brown sugar
125 ml (4 ¼ fl oz) vanilla yoghurt

In a small saucepan over a low heat, cook the rhubarb with the orange zest, orange juice and sugar for about 10 minutes, until tender; leave to cool. Transfer to a blender, add the yoghurt and process until smooth.

Makes 1 glass

HANDY TIP

To make the rhubarb pinker, add a few drops of red food colouring.

Makes 1 glass

variations

464 RHUBARB ICE-CREAM SHAKE

Make the Rhubarb and Orange Smoothie, replacing the vanilla yoghurt with 1 scoop of raspberry ice cream.
Interesting fact: Thought of as a fruit, rhubarb is actually a vegetable.

465 RHUBARB AND BANANA SMOOTHIE

Make the Rhubarb and Orange Smoothie, adding a small banana to the blender and replacing the yoghurt with 150 ml (5 fl oz) milk or almond milk.
Handy tip: The leaves of the rhubarb plant are toxic, so don't be tempted to add them to your smoothie.

466 RHUBARB AND COCONUT SMOOTHIE

Prepare the Rhubarb and Orange Smoothie, replacing the vanilla yoghurt with coconut yoghurt and adding a few drops of vanilla extract.
Handy tip: Rhubarb freezes well. Stew as directed above, then cool and pack in portions in resealable freezer bags.

467 RHUBARB AND STRAWBERRY SMOOTHIE

Make the Rhubarb and Orange Smoothie, adding 6 large strawberries to the blender along with the stewed rhubarb.
Nutritional tip: Rhubarb is high in vitamin K, calcium and potassium, all of which are good for the muscles, bones and nervous system.

468 RHUBARB AND PEAR SMOOTHIE

Make the Rhubarb and Orange Smoothie, replacing 60 g (2 oz) rhubarb with 1 peeled, cored and chopped firm pear. Replace the orange juice with apple juice.
Handy tip: Red-stemmed rhubarb is not necessarily sweeter than green rhubarb.

469 RHUBARB AND GINGER SMOOTHIE

Make the Rhubarb and Orange Smoothie, adding 1 teaspoon ground ginger powder to the rhubarb when cooking.
Handy tip: One tablespoon of crystallised ginger would be a good substitute for ground ginger.

470 RHUBARB AND CREAM SMOOTHIE

Make the Rhubarb and Orange Smoothie, replacing the yoghurt with single cream but do not add to the blender. Pour the rhubarb and orange mix into the glass and swirl in the cream.
Handy tip: A healthier alternative would be to use soya or oat cream.

471 Mexican Cactus Smoothie

Mexico's nopal cactus, also known as prickly pear or paddle cactus, is one of nature's most valuable foods. A glass of nopal cactus juice, *Licuado de Nopal,* is a favourite breakfast south of the border. Turn this into a smoothie and you have a healthy and sustaining snack at any time of the day.

INGREDIENTS

1 medium nopal cactus pad, spines removed, or 2 tsp nopal cactus powder

1 banana, peeled and chopped

125 ml (4 ¼ fl oz) plain yoghurt

300 ml (10 fl oz) orange juice, preferably freshly squeezed

Put the cactus pad or cactus powder into a blender, add the banana and yoghurt and process into a purée. Pour in the orange juice and process until blended. Pour into glasses and serve immediately.

Makes 2 glasses

HANDY TIP

If using fresh cactus pad, obviously, it is important that all the spines have been removed and that the pad is as young and fresh as possible.

Variations

472 JUICY CACTUS SMOOTHIE

Make the Mexican Cactus Smoothie, replacing the banana with 1 cucumber.
Nutritional tip: The pads of the nopal cactus contain antioxidants, dietary fibre, iron and vitamins A, B and C.

473 CACTUS AND PINEAPPLE SMOOTHIE

Make the Mexican Cactus Smoothie with 1 slice of pineapple rather than banana, using only 240 ml (8 fl oz) orange juice.
Shopping tip: Cactus pads are not readily available from supermarkets, but you can use the juice or powder.

474 CACTUS AND WATER-MELON SMOOTHIE

Make the Mexican Cactus Smoothie, replacing the banana with 150 g (5 ½ oz) cubed watermelon and using only 125 ml (4 ¼ fl oz) orange juice.

475 CACTUS AND STRAWBERRY SMOOTHIE

Make the Mexican Cactus Smoothie, replacing the banana with 150 g (5 ¼ oz) strawberries and using only 125 ml (4 ¼ fl oz) orange juice.

476 CACTUS AND LIME SMOOTHIE

Make the Mexican Cactus Smoothie, replacing the banana with 1 cucumber and using the juice of 2 limes and 240 ml (8 fl oz) filtered or mineral water. Add 1 teaspoon agave syrup, to sweeten (optional).

477 Australian Guada Bean Smoothie

Trailing guada bean plants that cling to huge trellises are a familiar sight in subtropical regions of Australia and South Africa, where they are cultivated instead of courgettes.

INGREDIENTS

2 guada beans, trimmed and chopped

50 g (1 ¾ oz) baby spinach leaves

1 apple, peeled, cored and quartered

2 tbsp white grape juice

Put all the ingredients in a blender and process until smooth. Pour into glasses and serve immediately.

Makes 2 glasses

HANDY TIP

The grape juice should sweeten this smoothie, but add a little honey or agave syrup if necessary.

variations

478 COURGETTE SMOOTHIE

Replace the guada beans with 115 g (4 oz) sliced young courgette.

Handy tip: Courgette and guada beans are interchangeable in most recipes.

479 Mega Iron Energy Juice

This deliciously sweet juice is concentrated with ingredients to help you boost your iron levels and give your energy levels a lift. It uses dried apricots, which need to be rehydrated before juicing.

INGREDIENTS

75 ml (2 ½ fl oz) apple juice

50 g (1 ¾ oz) dried apricots, chopped

2 carrots, trimmed

50 g (1 ¾ oz) baby spinach

1 cucumber

1-cm (½-inch) piece ginger, peeled

½ lime, peeled

1 tsp spirulina powder

Approximately 60 ml (2 fl oz) filtered or mineral water

1 tbsp pumpkin seeds, finely chopped

In a small bowl in the microwave, heat the apple juice until hot, not boiling, about 20 seconds. Add the apricots; let sit until cool.

Put the apricot mixture, carrots, spinach, cucumber, ginger and lime through the juice extractor. Stir in the spirulina and pour into glasses. Top off each glass with a little water to taste. Sprinkle over chopped pumpkin seeds and serve immediately.

Makes 2 glasses

SERVING TIP

This makes an excellent nutrient boost at lunchtime served with a light snack such as hummus, pita bread and olives.

Variations

480 COCONUT IRON ENERGY LIFT

Make the Mega Iron Energy Juice, replacing the water with coconut water.
Handy tip: Kelp powder can be used instead of spirulina.

481 EARL GREY IRON ENERGY LIFT

Make the Mega Iron Energy Juice, replacing the apple juice with strong Earl Grey tea. Add the apricots to the hot tea; leave to stand until cool.
Interesting fact: Earl Grey tea contains the oil from bergamot orange peel. It is this that gives the tea its distinctive smoky flavour and makes an ideal smoothie base.

482 DRIED FIG MEGA IRON LIFT

Make the Mega Iron Energy Juice, replacing the dried apricots with dried figs.
Handy tip: Dried fruits provide more concentrated sources of vitamins and minerals, but they do not juice without rehydration.

483 PRUNE MEGA IRON LIFT

Make the Mega Iron Energy Juice, replacing the dried apricots with stoned prunes.

Nutritional tip: Prunes (called plums in their non-dried form) are high in fibre and have a natural laxative effect.

484 BITTER MELON MEGA IRON LIFT

Make the Mega Iron Energy Juice, replacing the cucumber with 170 g (6 oz) bitter melon and omitting the lime.

Interesting fact: Bitter melon is a green-skinned fruit with smooth ridges, thick flesh and a very bitter taste. It is iron-rich and works nicely to balance out the sweetness in this juice.

485 PEAR MEGA IRON LIFT

Prepare the Mega Iron Energy Juice, replacing the apple juice with strong green tea and replacing the apricots with dried pear.

Handy tip: For added protein, add 1 tablespoon protein powder.

486 MEGA MEGA IRON LIFT

Prepare the Mega Iron Energy Juice, adding 2 teaspoons nutritional yeast and ½ teaspoon ground flaxseed.

Handy tip: Brewer's yeast can be used in place of nutritional yeast.

487 Brazilian Avocado Smoothie

This avocado smoothie is reminiscent of a vanilla milkshake and is hugely popular in Brazil. Avocado is one of the only fruits to contain fat, but luckily it's the healthy monounsaturated fat – the kind that lowers cholesterol.

INGREDIENTS

½ avocado, stoned and skinned
375 ml (12 ½ fl oz) vanilla soya milk
1 ½ to 3 tbsp liquid honey,
    or to taste
8 ice cubes

Put the avocado, soya milk, 1 ½ tablespoons of the honey and the ice cubes in a blender and process until smooth. Adjust the sweetness to taste. Pour into glasses and serve immediately.

Makes 2 glasses

HANDY TIP

If using regular milk, add ½ teaspoon vanilla extract.

Variations

488 AVOCADO AND ORANGE SMOOTHIE

Make the Brazilian Avocado Smoothie, replacing the soya milk with orange juice.
Interesting fact: Avocados will not ripen on the tree because the leaves supply a substance that prevents ripening. Avocados will store on the tree for up to 18 months. Once picked, they should be stored at room temperature until ripe, then in the fridge for 3 to 5 days.

489 CHOCOLATE AVOCADO SMOOTHIE

Make the Brazilian Avocado Smoothie, replacing the soya milk with chocolate soya milk or with dairy chocolate milk.
Nutritional tip: Avocado is good for the skin because it is a good source of biotin, which helps to prevent dry skin and brittle hair and nails.

490 PLAIN AVOCADO SMOOTHIE

Make the Brazilian Avocado Smoothie, replacing the vanilla soya milk with dairy milk and the honey with caster sugar.
Handy tip: Try omitting the sugar and adding a pinch of salt and 1 tablespoon coriander. The salt acts as a flavour enhancer.

491 AVOCADO AND MANGO SMOOTHIE

Make the Brazilian Avocado Smoothie, replacing the soya milk with coconut milk and adding 170 g (6 oz) chopped mango and 1 teaspoon lime juice.
Handy tip: If you don't have coconut milk, use orange juice instead.

492 AVOCADO AND BANANA SMOOTHIE

Prepare the Brazilian Avocado Smoothie, adding 1 small banana and ¼ teaspoon ground cinnamon to the blender.
Handy tip: This variation is indulgently good made with chocolate milk.

493 RICH AVOCADO SMOOTHIE

Prepare the Brazilian Avocado Smoothie, reducing the vanilla soya milk to 240 ml (8 fl oz) and adding 125 g (4 ½ oz) silken tofu.
Interesting fact: The avocado is an Aztec symbol of love and fertility – maybe because they grow in pairs on trees.

494 Strawberry and White chocolate Smoothie

Sometimes a little treat does you good and this is a lovely smoothie emboldened with the richness of the white chocolate.

INGREDIENTS

4 (25-g/1-oz) squares white chocolate

125 ml (4 ¼ fl oz) pomegranate juice

300 g (10 ½ oz) strawberries

125 ml (4 ¼ fl oz) whole milk or single cream

150 ml (5 fl oz) vanilla yoghurt

10 ice cubes

Put the chocolate in a small heatproof bowl and place over a saucepan of simmering water, stirring occasionally while the chocolate melts. Set aside to cool slightly. Add all the remaining ingredients to the blender, pour in the melted chocolate and blend until smooth.

Makes 2 glasses

HANDY TIP

White chocolate has a very low burning point of 44° C (110° F). Consequently, it is best melted over hot water and stirred while it melts. It is easy to ruin it in the microwave.

variations

495 DARK CHOCOLATE STRAWBERRY SMOOTHIE

Make the Strawberry and White Chocolate Smoothie, replacing the white chocolate with 2 tablespoons chocolate syrup.

Handy tip: Dark chocolate has a much more intense flavour than white chocolate, so it requires much less for a similar taste impact.

496 CHOCOLATE STRAWBERRY MEAL SMOOTHIE

Make each smoothie from 240 ml (8 fl oz) chocolate-flavoured nutritional milk drink, 150 g (5 ¼ oz) strawberries and 5 ice cubes. Thin with a little water, if required.

Serving tip: This can be a lovely change for someone recovering from illness and much nicer than synthetic, strawberry-flavoured drinks.

497 STRAWBERRY CHEESECAKE SMOOTHIE

Make the Strawberry and White Chocolate Smoothie, replacing the yoghurt with 125 ml (4 ¼ fl oz) ricotta cheese and adding ½ teaspoon grated orange zest, ¼ teaspoon vanilla extract and 1 tablespoon ground flaxseed.

Handy tip: Almond milk adds a lovely flavour to this smoothie, if used instead of milk.

498 STRAWBERRY PEPPER SMOOTHIE

Make the Strawberry and White Chocolate Smoothie, omitting the white chocolate. Replace the vanilla yoghurt with plain yoghurt and add ½ to 1 teaspoon freshly ground pink or black peppercorns and a sprig of mint.
Handy tip: A sprinkling of pepper on a bowl of strawberries is a classic flavour enhancer.

499 THE SIMPLEST STRAWBERRY SMOOTHIE

For each smoothie simply blend together 150 g (5 ¼ oz) strawberries and 240 ml (8 fl oz) milk.
Handy tip: For dairy-free, use rice milk or vanilla rice milk.

500 CLASSIC STRAWBERRY SMOOTHIE

Make the Strawberry and White Chocolate Smoothie, replacing the white chocolate with 1 peeled and chopped banana.
Serving tip: This is a winning smoothie choice for a children's sleepover treat.

501 STRAWBERRY PROTEIN RUNNER'S SMOOTHIE

Make the Classic Strawberry Smoothie variation, adding 2 tablespoons chocolate protein powder and 2 teaspoons flaxseed oil to the blender.
Handy tip: If using vanilla protein powder, use plain yoghurt.

Thirst Quenchers

When thirst strikes, fruit delights. This chapter is full of delicious fruit and vegetable drinks that take juicing and blending into another league. Some combinations are old favourites, while others combine the exotic with the mundane and the simple with the unexpected. These recipes will just get you started, but no doubt you will soon be experimenting and coming up with your own personal favourites. You can even start replacing your store-bought fizzy drinks with home-prepared pineappleade and other carbonated wonders. There are perfect drinks here to greet hot and thirsty visitors as well as ones that children will adore.

502 Luscious Summer Smoothie

Using frozen fruit straight from the freezer makes these smoothies quick to prepare and icy cold without the diluting effects of ice.

INGREDIENTS

250 g (8 ¾ oz) frozen mixed
   summer berries
2 tbsp liquid honey
300 ml (10 fl oz) fresh
   orange juice
60 ml (2 fl oz) Greek yoghurt

Pour all but a few frozen berries into the blender or food processor. Add the honey, orange juice and yoghurt. Process until smooth, adding a little more orange juice, if required. Pour into glasses and decorate with the reserved berries.

Makes 3 glasses

HANDY TIP

To keep you full for longer, add 60 ml (2 fl oz) oats to the blender with the other ingredients.

Variations

503 MINTY SUMMER GREEN SMOOTHIE

Make the Luscious Summer Smoothie, adding a small handful of mint leaves and 10 baby spinach leaves to the blender.
Handy tip: Adding mint always brightens up the flavour of fruits and vegetables. It is also good as a digestive aid.

504 CRANBERRY AND RASPBERRY SMOOTHIE

Make the Luscious Summer Smoothie, replacing the mixed berries with 120 g (4 ¼ oz) each of frozen cranberries and raspberries and adding a 5-cm (2-inch) piece of cucumber.
Handy tip: The cucumber makes this a slightly longer drink, perfect for hot days.

505 BLUEBERRY SMOOTHIE

Make the Luscious Summer Smoothie, replacing the mixed frozen berries with frozen blueberries and add a 5-cm (2-inch) piece of cucumber.
Serving tip: This makes a good drink for boosting energy; try it in the middle of the afternoon when you feel yourself flagging.

506 DAIRY-FREE PROTEIN SMOOTHIE

Make the Luscious Summer Smoothie, replacing the yoghurt with 60 g (2 oz) silken tofu.
Handy tip: Added protein from the tofu makes this smoothie into more of a meal.

507 STRAWBERRY SMOOTHIE

Make the Luscious Summer Smoothie, replacing the mixed summer berries with frozen strawberries.
Handy tip: Freeze strawberries when they are in season and you'll find many uses for them throughout the year.

508 FIZZY SUMMER CRUSH

Make the Luscious Summer Smoothie, replacing the orange juice with sparkling orange or sparkling water and omitting the yoghurt.
Nutritional tip: Read the labels carefully to select the sparkling orange that contains the least sugar.

509
SUMMER SMOOTHIE DESSERT

Make the Luscious Summer Smoothie, omitting the yoghurt. Fill the glasses with one-third of the smoothie, top each one with 1 tablespoon Greek yoghurt, repeat with the remaining mixture, ending with a layer of yoghurt garnished with the reserved fruit.
Handy tip: Turn your favourite smoothies into stunning desserts this way. Use nonfat yoghurt to reduce the calories and fat content, if desired.

510
LOW-FAT MANGO AND BERRY SMOOTHIE

Prepare the Luscious Summer Smoothie, replacing the orange juice with mango nectar or mango and orange juice and use nonfat or soya yoghurt in place of Greek yoghurt. Add up to 3 tablespoons wheat germ to the blender with the other ingredients.
Nutritional tip: Mango is a great source of vitamins and antioxidants, making this a good health-boosting smoothie.

511
BERRY SLUSH

Make the Luscious Summer Smoothie, replacing the yoghurt with 3 scoops of vanilla or raspberry frozen yoghurt and reducing the orange juice to 150 ml (5 fl oz).
Serving tip: Using frozen yoghurt instead of orange juice makes this drink really icy, which makes it particularly good to go in a thermos for an on-the-run snack.

512 Vegetable Juice

This is a ready-in-minutes meal in a glass: full of flavour, antioxidants, vitamins – especially vitamin C – and essential minerals such as iron.

INGREDIENTS

1 broccoli floret
2 celery stalks
1 carrot, trimmed
1 red pepper, cored and seeded

4 tomatoes
Small handful of parsley leaves
5 watercress stalks
Pinch of salt

Put all the ingredients through a juice extractor. Pour into a glass and serve immediately.

Serves 1

SERVING TIP

This juice settles if it is not drunk immediately, so serve with a swizzle stick or thick straw.

variations

514 VEGETABLE JUICE WITH A SPICY KICK

Make the Vegetable Juice, then add 1 teaspoon chili sauce and a generous grinding of black pepper.
Handy tip: For a sweeter alternative, use Thai sweet chili sauce.

515 VEGETABLE JUICE WITH A ZINGY KICK

Prepare the Vegetable Juice, then add 1 teaspoon lemon juice and 1 teaspoon lime juice.
Handy tip: Try this with 1 to 2 teaspoons grapefruit juice.

516 VEGETABLE JUICE WITH ROCKET KICK

Make the Vegetable Juice, replacing the watercress with rocket and adding ¼ of a peeled lemon.
Handy tip: Rocket is very easy to grow in a pot. Re-seed at regular intervals for a constant supply.

513 VEGETABLE JUICE 'VIRGIN MARY'

Prepare the Vegetable Juice, then add up to 1 ½ teaspoons Worcestershire sauce, a couple of dashes of Tabasco, a sprinkling of celery salt, a squeeze of lemon juice and a generous grinding of black pepper.

517 VEGETABLE JUICE WITH ALOE BOOST

Make the Vegetable Juice or any of the variations and add 1 tablespoon aloe vera juice.
Handy tip: If you have an aloe plant, cut off 2.5 cm (1 inch) of flesh and pass through the juice extractor.

518 Apple and Orange Juice

This is perhaps the most traditional and familiar of all fruit juice combinations – and with very good reason.

INGREDIENTS

3 apples, quartered
3 oranges, peeled

Put the apples and oranges through a juice extractor. Pour into a glass and serve immediately.

Makes 2 small glasses

HANDY TIP

Exploit the many and various flavours of apples. Look for unusual varieties at a farmers' market in the autumn since they have the added advantage of being locally grown.

Variations

519 PEAR AND ORANGE JUICE

Prepare the Apple and Orange Juice, omitting the apples and replacing them with 3 pears.
Handy tip: Use the pulp from the orange juice in orange muffins and quick breads.

520 PINEAPPLE AND ORANGE JUICE

Make the Apple and Orange Juice, replacing the apples with 225 g (8 oz) peeled pineapple chunks.
Handy tip: Pineapple is a member of the *Bromeliaceae* family, so named because they are rich in bromelain, an enzyme that reduces inflammation.

521 PINEAPPLE AND APPLE JUICE

Make the Apple and Orange Juice, replacing the oranges with 225 g (8 oz) peeled pineapple chunks.
Nutritional tip: Pineapples are high in manganese, an essential mineral important for metabolism, bones and the healing of wounds.

522 APPLE AND FENNEL JUICE

Make the Apple and Orange Juice, replacing the oranges with ¼ medium fennel bulb.
Serving tip: Fennel is good for bloating and other stomach upsets, making this a good drink when the stomach is feeling fragile.

523 APPLE AND BLACKBERRY JUICE

Make the Apple and Orange Juice, replacing the oranges with 150 g (5 ¼ oz) blackberries.
Handy tip: Try serving this juice warmed.

524 APPLE AND BROCCOLI JUICE

Make the Apple and Orange Juice, replacing the oranges with 6 broccoli florets.
Handy tip: This is a good juice to drink when you feel your energy flagging.

525 Pineappleade

This tangy twist on an old-fashioned sparkling fruit juice is perfect for pouring out of a tall jug on a long summer afternoon.

INGREDIENTS

¼ pineapple, peeled
60 ml (2 fl oz) sparkling water

Put the pineapple through a juice extractor. Pour into a glass and top off with sparkling water.

Makes 1 glass

HANDY TIP

Cut a few slices of pineapple skin off the fruit before juicing; you can use them for decorating glasses if you're making this for friends.

Variations

527 ORANGEADE

Make the Pineappleade, replacing the pineapple with 3 peeled oranges.
Handy tip: This is delicious made from mandarin and clementine oranges, too.

528 APPLEADE

Make the Pineappleade, replacing the pineapple with 3 quartered apples.
Handy tip: Children love bottled apple soda. Try this as a less expensive, healthier option.

529 CHERRYADE

Make the Pineappleade, replacing the pineapple with 150 g (5 ¼ oz) stoned cherries.
Handy tip: For a sweeter juice, top off with lemon-lime soda instead of water.

526 PINEAPPLEADE WITH LIME AND MINT

Make the Pineappleade, adding 8 mint leaves and ¼ peeled lime with the pineapple to the juice extractor. Sweeten with 1 teaspoon agave syrup, or to taste. Pour into an iced glass and top with fresh mint leaves.

530 PINEAPPLE GINGERADE

Make the Pineappleade, replacing the sparkling water with ginger beer.
Handy tip: This makes more fiery version.

531 Hibiscus Cooler

Known as *agua de Jamaica* in Mexico and *karkadé* in Egypt, this refreshing drink is a wonderful, rich red colour and is sour and sweet at the same time.

INGREDIENTS

500 ml (17 fl oz) water
240 ml (8 fl oz) hibiscus flowers, washed
160 g (5 ½ oz) cane sugar, broken into chunks
Ice, to serve
Filtered or mineral water, to serve
Agave syrup, to taste

In a saucepan, bring the water to a boil. Add the flowers and sugar, stir until the sugar is dissolved, then boil for 1 minute. Cover, cool and let sit for 30 to 60 minutes to infuse (do not exceed 2 hours). Drain through a cheesecloth, pressing the flowers to extract as much juice as possible. Pour into a bottle and keep cool.

To serve, put a few ice cubes in a glass and fill about halfway with the hibiscus syrup. Top off with mineral or filtered water. Use more or less syrup to taste and sweeten with a little agave syrup, if required.

Makes 2 glasses

HANDY TIP

Dried hibiscus (Jamaica) flowers are available in larger health food shops, international food shops and online.

Variations

532 HIBISCUS TEA COOLER

Make the Hibiscus Cooler, but when preparing the hibiscus syrup add 1 English breakfast tea bag to the boiling water with the flowers. Serve as directed with a squeeze of lemon and lime juice.
Handy tip: Green tea could be substituted for the English breakfast tea.

533 SPICED HIBISCUS COOLER

Make the Hibiscus Cooler, but when preparing the hibiscus syrup add a 2.5-cm (1-inch) piece of bashed ginger, a small cinnamon stick and the zest of ½ an orange to the boiling water with the flowers. Serve as directed, adding 2 tablespoons orange juice to each glass.

534 BERRY HIBISCUS COOLER

Make the Hibiscus Cooler, adding 60 ml (2 fl oz) blueberry juice (preferably freshly juiced) and 1 teaspoon lime juice to the glass before topping off with water.
Handy tip: If cane sugar is unavailable, substitute golden caster or a light brown sugar.

535 ORANGE HIBISCUS COOLER

Prepare the Hibiscus Cooler, adding the zest of 1 orange to the hibiscus flowers when making the syrup. To serve, add 2 tablespoons orange juice to the glass before topping off with water.

536   CITRUS HIBISCUS COOLER

To each glass of Hibiscus Cooler, add 1 teaspoon each lemon and lime juice and 2 tablespoons orange juice. Sweeten to taste with agave nectar.

Handy tip: Agave nectar is the best sweetener for juices – being liquid it blends in quickly and it has a very mild taste.

537   HIBISCUS POMEGRANATE COOLER

Make the Hibiscus Cooler, adding 60 ml (2 fl oz) pomegranate juice (preferably freshly juiced) and 2 tablespoons orange juice to the glass before topping off with water.

Handy tip: Wear an apron when making the syrup!

538   TROPICAL HIBISCUS TEA COOLER

Make the hibiscus tea syrup as instructed in the Hibiscus Tea Cooler recipe. Half fill a glass with hibiscus tea syrup and top off with equal quantities of pineapple juice and coconut water.

Nutritional tip: There is evidence emerging that hibiscus might be good for lowering blood pressure.

539   WATERMELON HIBISCUS COOLER

Make the Hibiscus Cooler, adding 60 ml (2 fl oz) watermelon juice (preferably freshly juiced) and 1 tablespoon lime juice before topping with water.

Handy tip: Freeze leftover watermelon juice as ice cubes.

540 Rambutan Smoothie

Look at the rambutan's coat of spiky red and yellow tendrils and you'll understand how it got its name – from the Malay word *rambut*, meaning hair. Under the hair is a brittle orange rind that is peeled away to reveal firm, white, translucent flesh. Sweet, juicy and delicately flavoured, rambutans combine well with two other prolific Malaysian fruits – papaya and pineapple – in this smoothie.

INGREDIENTS

8 rambutans, peeled and seeded

½ medium papaya, seeded and chopped

300 ml (10 fl oz) pineapple juice

Crushed ice

Put the fruit and pineapple juice in a blender and process until smooth. Pour into glasses over crushed ice and serve immediately.

Makes 2 glasses

HANDY TIP

Rambutans are available in two colours, red and yellow – either could be used in this smoothie.

variations

541 RAMBUTAN AND MANDARIN SMOOTHIE

Make the Rambutan Smoothie, replacing the pineapple juice with mandarin orange juice.
Shopping tip: Look for brightly coloured, firm, undamaged rambutan with firm spikes. Avoid any fruit that has turned black or has blackened spikes.

542 RAMBUTAN AND RUBY GRAPEFRUIT SMOOTHIE

Make the Rambutan Smoothie, replacing the pineapple juice with ruby grapefruit juice.
Handy tip: Ripe rambutans will store for 5 to 7 days in the fridge, preferably wrapped in a paper towel or perforated plastic bag.

543 RAMBUTAN AND STRAWBERRY SMOOTHIE

Make the Rambutan Smoothie, replacing the papaya with 150 g (5 ¼ oz) strawberries.
Nutritional tip: Malaysian traditional medicine uses rambutan for diabetes, hypertension and to increase energy levels.

544 LYCHEE AND PINEAPPLE SMOOTHIE

Make the Rambutan Smoothie, replacing the rambutans with 8 lychees.
Handy tip: You could make this with 150 g (5 ¼ oz) chopped pineapple and lychee juice in place of pineapple juice.

545 CUSTARD APPLE SMOOTHIE

Make the Rambutan Smoothie, replacing the rambutans with 240 ml (8 fl oz) custard apple pulp, seeds removed.
Handy tip: The best way to eat a custard apple is to just cut in half or pull it apart with your hands, then use a spoon to scoop out the flesh. Do not be put off by appearances – they are sweet and juicy and much nicer than they look.

546 JACKFRUIT SMOOTHIE

Make the Rambutan Smoothie, replacing the rambutans with 180 g (6 ½ oz) chopped jackfruit.
Handy tip: Jackfruit, rambutans and lychees are all available tinned or frozen in some international shops when it is unavailable fresh.

547 JACKFRUIT AND COCONUT SMOOTHIE

Make the Jackfruit Smoothie variation, replacing the pineapple juice with coconut water.
Handy tip: For a creamy version, use low-fat coconut milk.

548 DRAGONFRUIT SMOOTHIE

Make the Rambutan Smoothie, replacing the rambutans with 225 g (8 oz) dragonfruit flesh, scooped from the centre of a dragonfruit.
Handy tip: Only 60% of the dragonfruit is edible.

549 Lychee, Raspberry and Rose Water Fizz

The delicate scent of rose water adds an even more exotic note to the unusual combination of lychees and raspberries.

INGREDIENTS

300 g (10 ½ oz) peeled and stoned lychees

150 g (5 ¼ oz) raspberries

1 tsp rose water

125 ml (4 ¼ fl oz) sparkling water

Put the lychees and raspberries through a juice extractor. Stir in the rose water. Pour into a glass, top with sparkling water and serve immediately.

Makes 1 glass

HANDY TIP

Tinned lychees can be used in this recipe.

Variations

550 LYCHEE, STRAWBERRY AND ROSE WATER FIZZ

Make the Lychee, Raspberry and Rose Water Fizz, replacing the raspberries with strawberries.
Handy tip: Add a squeeze of lemon or lime if this combination is too sweet for your taste.

551 LYCHEE, BLUEBERRY AND ROSE WATER FIZZ

Make the Lychee, Raspberry and Rose Water Fizz, replacing the raspberries with blueberries.
Serving tip: This would make a delicious post-exercise drink.

552 LYCHEE, REDCURRANT AND ROSE WATER FIZZ

Make the Lychee, Raspberry and Rose Water Fizz, replacing the raspberries with redcurrants.
Handy tip: Redcurrants can be difficult to get hold of but are often found at farmers' markets when in season.

553 LYCHEE, BLACKBERRY AND ROSE WATER FIZZ

Make the Lychee, Raspberry and Rose Water Fizz, replacing the raspberries with blackberries.
Shopping tip: Lychees freeze well; add one as a garnish.

554 Black Grape Juice

Mild, sweet grape juice forms the background of this delicious juice. This combination of fruits has anti-ageing properties, too.

INGREDIENTS

300 g (10 ½ oz) red grapes
150 g (5 ¼ oz) blackcurrants or
   blackberries
1 apple, quartered

Process the fruit through a juice extractor. Pour into glasses and serve immediately.

Makes 1 glass

HANDY TIP

It is best to remove the stalks from the blackcurrants and grapes before juicing.

Variations

555 BLACK AND BLUE GRAPE JUICE

Make the Black Grape Juice, adding 75 g (2 ½ oz) blueberries to the other berries.
Handy tip: There are about 15 medium grapes in 225 g (8 oz).

556 BRIGHT RED GRAPE JUICE

Make the Black Grape Juice, replacing the blackcurrants or blackberries with 75 g (2 ½ oz) each of cranberries and stoned cherries.
Nutritional tip: Cranberries are great for keeping the urinary tract flowing freely.

557 GLOWING GRAPE JUICE

Make the Bright Red Grape Juice, replacing the apple with 1 large trimmed carrot.
Handy tip: The carrot in this juice should provide sufficient sugar to sweeten, but add a little agave syrup or liquid honey if the cranberries are too sour.

558   PINK GRAPE JUICE

Make the Black Grape Juice, replacing the blackcurrants or blackberries with the seeds from 1 large pomegranate.

Serving tip: Pomegranate is a relatively pale juice, so this is a particularly pretty drink to serve with a few delicate canapés.

559   PURPLE GRAPE JUICE

Make the Black Grape Juice, replacing the blackcurrants or blackberries with 4 stoned black plums.

Handy tip: Four large plums weigh about 450 g (1 lb).

560   DEEP PURPLE GRAPE JUICE

Make the Purple Grape Juice variation, adding 1 small beetroot.

Handy tip: All these grape-based drinks could be diluted down with a little still or sparkling water.

561 Sparkling Passion Juice

variations

This passion fruit drink gives you a boost of energy – just the thing for a Valentine's day celebration meal.

INGREDIENTS

4 oranges
4 passion fruit, halved
Watermelon ice cubes, optional
  (see page 10)
Sparkling water

Juice the oranges through a citrus press, or peel and process in the juice extractor. Spoon out the pulp from the passion fruit and stir into the orange juice. Drop 3 or 4 watermelon ice cubes into glasses, if desired and pour the combined juice into glasses filling halfway. Top off with sparkling water.

Makes 2 glasses

HANDY TIP

If you dislike the passion fruit seeds in your drink, pass the pulp through a nonmetallic sieve.

562 NEW ZEALAND SPARKLER

Make the Sparkling Passion Juice, replacing the passion fruit with 3 kiwi fruit. Process the peeled oranges and peeled kiwi fruit through the juice extractor.
Serving tip: For a special occasion make any of these sparklers with sparkling grape juice instead of sparkling water and serve in a champagne flute with a sugared rim.

563 CHERRY SPARKLER

Prepare the Sparkling Passion Juice, replacing the passion fruit with 150 g (5 ¼ oz) stoned cherries.
Nutritional tip: In general, the darker the cherry, the more concentrated the nutritional benefits.

564 ORANGE, RASPBERRY AND ROSEMARY SPARKLER

Prepare the Sparkling Passion Juice, replacing the passion fruit with 150 g (5 ¼ oz) raspberries and adding the leaves of 1 sprig of rosemary to the processor.
Handy tip: For an unusual twist, omit the rosemary and add 1 to 2 teaspoons of a herb syrup such as rosemary or basil, or try a spicy cardamom or cinnamon syrup (see page 252).

Sparkling Passion Juice is a healthy alternative to shop-bought fizzy drinks

565 SOURSOP SPARKLER

Prepare the Sparkling Passion Juice, replacing the passion fruit with 240 ml (8 fl oz) soursop pulp or 125 ml (4 ¼ fl oz) soursop juice. In place of 4 oranges, use 2 oranges and the peeled and stoned flesh of ½ a mango.

Handy tip: Also known by its Spanish name, *guanábana*, it is easy to peel back the green skin on this fruit to expose the creamy flesh.

566 MANGO LIME SPARKLER

Prepare the Sparkling Passion Juice, replacing the passion fruit with ½ a lime (peeled) and the stoned flesh of 1 small mango. Process the peeled oranges, peeled lime and mango through the juice extractor.

Handy tip: Mango and orange juice is a common commercial juice combination; if pressed for time, use a good-quality juice to make your sparkler.

567 PAPAYA LIME SPARKLER

Make the Sparkling Passion Juice, replacing the passion fruit with ½ a medium papaya and ½ a lime. Process the peeled oranges, peeled papaya and peeled lime through the juice extractor.

Handy tip: Papaya seeds do not have to be removed before juicing.

568 Nectarine and Raspberry Juice

The sunny flavour of this juice is a perfect remedy for days when the weather is anything but tropical.

INGREDIENTS

3 nectarines, halved
    and stoned
150 g (5 ¼ oz) raspberries

Put the nectarines and raspberries through a juice extractor. Pour into a glass and serve immediately.

Makes 1 glass

HANDY TIP

You can use the pulp from this juice in muffin batter.

Variations

570 NECTARINE AND BLACKBERRY JUICE

Make the Nectarine and Raspberry Juice, replacing the raspberries with the same amount of blackberries.
Serving tip: Serve with thin nectarine wedges tucked over the rim of the glass.

571 NECTARINE AND BLUEBERRY JUICE

Make the Nectarine and Raspberry Juice, replacing the raspberries with the same amount of blueberries.
Shopping tip: Avoid nectarines with green, unripe patches.

569 NECTARINE AND STRAWBERRY JUICE

Make the Nectarine and Raspberry Juice, replacing the raspberries with 5 large strawberries.
Handy tip: Nectarines are slightly sweeter than peaches, so use peaches if this is too sweet for your liking.

NECTARINE AND PLUM JUICE

Make the Nectarine and Raspberry Juice, replacing the raspberries with 3 halved and stoned purple plums.

573 NECTARINE AND APRICOT JUICE

Make the Nectarine and Raspberry Juice, replacing the raspberries with 2 halved and stoned apricots. Top off the glasses with about 60 ml (2 fl oz) filtered or mineral water.

574 Papaya Tropical Smoothie

Fragrant papaya is mixed with fresh orange to form a deliciously bright smoothie that will take you to a tropical island, whatever the weather.

INGREDIENTS

150 g (5 ¼ oz) fresh papaya, peeled, seeded and chopped
½ medium banana, peeled and chopped

240 ml (8 fl oz) orange juice, preferably freshly squeezed
1 tsp lime juice, preferably freshly squeezed

Put all the ingredients in a blender and process until smooth. Pour into glasses and serve immediately.

Makes 1 large or 2 small glasses

HANDY TIP

To prepare a papaya, cut in half lengthwise, scoop out the seeds with a teaspoon, then, using a sharp knife, cut the flesh away from the skin.

variations

575 PAPAYA AND ORANGE SMOOTHIE

Make the Papaya Tropical Smoothie, omitting the banana and adding 2 teaspoons of honey.
Shopping tip: To buy a ripe papaya look for one that is yellow and red in colour and that gives slightly when squeezed gently.

576 PAPAYA AND MANGO SMOOTHIE

Make the Papaya and Orange Smoothie, replacing the orange juice with mango juice.
Handy tip: Papaya seeds can be eaten and have a peppery flavour to them. They are particularly good in salads.

PAPAYA, PINEAPPLE AND CHERRY SMOOTHIE

Make the Papaya and Orange Smoothie, replacing the orange juice with pineapple juice and adding 50 g (1 ¾ oz) stoned cherries.
Nutritional tip: Papayas enzymes reduce inflammation.

578 Orange Froth

The addition of egg white adds texture to this otherwise simple juice. With so few ingredients, the orange juice does really need to be freshly squeezed and bursting with flavour. Don't forget that uncooked egg white isn't for anyone with a compromised immune system or pregnant women.

INGREDIENTS

240 ml (8 fl oz) freshly squeezed
    orange juice
60 ml (2 fl oz) lime juice
1 tsp honey, optional
1 egg white
3 ice cubes

Combine the orange juice, lime juice, honey (if using), egg white and ice cubes in the blender and process on low until the ice is almost broken up, then process on high until smooth. Pour into glasses and serve immediately.

Makes 1 large or 2 small glasses

NUTRITIONAL TIP

Egg whites are high in protein but low in fat and calories.

Variations

579 ORANGE AND RASPBERRY FROTH

Make the Orange Froth, reducing the orange juice to 175 ml (6 fl oz) and adding the juice from 75 g (2 ½ oz) raspberries.
Serving tip: Make the Orange Froth, then drizzle in the raspberry juice and serve without stirring along with a swizzle stick.

580 ORANGE AND KIWI FROTH

Make the Orange Froth, reducing the orange juice to 175 ml (6 fl oz) and adding the juice from 2 kiwi fruit.
Interesting fact: Although associated with New Zealand, kiwi fruit originated in China, where they were called *yáng táo*. They were brought to New Zealand by missionaries in the early 20th Century.

581 ORANGE AND MANGO FROTH

Make the Orange Froth, reducing the orange juice to 150 ml (5 fl oz) and adding the juice of ½ a peeled and stoned mango.
Serving tip: Serve this refreshing juice to accompany grilled salmon or chicken.

582 ORANGE AND CHERRY FROTH

Prepare the Orange Froth, reducing the orange juice to 175 ml (6 fl oz) and adding the juice from 75 g (2 ½ oz) fresh red or black stoned cherries.
Serving tip: Because this juice contains some protein it is a good booster to give to a child who is under the weather.

583 PINEAPPLE FROTH

Prepare the Orange Froth, replacing the orange juice with pineapple juice and using only 2 tablespoons lime juice.
Handy tip: Try drinking pineapple juice instead of taking an antacid. It contains a protein called bromelain, which helps to break down proteins and the small residue of dietary fibre helps unclog the digestive tract.

584 PINEAPPLE AND COCONUT FROTH

Make the Pineapple Froth variation, adding 2 tablespoons creamed coconut.
Serving tip: Being both astringent and creamy and fluffy, this makes an excellent drink to serve with a spicy Mexican or Indian meal.

585 Midsummer Melon Quencher

The star of these simple drinks is the melon. Melons make a wonderful mild juice that, served cold, will quench a thirst in moments. The nutrients from melons are absorbed quickly, making them perfect for an after-exercise treat.

INGREDIENTS

½ honeydew or cantaloupe melon, peeled and seeded
100 g (3 ½ oz) mixed summer berries
Crushed ice

Process the melon and berries through a juice extractor. Stir to mix and pour into a glass over crushed ice. Serve immediately.

Makes 1 glass

HANDY TIP

Don't gulp down freshly squeezed juices. Sip them and allow the juices to linger in the mouth. Not only do you really appreciate their flavours, but they mix the enzymes in the saliva.

Variations

586 MELON AND STRAWBERRY QUENCHER

Prepare the Midsummer Melon Quencher, replacing the mixed summer berries with strawberries.
Shopping tip: Ripe melons feel heavier than unripe ones.

587 MELON AND BLUEBERRY QUENCHER

Prepare the Midsummer Melon Quencher, replacing the mixed summer berries with blueberries.
Serving tip: This juice has a spectacular colour and makes a delicious drink to welcome guests with after they have driven through the heat of the day.

588 MELON AND PEAR QUENCHER

Prepare the Midsummer Melon Quencher, replacing the mixed summer berries with 1 ripe pear and 10 fresh mint leaves.
Handy tip: You may need to add a little lemon or lime juice if this quencher is too sweet for your taste.

590 MELON AND GRAPE QUENCHER

Prepare the Midsummer Melon Quencher, replacing the mixed summer berries with seedless red or green grapes.

Serving tip: Serve this variation with lamb kebabs or a similar Mediterranean lamb dish.

591 MIDSUMMER MELON SMOOTHIE

Put the melon and mixed summer berries in a blender with 75 ml (2 ½ fl oz) plain yoghurt and 75 ml (2 ½ fl oz) apple juice.

Handy tip: Other juices, such as a red berry juice or pear juice, could be used instead of apple juice in this variation.

589 MELON AND GUAVA QUENCHER

Prepare the Midsummer Melon Quencher, replacing the mixed summer berries with 2 peeled and halved guavas.

Handy tip: Melon juice is good for skin conditions such as eczema.

592 MIDSUMMER MELON FIZZ

Make the Midsummer Melon Quencher, adding 240 ml (8 fl oz) sparkling apple juice to the prepared juice.

Handy tip: Replace the sparkling apple juice with sparkling water to reduce the fructose and calories.

593 Wild Berry Shrub Syrup

Fruit shrub drinks are based on very old country recipes dating back to the cordials found in medieval Europe and probably much further back in the Middle East. Basic Raspberry Vinegar is found in *Mrs Beeton's Book of Household Management*, where it is described as 'an excellent drink in cases of fevers and colds'. Make with foraged wild berries, but be sure you know what you are picking.

INGREDIENTS

120 g (4 ¼ oz) fresh-picked wild berries (blackberries, elderberries, blueberries, raspberries, lingonberries, etc.)

240 ml (8 fl oz) cider or white wine vinegar

Approximately 250 g (8 ¾ oz) granulated sugar

Put the berries in a large glass jar or nonmetallic bowl and lightly crush using a fork or potato masher. Add the vinegar and stir to combine. Cover and leave in the fridge or a cool place for at least 24 hours and up to one week, occasionally shaking the jar or stirring the mixture.

Drain the fruity vinegar through a fine mesh sieve or cheesecloth into a measuring cup. Pour the strained liquid into a saucepan along with an equal volume of sugar. Stir over a low heat until the sugar has dissolved, then bring to the boil and simmer for 5 minutes. Allow to cool, then pour into a sterilised bottle.

Makes about 375 ml (12 ½ fl oz) syrup

HANDY TIP

The leftover fruit pulp may be mixed into 500 ml (17 fl oz) of white wine or distilled white vinegar, covered and left for two weeks. Drain through a fine mesh sieve or muslin cloth and bottle. Use as the vinegar base in other fruit shrubs or in salad dressings.

Variations

594 ICE-COLD BERRY SHRUB SYRUP

Put 1 tablespoon Wild Berry Shrub Syrup in a tall glass and add ice-cold filtered or mineral water, adjusting the quantity of syrup to taste. Serve over crushed ice.
Handy tip: It is worth doubling up the quantities when making shrub syrups, or making two flavours at a time.

595 ICE-COLD SPARKLING SHRUB SYRUP

Put 1 tablespoon Wild Berry Shrub Syrup in a tall glass and top off with sparkling water, adjusting the quantity of syrup to taste. Serve over ice cubes.
Handy tip: Add the water very slowly, as the vinegar and carbon dioxide in the water can have a volcanic reaction.

596 ICE-COLD GINGER BERRY SHRUB SYRUP

Put 1 tablespoon Wild Berry Shrub Syrup in a tall glass and top off with ginger beer, adjusting the quantity of syrup to taste. Serve over ice cubes.
Serving tip: Drizzle neat shrub syrup over vanilla ice cream for a surprisingly delicious dessert.

597 ICED APPLE BERRY SHRUB SYRUP

Put 1 tablespoon Wild Berry Shrub Syrup in a tall glass and top off with sparkling apple juice, adjusting the quantity of syrup to taste. Serve over ice cubes.
Serving tip: Shrub syrups make excellent gifts.

598 HOT BERRY SHRUB SYRUP

Stir 1 teaspoon Wild Berry Shrub Syrup into 240 ml (8 fl oz) of boiling water, adding a little more or less to taste.
Serving tip: This is great made up in a flask and taken on a bracing walk or as a nonalcoholic alternative to mulled wine.

599 CHERRY AND VANILLA SHRUB SYRUP

Make the Wild Berry Shrub Syrup, replacing the wild berries with stoned cherries and inserting a vanilla bean into the shrub syrup as it infuses.
Handy tip: This does not require a new vanilla bean; use one that has already been scraped of its seeds.

600 PLUM AND CINNAMON SHRUB SYRUP

Make the Wild Berry Shrub Syrup, replacing the wild berries with 10 halved medium plums and inserting a cinnamon stick into the shrub syrup as it infuses.

601 STRAWBERRY AND BALSAMIC SHRUB SYRUP

Make the Wild Berry Shrub Syrup, replacing the wild berries with strawberries and the cider or wine vinegar with white balsamic vinegar.

602 DELICATE PEAR SHRUB SYRUP

Make the Wild Berry Shrub Syrup, replacing the wild berries with a large ripe pear. Chop the pear into very small pieces, add 60 g (2 oz) sugar and leave for 30 minutes to release the liquid. Proceed as in the main recipe.

603 Blueberry Syrup

This is a wonderful syrup to have on hand to make lovely, refreshing drinks. Because they are made with a boiled sugar syrup they will keep in a cool, dark place for about six months. To use, simply pour about 2 tablespoons of the syrup into a glass and top up with still or sparkling water.

INGREDIENTS

600 g (1 ¼ lb) fresh blueberries
750 ml (1 pt 6 fl oz) water
Zest of 1 lemon, cut in strips
500 g (1 lb 1 ½ oz) raw or
   granulated sugar
Juice ½ lemon

Put the blueberries in a large saucepan and break up with a potato masher. Add 240 ml (8 fl oz) water and the lemon zest strips, then bring to the boil over a medium-high heat, stirring. Boil for 5 minutes; remove from heat and leave to cool. Drain the mixture through a fine nonmetallic sieve or cheesecloth.

In a clean saucepan, combine the remaining water with the sugar, dissolving it over a low heat, stirring. Increase the heat and boil for about 20 minutes until the mixture reaches 110°C (230°F). Carefully stir in the blueberry mixture and boil for 2 minutes, then add in the lemon juice. Leave to cool. Transfer to sterilised bottles. Keep in a cool place for up to six months.

Makes about 600 ml (1 pt) syrup

HANDY TIP

Remove the lemon zest from the lemon with a vegetable peeler.

variations

604 BLUEBERRY AND LIME SYRUP

Prepare the Blueberry Syrup, replacing the lemon zest with lime zest and using the juice of a whole lime.
Handy tip: Freshly picked blueberries are very high in pectin. Let them rest in a cool place for a couple of days before processing or the mixture might set.

605 BLUEBERRY AND BASIL SYRUP

Begin making the Blueberry Syrup. After the blueberries have cooked, add 6 sprigs of basil, including the leaves and stems and allow to infuse while the berry mixture is cooling. Proceed with the instructions for the Blueberry Syrup.
Handy tip: This method works just as well with other herbs such as thyme or rosemary.

606 STRAWBERRY, CARDAMOM AND PEPPERCORN SYRUP

Make the Blueberry Syrup, replacing the blueberries with strawberries and replacing the lemon with the zest and juice of ½ an orange. Add 12 crushed cardamom pods and 1 teaspoon pink or black peppercorns to the strawberries when cooking.
Handy tip: Because the strawberries are cooked, you don't have to use the finest strawberries.

607 STRAWBERRY AND ROSE WATER SYRUP

Make the Blueberry Syrup, replacing the blueberries with strawberries and replacing the lemon with the zest and juice of ½ an orange. Stir 2 to 4 teaspoons rose water into the finished syrup with the orange juice. Add little by little, to taste.
Serving tip: Wedge slices of star fruit among ice cubes to serve.

608 SOUR CHERRY SYRUP

Prepare the Blueberry Syrup, replacing the blueberries with sour cherries.
Handy tip: If you can't get fresh wild cherries, you can rehydrate dried sour cherries.

609 RASPBERRY SYRUP

Make the Blueberry Syrup, replacing the blueberries with raspberries.
Handy tip: Raspberries work well with lime, use the zest and juice of a whole lime. They also work with orange – use the zest and juice of ½ an orange.

610 Apple and Blueberry Refresher

Even if you do not make your own syrup, there is a range of commercially available fruit syrups on the market and they make great instant drinks. Combined with fruit juices, you can make some really lovely, refreshing combinations.

INGREDIENTS

Crushed ice

2 tbsp blueberry syrup (see page 176)

Approximately 500 ml (17 fl oz) apple juice

Divide the crushed ice between two glasses and pour over the syrup. Top off each glass with apple juice and stir well.

Makes 2 glasses

SERVING TIP

Put a layer of blueberries in the base of each glass.

variations

611 SOUR CHERRY WATERMELON REFRESHER

Make the Apple and Blueberry Refresher using Sour Cherry Syrup (see page 177) and watermelon juice.
Shopping tip: If you see unusual juices in the market, don't be timid – try them out.

612 PEACH AND CRANBERRY REFRESHER

Make the Apple and Blueberry Refresher using peach syrup and cranberry juice.
Handy tip: Roll a small sprig of rosemary between the palms to slightly crush it and then add it to the drink for a hint of herb flavour.

613 RASPBERRY, TANGERINE AND LIME REFRESHER

Make the Apple and Blueberry Refresher using raspberry syrup (see page 177), tangerine juice and 1 tablespoon lime juice.
Serving tip: Bulk this one up using 2 L (3 ½ pt) orange juice and 125 ml (4 ¼ fl oz) syrup for a party.

614 RASPBERRY AND LYCHEE REFRESHER

Make the Apple and Blueberry Refresher using raspberry syrup (see page 177) and lychee juice.
Serving tip: Serve this variation with a Thai meal.

615 Citrus cordial

This drink tastes nothing like the drinks made from commercial cordials. It is so simple to make, economical and a great drink for the whole family. You know that it is preservative-free, too.

INGREDIENTS

3 oranges

3 lemons

1 L (1 ¾ pt) boiling water

900 g (2 lb) granulated sugar

2 tbsp citric acid

Shred the zest from the oranges and lemons, then juice through a citrus press or juice extractor. In a large heatproof jug or bowl, mix the juice with the grated rinds. Pour over the boiling water and add the sugar and citric acid. Stir until dissolved, leave to cool and infuse for 24 hours. Drain through a fine mesh nonmetallic sieve and place in a sterilised bottle.

Makes about 1 L (1 ¾ pt) which is 30-60 glasses when diluted, depending on taste.

HANDY TIP

To get more juice from citrus fruit, warm in the microwave for 10 to 20 seconds.

variations

616 MANDARIN CORDIAL

Make the Citrus Cordial, replacing the oranges and 2 of the lemons with the zest and juice of 8 large mandarin oranges.
Handy tip: Clementines could be used in this variation instead of mandarins.

617 PASSION CITRUS CORDIAL

Make the Citrus Cordial, adding the pulp of 3 passion fruits when adding the grated citrus rinds.
Serving tip: This is particularly good served with sparkling water at a barbecue. The flavours contrast well with the smoky food.

618 LEMON CORDIAL

Make the Citrus Cordial, omitting the oranges and using the zest of 3 lemons and the juice of 6 lemons.
Handy tip: Shred the zest from the remaining lemons and keep in a small airtight container in the freezer for later use in cooking.

619 LEMON AND RASPBERRY CORDIAL

Make the Lemon Cordial variation, adding 300 g (10 ½ oz) raspberries.

620 SPICED BERRY CORDIAL

Make the Citrus Cordial using the zest and juice of
1 lemon and 1 orange and adding 300 g (10 ½ oz)
blackberries. Add 3 whole cloves; 3 cardamom pods,
lightly crushed; 2 pink or black peppercorns;
two 7.5-cm (3-inch) cinnamon sticks and 1 bay leaf.

621 ELDERFLOWER CORDIAL

Prepare the Citrus Cordial, omitting the oranges.
Finely slice 2 lemons and use 75 g (2 ½ oz) citric acid,
1.5 kg (3 ¼ lb) sugar and 20 large elderflower heads.
Proceed as directed. Drain through a cheesecloth or
through coffee filters to capture the pollen.

622 GRAPEFRUIT, GINGER AND LEMONGRASS CORDIAL

Make the Citrus Cordial, replacing the oranges and lemons
with the zest of 1 grapefruit and the juice of 2 grapefruits.
Add 2 stalks fresh lemongrass and a 5-cm (2-inch) piece
finely sliced, unpeeled ginger.

623 LIME CORDIAL

Make the Citrus Cordial, replacing the oranges and
lemons with the zest of 5 limes and the juice of 10 limes.
Handy tip: This is delicious with a dash of mint syrup
(see page 252).

624 TROPICAL CORDIAL

Make the Citrus Cordial using only 1 orange and
1 lemon, the pulp of 1 passion fruit and 225 g (8 oz)
freshly crushed pineapple.

Milkshakes and Frozen Drinks

These are indulgent drinks that make you feel happy. Some are high in calories, but healthy options are plentiful and nonetheless enjoyable for it. The entire repertoire of frozen drinks are given in this chapter. There are milkshakes and frappés, frozen smoothies and frosted smoothies, slushies and cream sodas. There are some drinks based on ice cream, some on sorbets or sherbets and a selection that use frozen yoghurts. No collection would be complete without the perfect, classic vanilla shake and its cousins, the banana shake and the Belgian chocolate shake, but there are more unusual combinations to be discovered too.

625 Classic Vanilla Shake

These shakes are miraculously wonderful for something so simple and form the basis of most of the other shakes that follow. The vanilla is the star in these shakes, so it is important to buy the very best ice cream and the very best vanilla extract you can find.

INGREDIENTS

240 ml (8 fl oz) vanilla
   ice cream
½ tsp vanilla extract
1 to 2 tsp sugar, optional
75 to 125 ml (2 ½ to 4 ¼ fl oz)
   whole milk

Put the ice cream, vanilla extract, sugar (if using) and 75 ml (2 ½ fl oz) milk into a blender and process on low for 30 seconds. Stir and process on high until smooth and whipped, adding a little more milk until thick enough to your liking. Pour into a glass and serve immediately.

Makes 1 glass

HANDY TIP

The addition of sugar does depend on the sweetness of the ice cream, so taste a little first before adding the sugar.

Variations

 REALLY RICH VANILLA SHAKE

Make the Classic Vanilla Shake using single cream instead of whole milk.
Serving tip: Serve topped with whipped cream and chocolate syrup.

 VANILLA AND OREO SHAKE

Make the Classic Vanilla Shake, adding 3 Oreo biscuits or other chocolate sandwich biscuits to the blender with the other ingredients.
Handy tip: Instead of adding biscuits, you could use a biscuit-flavoured ice cream.

 STRAWBERRY SWIRL

Purée 8 medium strawberries and add ¼ teaspoon grated orange zest. Remove the strawberry purée from the blender and make the Classic Vanilla Shake. Pour one-third of the shake into the glass, add a third of the strawberry mixture, swirl slightly with a spoon and repeat two more times.
Handy tip: Instead of swirling the strawberry through the milkshake, top the milkshake with the strawberry purée and garnish with mint.

 VANILLA AND SALTED CARAMEL SHAKE

Make the Classic Vanilla Shake, adding 1 tablespoon salted caramel sauce to the blender with the other ingredients. Top with crumbled pretzels and a drizzle of caramel sauce.
Handy tip: Salted caramel sauce is sometimes called fleur de sel caramel sauce.

 COCONUT SHAKE

Make the Classic Vanilla Shake, replacing the vanilla ice cream with coconut ice cream and top with a wedge of pineapple.
Serving tip: Add 2 tablespoons plain chocolate shavings after blending and decorate with additional chocolate shavings.

 APPLE PIE SHAKE

Add 225 g (8 oz) stewed apple or apple sauce to the ingredients plus ¼ teaspoon cinnamon and a pinch of nutmeg, then proceed as directed in the Classic Vanilla Shake recipe. Top with crumbled digestive biscuits and cinnamon sugar.
Handy tip: If preferred, use a fresh apple. Put one peeled, cored and chopped apple in the blender with half of the milk, then proceed as directed.

632 PEACH AND VANILLA SHAKE

Put one peeled, stoned and chopped peach in the blender with 2 tablespoons orange juice. Process until smooth. Add the remaining ingredients from the Classic Vanilla Shake recipe and proceed as directed.
Handy tip: Using tinned peaches in this shake is fine, but nothing really substitutes for fresh fruit.

633 DAIRY-FREE CLASSIC VANILLA SHAKE

Make the Classic Vanilla Shake, replacing the vanilla ice cream with dairy-free ice cream and the milk with soya or almond milk.
Handy tip: Dairy-free ice creams are made from soya, coconut, almond, or rice milk. They all vary in taste and consistency, but most make good shakes.

634 SKINNY VANILLA SHAKE

Mix together 175 ml (6 fl oz) unsweetened almond milk, ½ teaspoon vanilla extract and sweetener, to taste. Pour into a plastic container and transfer to the freezer; let freeze, about 2 hours. Process along with an additional 175 ml (6 fl oz) almond milk until smooth.
Handy tip: If you use vanilla almond milk, add just a few more drops of vanilla – the intense cold masks the delicate flavour of the vanilla.

635 Banana Milkshake

This milkshake, the one that we all grew up on, never loses its charm. It is best to use really ripe bananas, when they are at their most flavoursome, for this shake.

INGREDIENTS

1 banana, peeled and quartered
300 ml (10 fl oz) vanilla ice cream
2 tbsp milk

Put all the ingredients into a blender and process on low for 30 seconds; stir and process on high until smooth and whipped. Pour into a glass and serve immediately.

Makes 1 glass

SERVING TIP

Just because you are making this at home doesn't mean you can't have it all – just add whipped cream and a scattering of chocolate chips or nuts and maybe even a cherry!

Variations

636 BANANA MALT SHAKE

Make the Banana Milkshake, adding 1 tablespoon malt powder to the ingredients before blending.
Interesting fact: Malt powder is a fine pale-coloured powder with a sweet, slightly nutty flavour. It is made from ground, kiln-dried, sprouted grain, most commonly barley.

637 BANANA AND PEANUT BUTTER MALT SHAKE

Make the Banana Milkshake, adding 1 tablespoon malt powder and 1 tablespoon peanut butter to the ingredients before blending.
Handy tip: If using crunchy peanut butter, you may want to buy some bigger straws.

638 BANANA AND CHOCOLATE MALT SHAKE

Make the Banana Milkshake, replacing the vanilla ice cream with the same quantity of chocolate ice cream. Also add 1 tablespoon malt powder to the ingredients before blending.

639 BANANA AND CHOCOLATE MILKSHAKE

Make the Banana Milkshake, replacing the vanilla ice cream with the same quantity of chocolate ice cream.

640 BANOFFEE SHAKE

Make the Banana Milkshake, replacing the vanilla ice cream with toffee ice cream and topping the shake with whipped cream and mini chocolate chips.
Serving tip: Serve this as dessert with a few sliced bananas at the base of the glass and drizzle a little caramel sauce through the shake as you pour it into the glass.

641 SPICED BANANA SHAKE

Make the Banana Milkshake, adding ¼ teaspoon pumpkin pie or apple pie spice with the other ingredients before blending.
Handy tip: You could replace the spice mix with a generous pinch each of ground cinnamon and nutmeg.

642 COFFEE BANANA SHAKE

Make the Banana Milkshake, replacing the vanilla ice cream with coffee ice cream.
Handy tip: If you haven't got coffee ice cream, you can add 2 tablespoons instant coffee powder to the blender. If using granules, dissolve in a little hot water and cool before adding.

643 MOCHA BANANA SHAKE

Make the Banana Milkshake, replacing the vanilla ice cream with coffee ice cream and stirring in 1 tablespoon chocolate syrup.

644 HONEY BANANA SHAKE

Add 2 tablespoons liquid honey, 1 tablespoon lemon juice and a pinch of ground nutmeg to the blender when making the Banana Milkshake.

645 Raspberry and White Chocolate Milkshake

One of life's simple pleasures – raspberry and white chocolate is a match made in heaven. Choose the best-quality ice cream you can find, as it makes a real difference here.

INGREDIENTS

120 g (4 ¼ oz) raspberries
300 ml (10 fl oz) white chocolate ice cream
2 tbsp milk

Put all the ingredients into a blender and process on low for 30 seconds, then stir and blend on high until smooth. Pour into a glass and serve immediately.

Makes 1 glass

HANDY TIP

It is the coldness that will give you that thick, creamy consistency, so ensure everything is as cold as possible – ice cream, utensils, blender, milk and flavourings.

Variations

647 WHITE CHOCOLATE MILKSHAKE

Make the Raspberry and White Chocolate Milkshake, omitting the raspberries and increasing the quantity of ice cream to 375 ml (12 ½ fl oz).
Handy tip: Avoid using light ice creams.

648 WHITE CHOCOLATE MALT SHAKE

Make the Raspberry and White Chocolate Milkshake, omitting the raspberries and increasing the quantity of ice cream to 375 ml (12 ½ fl oz). Add 1 tablespoon malt powder to the other ingredients before blending.

649 DOUBLE CHOCOLATE MILKSHAKE

Prepare the Raspberry and White Chocolate Milkshake, omitting the raspberries and adding 125 ml (4 ¼ fl oz) white chocolate ice cream and 1 tablespoon chocolate chips to the other ingredients before blending.

650 CHERRY AND WHITE CHOCOLATE SHAKE

Prepare the Raspberry and White Chocolate Milkshake, replacing the raspberries with stoned cherries.
Handy tip: Big, rich, red cherries look fantastic.

646 RASPBERRY AND WHITE CHOCOLATE MALT SHAKE

Make the Raspberry and White Chocolate Milkshake adding 1 tablespoon malt powder to the other ingredients before blending.

651 BLUEBERRY AND WHITE CHOCOLATE SHAKE

Prepare the Raspberry and White Chocolate Milkshake, replacing the raspberries with blueberries.
Handy tip: Dip blueberries in melted white chocolate to garnish

652 Pear, chocolate and Ginger Milkshake

Pear with chocolate is an inspired combination that has consistently found favour. This smooth shake is sure to become one of your favourites. It also makes a great iced dessert if served in smaller glasses.

INGREDIENTS

2.5-cm (1-inch) piece fresh
  ginger, peeled
1 ripe pear, peeled, cored
  and chopped

300 ml (10 fl oz) chocolate
  ice cream
2 tbsp milk

Shred the ginger and put in the blender with all the other ingredients. Process on low for 30 seconds, stir, then blend on high until smooth and whipped. Pour into a glass and serve immediately.

Makes 1 glass

HANDY TIP

Pears should be really ripe or the resulting shake may have a gritty texture. Tinned pears are better than unripe fresh pears.

variations

653 INDULGENT PEAR, CHOCOLATE AND GINGER MILKSHAKE

Make the Pear, Chocolate and Ginger Milkshake and top the milkshake with 1 crumbled ginger snap just before serving.
Handy tip: A dark-chocolate biscuit also works well with this flavour combination.

654 PEAR, CHOCOLATE AND GINGER MALT SHAKE

Make the Pear, Chocolate and Ginger Milkshake and add 1 tablespoon malt powder to the other ingredients before blending.
Handy tip: If you don't want to use fresh ginger, try using crystallised ginger, which is sweetened.

655 PEAR AND CHOCOLATE MILKSHAKE

Omit the ginger when preparing the Pear, Chocolate and Ginger Milkshake.
Nutritional tip: Pears are a good source of fibre and vitamin C.

656 Many Berry Shake

This delicious shake is made in a moment and using fruit straight from the freezer means that it makes the ideal after-school (or after-work!) treat.

INGREDIENTS

240 ml (8 fl oz) vanilla ice cream
40 g (1 ½ oz) mixed frozen berries
75 ml (2 ½ fl oz) milk

Put all the ingredients into a blender and process on low for 30 seconds. Stir, then blend on high until smooth and whipped. Pour into a glass and serve immediately.

Makes 1 glass

HANDY TIP

If your ice cream is even a little bit soupy, you won't make a really thick shake. It must be really well frozen.

Variations

657 BERRY CHOCOLATE SHAKE

Make the Many Berry Shake, replacing the vanilla ice cream with chocolate ice cream.
Serving tip: It is a good idea to offer a jug of filtered or mineral water with a milkshake.

658 DOUBLE BERRY SHAKE

Make the Many Berry Shake, replacing the vanilla ice cream with strawberry ice cream.
Handy tip: If your shake isn't thick enough, put it in the freezer for 15 to 20 minutes after blending.

659 STRAWBERRY AND ROSE WATER SHAKE

Make the Many Berry Shake, replacing the mixed berries with frozen strawberries and adding 1 teaspoon rose water to the blender with the other ingredients.
Serving tip: Garnish with a few freshly ground cardamom seeds.

BLUEBERRY VANILLA SHAKE

Prepare the Many Berry Shake, replacing the mixed berries with frozen blueberries and adding ¼ teaspoon vanilla extract.

Handy tip: If using fresh blueberries, chill in the fridge before use.

BLUEBERRY AND PEACH SHAKE

Make the Blueberry Vanilla Shake variation and add 1 peeled, stoned and chopped peach to the blender.

Serving tip: Divide in two and serve as two children's desserts or as little sweet dessert treats for adults.

BLUEBERRY ALMOND SHAKE

Make the Blueberry Vanilla Shake variation and add 2 tablespoons grated almond paste and a few drops almond extract, to taste.

Handy tip: Add the almond extract to the finished shake, that way you adjust to your liking – do not be tempted to be heavy handed with the drops or the shake will be bitter.

663 Dairy-Free Banana Shake

Using frozen watermelon and frozen banana gives the iciness without the lactose or calories – and the watermelon is almost tasteless. These milkshakes are so good for you, they don't have to be kept as a treat.

INGREDIENTS

300 g (10 ½ oz) frozen watermelon cubes

1 banana, peeled and frozen

125 to 175 ml (4 ¼ to 6 fl oz) vanilla soya or rice milk

A few drops vanilla extract, optional

Put all the ingredients, except the vanilla extract, into a blender and process on low until the fruit is puréed. Stir, then blend on high until smooth and whipped. Add vanilla extract to taste. Pour into a glass and serve immediately.

Makes 1 glass

HANDY TIP

Freeze fruit when it is at its ripest and most flavoursome.

Variations

664 CHOCOLATE DAIRY-FREE SHAKE

Make the Dairy-Free Banana Shake, adding 2 tablespoons unsweetened cocoa powder and sweetening to taste with 1 to 2 teaspoons chocolate syrup, liquid honey or agave syrup.
Handy tip: For a speckled chocolate shake, use 60 ml (2 fl oz) plain chocolate chips instead of the cocoa power.

665 PROTEIN-BOOSTED CHOCOLATE DAIRY-FREE SHAKE

Make the Dairy-Free Banana Shake, omitting the vanilla extract and adding 1 heaping scoop of chocolate-flavoured protein powder and 2 teaspoons unsweetened cocoa powder.
Handy tip: Add a couple of ice cubes to thicken the shake.

666 DAIRY-FREE MAPLE SHAKE

Make the Dairy-Free Banana Shake and add 2 tablespoons of maple syrup to the blender with the other ingredients.
Handy tip: Using good-quality ingredients will result in good-quality shakes, so don't compromise on the maple syrup.

667 Belgian chocolate shake

Few people can resist a large glass of iced liquid chocolate topped with even more chocolate or other sweet temptations. Serious chocoholics will want to use Belgian chocolate ice cream, while others may prefer a lighter textured ice cream.

INGREDIENTS

240 ml (8 fl oz) whole milk
125 ml (4 ¼ fl oz) Belgian
   chocolate ice cream

Put the milk and ice cream into a blender and process on low for 30 seconds. Stir and blend on high until smooth and whipped. Pour into a glass and serve immediately.

Makes 1 glass

HANDY TIP

Make your ice cubes from chocolate milk to reduce the diluting effect of ice.

Variations

CHOCOLATE, CHOCOLATE CHIP SHAKE

Prepare the Belgian Chocolate Shake, adding 2 tablespoons chocolate chips after the initial blending so that they retain some texture.

Handy tip: For a really textured shake, add mini chocolate chips and stir into the finished shake.

CHOCOLATE ORANGE SHAKE

Peel, seed and chop one orange and add it to the blender with the other ingredients when making the Belgian Chocolate Shake.

Handy tip: For a stronger flavour, add a few drops of orange oil or orange extract.

NEAPOLITAN SHAKE

Make the Belgian Chocolate Shake. Stir 60 ml (2 fl oz) chopped strawberries into the finished shake by hand. Top with a scoop of vanilla ice cream, more sliced strawberries and toasted almonds.

Handy tip: This is great topped with strawberry syrup. (See page 176 for instructions on making syrups.)

ROCKY ROAD SHAKE

Make the Belgian Chocolate Shake, adding 2 tablespoons mini marshmallows and 2 tablespoons mixed chopped nuts to the blender. Top with more of the marshmallows and chopped nuts.

Handy tip: Toasted marshmallows could be used instead of mini marshmallows. Thread 3 marshmallows on a skewer and hold over a gas range until evenly charred. Top the finished shake with another toasted marshmallow.

CHOCOLATE PRALINE SHAKE

Make the Belgian Chocolate Shake. Stir 3 tablespoons finely chopped praline and top with additional praline bits.

Handy tip: To make praline, combine 115 g (4 oz) sugar and 2 tablespoons water in a saucepan over low heat. Cook, stirring until sugar has dissolved. Increase heat, bring to the boil, then boil without stirring for 5 minutes until golden. Let sit for 2 minutes, then add 60 g (2 oz) slivered almonds, pour onto a baking sheet lined with waxed paper, cool, then break into pieces.

PEPPERMINT CHOCOLATE SHAKE

Make the Belgian Chocolate Shake adding 1 or 2 drops (no more) of peppermint extract with the other ingredients. Top with crushed after-dinner mints; the ones with the crunchy minty bits are the best.

Serving tip: Serve in espresso cups with coffee spoons instead of chocolates after a meal.

Serve this shake with ice cubes made from chocolate milk for double chocolate decadence

SPICED CHOCOLATE PUMPKIN SHAKE

Make the Belgian Chocolate Shake, adding 2 tablespoons pumpkin purée, ¼ teaspoon ground cinnamon and a pinch each of ground cayenne pepper, ground ginger and ground cloves to the blender.

Handy tip: Omit the cayenne if you want the spice without the heat.

CHOCOLATE AND PECAN BUTTER SHAKE

Make the Belgian Chocolate Shake, adding up to 60 ml (2 fl oz) pecan butter. Top with a few pecans and a drizzle of maple syrup.

Handy tip: You can make this variation using almond, cashew, or plain old peanut butter instead of pecan butter.

CHOCOLATE BAR SHAKE

Make the Belgian Chocolate Shake, adding 1 tablespoon butterscotch sauce to the blender with the other ingredients. Stir 2 tablespoons finely chopped flavoured chocolate into the finished shake. Top with a scoop of vanilla ice cream, a drizzle of butterscotch sauce and chopped toasted almonds.

Handy tip: This works well with orange-flavoured chocolate or coconut-flavoured white chocolate.

677 strawberry and kiwi shake

Choose complementary flavours and good-quality ripe fruit to make a perfect shake every time. For a really smooth shake, purée the fruit in the blender, then press through a nonmetallic sieve. These fruit shakes are very adaptable and work well with fruit-flavoured ice creams, sherbets or sorbets.

INGREDIENTS

125 ml (4 ¼ fl oz) vanilla ice cream
125 ml (4 ¼ fl oz) whole milk
1 kiwi fruit, peeled and chopped

50 g (1 ¾ oz) strawberries
1 tbsp lime juice
Slices of kiwi and strawberry and mint leaves, to garnish

Put all the ingredients into a blender and process on low for 30 seconds, then stir and blend on high until smooth and whipped. Pour into a glass and serve immediately. Garnish with fresh fruit and mint leaves.

Makes 1 glass

HANDY TIP

The addition of lemon or lime often brings out the flavour of the fruit. Adjust to suit your own taste.

678 ORANGE, STRAWBERRY AND KIWI SHAKE

Make the Strawberry and Kiwi Shake, replacing the vanilla ice cream with strawberry sherbet and the milk with orange juice. **Nutritional tip:** This shake is fat-free if made with sorbet.

variations

679 CANTALOUPE AND RASPBERRY SHAKE

Make the Strawberry and Kiwi Shake, replacing the strawberries with raspberries and the kiwi with 85 g (3 oz) chopped cantaloupe.

MANGO AND RASPBERRY SHAKE

Make the Strawberry and Kiwi Shake, replacing strawberries with raspberries and the kiwi with 85 g (3 oz) chopped mango.

NECTARINE AND STRAWBERRY SHAKE

Prepare the Strawberry and Kiwi Shake, replacing the kiwi with one stoned, peeled and chopped small nectarine.
Serving tip: This variation makes a deliciously tempting brunch treat.

682 Frosted Berry Shake

Many old-fashioned milkshakes do not use ice cream; the frozen fruit provides the thickness.

INGREDIENTS

75 g (2 ½ oz) frozen summer berries

1 tbsp liquid honey or agave syrup, or more to taste

240 ml (8 fl oz) whole milk

Frozen berries and fresh mint leaves, to garnish

Put the berries straight into the blender from the freezer. Process with the other ingredients on low until almost smooth, then on high until smooth and creamy. Add more honey or syrup, if needed, then serve, garnished with berries and mint.

Makes 1 glass

HANDY TIP

You can sweeten this with a raspberry syrup.

variations

ALMOND AND STRAWBERRY SHAKE

Make the Frosted Berry Shake, replacing the summer berries with frozen strawberries and the milk with almond milk.
Nutritional tip: Any nondairy milk, such as rice milk or soya milk, would make this lactose-free.

COCONUT AND SUMMER BERRY SHAKE

Make the Frosted Berry Shake, replacing the milk with low-fat coconut milk. Garnish with toasted unsweetened flaked coconut.
Handy tip: Coconut burns very quickly when toasting.

BLACKBERRY AND ORANGE SHAKE

Make the Frosted Berry Shake, replacing the summer berries with blackberries and using 125 ml (4 ¼ fl oz) coconut milk and 125 ml (4 ¼ fl oz) orange juice instead of whole milk.

686 Black cherry and orange cooler

What a fantastic cooler! These drinks are based on two ingredients: a fruit sorbet and a fruit juice. They are perfect for a quick fix on a summer day. It's easy to swap different fruits and juices in and out, depending on what you have at hand.

INGREDIENTS

240 ml (8 fl oz) orange juice, preferably freshly squeezed

240 ml (8 fl oz) black cherry sorbet

Crushed ice

Orange slices, to garnish

Put the orange juice and black cherry sorbet into the blender and process until smooth. Pour over crushed ice and decorate with orange slices.

Makes 1 glass

HANDY TIP

It really is worth using freshly squeezed orange juice. When there are only two ingredients, they really should be the best ones possible.

Variations

688 PINEAPPLE AND MANGO COOLER

Make the Black Cherry and Orange Cooler, replacing the black cherry sorbet with mango sorbet and the orange juice with pineapple juice.
Handy tip: Mango sorbet can be made by simply churning a large tin of mango pulp with a little lime juice in an ice-cream maker.

689 PRICKLY PEAR AND ORANGE COOLER

Make the Black Cherry and Orange Cooler, replacing the black cherry sorbet with prickly pear sorbet.
Handy tip: There are an amazing variety of sorbets on the market. Buy unusual ones when you see them and whip up fantastic-tasting cooler combinations.

690 DRIED APRICOT AND ORANGE COOLER

Cook 10 dried apricots in a little water until soft; leave to cool. Purée in a blender with 3 tablespoons of the cooking liquor. Add 240 ml (8 fl oz) orange juice and 240 ml (8 fl oz) lemon sorbet. Drain through a nonmetallic sieve into a glass.
Handy tip: Dried apricots have a more intense apricot taste than the fresh fruit.

687 CRANBERRY AND ORANGE COOLER

Make the Black Cherry and Orange Cooler, replacing the black cherry sorbet with orange sorbet and the orange juice with cranberry juice.
Nutritional tip: These coolers are fat-free.

691 LIME AND BERRY COOLER

Make the Black Cherry and Orange Cooler, replacing the black cherry sorbet with lime sorbet and the orange juice with berry juice.

692 Skinny Mango Shake

Even if you are watching your weight, that doesn't mean that you can't have any kind of creamy milkshake. These almond milkshakes are very delicious and the frozen banana provides the thick texture you crave in a milkshake.

INGREDIENTS

½ large mango, stoned, peeled and chopped

1 frozen banana

240 ml (8 fl oz) vanilla almond milk

Put the mango chunks and the banana, straight from the freezer, into the blender. Add the almond milk and process on low until almost smooth, then process on high until smooth and creamy. Pour into a glass and serve immediately.

Makes 1 glass

HANDY TIP

Peel your bananas and cut into pieces before freezing them. Then, simply put the bananas into a resealable freezer bag and remove the air.

693 SKINNY PINEAPPLE SHAKE

Make the Skinny Mango Shake, replacing the mango with 150 g (5 ¼ oz) chopped pineapple and drain into the glass through a nonmetallic sieve, if desired.
Handy tip: Use frozen bananas straight from the freezer.

694 SKINNY BLUEBERRY SHAKE

Make the Skinny Mango Shake, replacing the mango with 150 g (5 ¼ oz) blueberries.
Shopping tip: Buy very ripe or brown bananas on sale and then freeze for later use.

695 Passion Fruit Frozen Yoghurt Smoothie

Whether you buy frozen yoghurt or make your own, the resulting smoothies are rich and creamy but cleaner-tasting than shakes made with ice cream. These are so good and healthy, you could even have one for a mid-morning snack.

INGREDIENTS

1 passion fruit, halved
125 ml (4 ¼ fl oz) frozen vanilla or
    pineapple yoghurt
125 ml (4 ¼ fl oz) orange juice,
    preferably freshly squeezed

Scoop the pulp from the passion fruit and press through a nonmetallic sieve into the blender. Add the frozen yoghurt and juice and process on low until almost smooth, then process on high until smooth and creamy. Pour into a glass and serve immediately.

Makes 1 glass

SERVING TIP

To make your own frozen yoghurt: Sweeten 500 ml (17 fl oz) plain yoghurt with liquid honey or sweetener. (You need to oversweeten slightly because frozen foods taste less sweet.) Add chopped fruit or vanilla extract to taste and churn in an ice cream maker until set. Transfer to a plastic container and freeze until firm.

Variations

696 PASSION FRUIT AND PEACH FROZEN YOGHURT SMOOTHIE

Make the Passion Fruit Frozen Yoghurt Smoothie, replacing the vanilla or pineapple frozen yoghurt with peach frozen yoghurt.
Handy tip: Most frozen yoghurts contains sweeteners, so there is no need to add any more sugar to these smoothies. Choose a frozen yoghurt sweetened with honey for preference.

697 CHOCO-PASSION FROZEN YOGHURT SMOOTHIE

Make the Passion Fruit Frozen Yoghurt Smoothie, replacing the vanilla or pineapple frozen yoghurt with chocolate-flavoured frozen yoghurt.
Handy tip: If you haven't got chocolate frozen yoghurt, add 1 tablespoon chocolate-flavoured syrup to the blender with the other ingredients.

698 PASSION FRUIT AND LIME FROZEN YOGHURT SMOOTHIE

Make the Passion Fruit Frozen Yoghurt Smoothie, replacing the vanilla or pineapple frozen yoghurt with lime frozen yoghurt.
Nutritional tip: Soya-based frozen yoghurts are available for those with lactose allergies and vegans.

TROPICAL FROZEN YOGHURT SMOOTHIE

Make the Passion Fruit Frozen Yoghurt Smoothie, replacing the orange juice with pineapple juice and using coconut frozen yoghurt instead of vanilla or pineapple yoghurt. Top with slices of star fruit.
Nutritional tip: Frozen yoghurt is lower in fat than ice cream because it uses milk rather than cream. However, since frozen yoghurts contain sugar, they may not be as low in calories as one might expect.

BERRY PASSIONATE FROZEN YOGHURT SMOOTHIE

Make the Passion Fruit Frozen Yoghurt Smoothie, replacing the vanilla or pineapple frozen yoghurt with berry frozen yoghurt and the orange juice with cranberry juice.
Nutritional tip: Add a scoop of protein powder to these smoothies if using as a meal replacement.

PASSION FRUIT CHEESECAKE SMOOTHIE

Make the Passion Fruit Frozen Yoghurt Smoothie, replacing half the frozen yoghurt with 60 ml (2 fl oz) chilled mascarpone cheese.
Handy tip: This variation could also be made with reduced-fat cream cheese.

702 Vietnamese Papaya Shake

This simple milkshake is characterised by the addition of sweetened condensed milk, so popular in tropical climates. This makes really rich, sweet creamy shakes that could become quite addictive!

INGREDIENTS

3 tablespoons sweetened condensed milk

5-cm (2-inch) piece banana

90 g (3 oz) chopped papaya

125 ml (4 ¼ fl oz) coconut milk

6 ice cubes

Put the ingredients into a blender and process on low until almost smooth, then process on high until smooth and creamy. Pour into a glass and serve immediately.

Makes 1 glass

INTERESTING FACT

Coconut milk is made from simmering one part grated coconut in one part water. Coconut cream is made from simmering four parts grated coconut in one part water. These methods provide very different consistencies and flavours, so do not confuse the two.

variations

703 VIETNAMESE PAPAYA MILKSHAKE

Prepare the Vietnamese Papaya Shake, replacing the coconut milk with whole dairy milk.
Interesting fact: In a tropical climate, condensed milk is easier to store than fresh milk and is popular in cooking throughout this belt of the globe.

704 GUAVA AND PEACH VIETNAMESE SHAKE

Prepare the Vietnamese Papaya Shake, replacing the papaya with 1 small peeled, stoned and chopped peach and add 60 ml (2 fl oz) guava nectar.
Handy tip: Removing the seeds from the guava is time consuming, so guava nectar makes a good, quick alternative, or use the seeded flesh from one small guava.

705 VIETNAMESE DRAGONFRUIT SHAKE

Prepare the Vietnamese Papaya Shake, replacing the papaya with the pulp from 1 dragonfruit.
Interesting fact: Dragon fruit develops on a cactus that flowers for only one night per cycle. It must be pollinated by passing moths or bats during that one night.

706 VIETNAMESE MANGO SHAKE

Prepare the Vietnamese Papaya Shake, replacing the papaya with chopped fresh mango.
Serving tip: This would make the perfect finale to a Vietnamese or Thai meal.

707 Frosted Peach Smoothie

Based on frozen fruit, these frosted smoothies make healthy alternatives to ice cream-based shakes without losing any of the flavour or joy.

INGREDIENTS

100 g (3 ½ oz) frozen sliced peaches
150 ml (5 fl oz) pomegranate juice
3 tbsp low-fat Greek yoghurt
3 ice cubes

Put the ingredients in a blender and process on a low speed until almost smooth. You may wish to add a bit more pomegranate juice if it appears too thick for your taste. Process on high until smooth. Pour into a glass and serve.

Makes 1 glass

HANDY TIP

If you don't have frozen peaches, drain a tin of peach slices and pop them in the freezer for an hour.

Variations

708 MINTED STRAWBERRY AND PEACH FROSTED SMOOTHIE

Follow the recipe for Frosted Peach Smoothie, adding 10 mint leaves and 5 frozen strawberries to the blender with the other ingredients.
Handy tip: Having frozen fruit in the freezer enables you to have a ready supply of fruit without running the risk of it spoiling.

709 RASPBERRY AND CRANBERRY FROSTED SMOOTHIE

Make the Frosted Peach Smoothie, replacing the peaches with frozen raspberries and adding a 5-cm (2-inch) piece of cucumber to the blender.
Handy tip: The cucumber makes this a slightly more watery drink, perfect for quenching thirst on hot days.

710 BLUEBERRY FROSTED SMOOTHIE

Make the Frosted Peach Smoothie, replacing the peaches with frozen blueberries.
Serving tip: This makes a good drink for boosting energy after exercise.

TOFU AND PEACH FROSTED SMOOTHIE

Make the Frosted Peach Smoothie, replacing the yoghurt with 3 tablespoons silken tofu.

Serving tip: Because of the added protein in this smoothie, it makes a good lunchtime drink to boost energy levels for the rest of the day.

PEACH AND BERRY FROSTED SMOOTHIE

Make the Frosted Peach Smoothie using only 50 g (1 ¾ oz) peach slices and adding 50 g (1 ¾ oz) raspberries, blackberries or blueberries.

Handy tip: Look out for fresh berries that are on the last day of sale; they are often a good price and can be frozen at home for later use.

PEACH SMOOTHIE DESSERT

Make the Frosted Peach Smoothie, omitting the yoghurt. Take two glasses and crumble an oatcake into the base. Top with alternative layers of smoothie and layers of Greek-style yoghurt, ending with a layer of yoghurt.

Handy tip: Greek-style yoghurt is chosen for its creamy taste, but, consequently, it is relatively high in calories. Try a fat-free version for a healthier dessert.

PEACH AND MANGO FROSTED YOGHURT SMOOTHIE

Prepare the Frosted Peach Smoothie, replacing the pomegranate juice with mango nectar or mango and orange juice and replacing the Greek yoghurt with 125 ml (4 ¼ fl oz) frozen vanilla yoghurt.

Nutritional tip: Mango is a great source of vitamins and antioxidants, making this a particularly health-boosting smoothie.

715 Pineapple Cream Soda

Fruit juice sodas were the craze more than a century ago and are still just as delicious, creamy and refreshing. The fruit versions are based on tangy juices such as pineapple, orange and cranberry, which are then blended with ice cream and soda water.

INGREDIENTS

1 tbsp double cream
150 ml (5 fl oz) pineapple juice, preferably fresh
Soda water

125 ml (4 ¼ fl oz) vanilla ice cream
Maraschino cherries

Put the cream in a tall glass and add the juice. Add sufficient soda water to three-quarters fill the glass. Add the ice cream, then top off with more soda water. Top with maraschino cherries.

Makes 1 glass

HANDY TIP

Club soda and soda water are interchangeable; however club soda often contains table salt or other slightly salty additives.

Variations

717 CRANBERRY CREAM SODA

Make the Pineapple Cream Soda, replacing the pineapple juice with cranberry juice and using a cranberry or raspberry ice cream, if available.
Serving tip: Serve with a long-handled parfait spoon to use as a mixer and to pick off pieces of the ice cream from within the drink.

718 CHERRY CREAM SODA

Make the Pineapple Cream Soda, replacing the pineapple juice with sour cherry juice and adding a couple of drops of almond extract.
Handy tip: If you don't want to add the cream, use 1 tablespoon raspberry syrup (page 177) in the base of the glass.

719 ORANGE-LIME CREAM SODA

Make the Pineapple Cream Soda, replacing the pineapple juice with freshly squeezed orange juice plus 1 tablespoon freshly squeezed lime juice.
Handy tip: Use orange soda instead of soda water for a more intense orange flavour and a little extra sweetness.

716 PINEAPPLE SODA

Make the Pineapple Cream Soda, omitting the cream and replacing the ice cream with pineapple or orange sorbet.
Serving tip: Look out for old-fashioned, 475-ml (16-oz) ice-cream soda glasses at garage sales, antique shops and charity shops.

720 CITRUS SODA

Make the Orange-Lime Cream Soda variation, omitting the cream and replacing half of the vanilla ice cream with lemon sorbet.
Handy tip: If you put the ice cream into the glass first, the drink is called a float.

721 Mexican Avocado Milkshake

Avocados are a fruit and combine well with honey or sugar to make surprisingly delicious shakes.

INGREDIENTS

1 avocado, skinned, halved
  and stoned
240 ml (8 fl oz) milk
6 ice cubes

1 to 2 tablespoons
  liquid honey
A few drops vanilla extract,
  optional

Put the avocado, milk, ice cubes and 1 tablespoon honey into a blender and process on low until it's almost smooth and the ice is almost crushed, then process on high until smooth and creamy. Adjust the sweetness and add vanilla to taste. Pulse to combine the additional sweetener, then allow to sit for 10 to 15 minutes in the fridge to let the flavours develop (although this is not essential). Pour into glasses to serve.

Makes 2 to 3 glasses

Shopping Tip

Avocados have to be very ripe for this shake, but they should be firm and blemish-free with no black spots. They should give slightly when pressed with the thumb.

723 VIETNAMESE AVOCADO SHAKE

Make the Mexican Avocado Milkshake, omitting the honey. Use only 125 ml (4 ¼ fl oz) of the milk and add 75 ml (2 ½ fl oz) sweetened condensed milk.
Interesting fact: This drink is called *sinh to bo* in Vietnamese, where it is perhaps the most common recipe made with avocados.

722 AVOCADO ICE-CREAM SHAKE

Make the Mexican Avocado Milkshake, omitting the honey. Add 125 ml (4 ¼ fl oz) vanilla ice cream and 1 teaspoon lime juice when blending.

724 AVOCADO AND BANANA SHAKE

Make the Mexican Avocado Milkshake, omitting the honey and adding 1 peeled and chopped banana with the other ingredients.
Handy tip: Choose a banana that is not too ripe.

variations

AVOCADO AND CHOCOLATE SHAKE

Prepare the Mexican Avocado Milkshake, adding a drizzle of chocolate syrup through the shake as you pour it into the glasses.
Serving tip: Instead of drizzling the chocolate syrup through the shake, you could drizzle it down the inside of the glass before adding the shake.

AVOCADO AND COFFEE SHAKE

Make the Mexican Avocado Milkshake, adding a cooled shot of espresso coffee with the other ingredients.
Handy tip: The coffee and chocolate variations work well with the Avocado Ice-Cream Shake, the Avocado and Banana Shake and the Vietnamese Avocado Shake variations, too.

727 Marzipan, cherry shake

In Sicily, bakeries make a special almond paste that is sold to be made into a drink. That is the inspiration for this sumptuous iced drink.

INGREDIENTS

150 g (5 ¼ oz) halved, stoned cherries
2 tbsp marzipan
125 ml (4 ¼ fl oz) milk
6 ice cubes

Put the ingredients into a blender and process on low until almost smooth and the ice almost crushed, then on high until smooth and creamy. Pour into a glass and serve immediately.

Makes 1 glass

HANDY TIP

If your blender can't handle ice cubes, use 125 ml (4 ¼ fl oz) crushed ice instead.

MARZIPAN AND CLEMENTINE SHAKE

Make the Marzipan, Cherry Shake, omitting the cherries and using 1 large clementine, peeled, seeded and segmented. Put the clementine in the blender and process until smooth; taste and sweeten with liquid honey if needed. Add the remaining ingredients and proceed as directed.
Handy tip: Remove the clementine pith and seeds.

MARZIPAN, CLEMENTINE AND CHOCOLATE SHAKE

Make the Marzipan and Clementine Shake variation and add 1 tablespoon plain chocolate chips.
Interesting fact: This is the liquid version of German marzipan sweets. These are small chocolate-coated logs of marzipan wrapped in gorgeous coloured papers.

MARZIPAN AND RASPBERRY SHAKE

Make the Marzipan Cherry Shake, replacing the cherries with 150 g (5 ¼ oz) raspberries.
Handy tip: Listen to the machine when blending ice, as you can hear when the ice is crushed.

731 Strawberry Frappé

The frappé is a soda fountain favourite made from syrup, ice cream and ice cubes blended until smooth, creamy and frothy. With the huge growth in flavoured syrups now on the market, there is an endless variety of frappés to be discovered. Sometimes though, the oldies are the best and the strawberry one is particularly delicious.

INGREDIENTS

6 medium strawberries
2 tbsp strawberry syrup
½ tsp lime juice
4 ice cubes
125 ml (4 ¼ fl oz) strawberry or
    vanilla ice cream
Soda water

Put all the ingredients except the soda water in the blender and process on low until almost smooth and the ice almost crushed, then process on high until smooth and creamy. Pour into a chilled glass and top off with soda water.

Makes 1 glass

SERVING TIP

Serve in a tall, thin glass that has been chilled in the fridge, with a parfait spoon or swizzle stick for mixing.

Variations

732 STRAWBERRY SORBET FRAPPÉ

Make the Strawberry Frappé, replacing the ice cream with strawberry sorbet.
Serving tip: Serve with a flourish of fresh fruit slices and mint or lemon balm leaves.

733 MAPLE FRAPPÉ

Make the Strawberry Frappé, omitting the strawberries and replacing the strawberry syrup with 2 tablespoons maple syrup. You can replace the soda water with milk, if desired.
Interesting fact: In soda fountains, frappés were often made with milk in preference to soda water.

734 CHOCOLATE AND PEAR FRAPPÉ

Make the Strawberry Frappé, replacing the strawberries with a ripe pear and the strawberry syrup with chocolate syrup.
Serving tip: This frappé looks attractive served with a cinnamon stick.

735 COFFEE AND PEAR FRAPPÉ

Make the Strawberry Frappé, replacing the strawberries with a ripe pear, the strawberry syrup with hazelnut coffee syrup and the vanilla ice cream with coffee ice cream.

Handy tip: For an indulgent treat, top with a scoop of vanilla ice cream drizzled with toffee syrup.

736 MELON AND PEPPERMINT FRAPPÉ

Make the Strawberry Frappé, replacing the strawberries with 85 g (3 oz) melon chunks, the strawberry syrup with peppermint syrup and the ice cream with lemon sorbet.

Serving tip: For a really pretty effect, you can put the fruit syrup in the base of the glass, but be sure to provide a long-handled spoon or swizzle stick.

737 BLUEBERRY AND GRAPE FRAPPÉ

Make the Strawberry Frappé, replacing the strawberries with 75 g (2 ½ oz) blueberries and the strawberry syrup with blueberry syrup. Stir in 1 teaspoon lime juice and top off with sparkling grape juice.

Handy tip: White or red sparkling grape juice would work in this recipe.

738 Mango and Melon Slushy

Fruit slushies make fabulous snacks for big and little kids alike. They are very simply based on a frozen fruit purée blended with a fresh juice.

INGREDIENTS

¼ cantaloupe or galia melon, peeled, seeded and chopped

1 mango, stoned, peeled and chopped

240 ml (8 fl oz) apple juice

Put the melon and mango in a food processor and blend until smooth. Put in a plastic container and transfer to the freezer for 1 hour.

Take the frozen fruit purée and put in the blender with the apple juice and process until smooth. Serve immediately.

Makes 2 glasses

HANDY TIP

The purée can be partially or totally frozen to make a slushy.

739 PASSION FRUIT AND MANGO SLUSHY

Make the Mango and Melon Slushy, replacing the apple juice with passion fruit juice and adding 1 tablespoon lime juice.

variations

740 PASSION FRUIT, MANGO AND COCONUT SLUSHY

Make the Passion Fruit and Mango Slushy variation, mixing 60 ml (2 fl oz) coconut milk into the mango and melon purée before freezing.
Handy tip: If you have frozen coconut milk ice cubes, you can use 4 of them instead.

741 POMEGRANATE AND MANGO SLUSHY

Make the Mango and Melon Slushy, replacing the apple juice with pomegranate juice.
Handy tip: Pouring the purée into a metal roasting tin that has been previously frozen will speed up freezing.

cactus juice pairs beautifully with melon to make the Melon and Cactus Juice Slushy

742 MANGO AND KIWI SLUSHY

Make the Mango and Melon Slushy, replacing the melon with 1 peeled and chopped kiwi fruit.

Handy tip: For preference use cloudy organic apple juice.

743 MELON AND CACTUS JUICE SLUSHY

Make the Mango and Melon Slushy, omitting the mango and using ½ a melon. Replace the apple juice with cactus (prickly pear) juice.

Handy tip: If you are making your own cactus juice, you can burn off the cactus pear spikes by stabbing the pear with a fork then holding over a gas flame or candle.

744 Apricot and Mandarin Smoothie

The rich flavour of the apricots combined with the mandarin frozen yoghurt is stunning. It indicates how successful combining a tin of fruit with a well-flavoured frozen yoghurt can be. Opening a tin isn't necessarily a compromise; tinned fruits make excellent nutritious smoothies. When fruits are tinned they do not lose any of their nutrients because the lack of exposure to oxygen halts the decomposition process until the tin is opened again.

INGREDIENTS

1 (410-g/15-oz) tin apricots in natural juices

240 ml (8 fl oz) mandarin or orange frozen yoghurt

1 to 2 tsp liquid honey, optional

Put 10 apricot halves in the blender. Drain the juice and make up to 240 ml (8 fl oz) with the natural juice; add to the blender, then process until smooth. Add the frozen yoghurt and honey, if using, then process on high until smooth and creamy. Pour into a glass and serve immediately.

Makes 1 glass

HANDY TIP

For a silky smooth smoothie, pass the apricot purée through a nonmetallic sieve and return to the blender.

745 PEACH AND MANDARIN SMOOTHIE

Make the Apricot and Mandarin Smoothie, replacing the apricots with 240 ml (8 fl oz) tinned peach slices.

746 MIXED TROPICAL FRUIT SMOOTHIE

Make the Apricot and Mandarin Smoothie, replacing the apricots with 240 ml (8 fl oz) tinned tropical fruit salad.

Shopping tip: Compare labels and buy the tinned fruit with the lowest sugar levels.

747 Green Juice Slushy

Here is a tempting way to get vegetables down anyone suspicious of green drinks. It is a lovely sweet and savoury slushy that would make a good dinnertime starter as well as a refreshing snack.

INGREDIENTS

2 apples, quartered
50 g (1 ¾ oz) baby spinach
½ cucumber

2.5-cm (1-inch) piece ginger, peeled
240 ml (8 fl oz) pineapple juice
Squeeze of lime juice

Put the apple, spinach, cucumber and ginger through a juice extractor. Put in a plastic container and transfer to the freezer for 1 hour.

Take the frozen fruit purée and put it in the blender with the pineapple juice and process until smooth. Top off with a squeeze of lime juice and serve immediately.

Makes 1 large or 2 small glasses

HANDY TIP

The larger the base of the freezing container, the thinner the layer of juice will be and the quicker it will freeze.

Variations

748 GREEN JUICE COOLER

Make the Green Juice Slushy through to making the fruit juice purée. Transfer the frozen juice purée into a blender, add 125 ml (4 ¼ fl oz) lemon-lime sorbet and process until smooth. Pour into glasses and serve immediately.
Handy tip: If children run off halfway through drinking iced drinks, pop the drinks in the freezer until the kids reappear ready for more.

749 CARROT AND PINEAPPLE SLUSHY

Make the Green Juice Slushy, replacing the apples and spinach with the juice of 5 trimmed medium carrots. Use only a 5-cm (2-inch) piece of cucumber.
Handy tip: Cut away any green bits from the carrots as they contain toxins that are harmful to humans.

750 HERBY TOMATO SLUSHY

Juice 2 medium tomatoes, a 5-cm (2-inch) piece of cucumber, 5 sprigs of basil, mint, parsley, or rocket and freeze as directed in the Green Juice Smoothie recipe. Add to the blender with the juice of 2 more ripe tomatoes. Season with salt and pepper and Worcestershire or chili sauce.

751 HERBY AVOCADO SLUSHY

Make the Herby Tomato Slushy variation, adding the flesh of ½ an avocado and a squeeze of lemon juice to the blender with the frozen tomato mixture.
Handy tip: Ensure the avocado is chilled before blending.

Perfect for Parties

Everyone loves a party, but those who don't wish to drink alcohol so often get only a poor selection of unimaginative, commercially produced drinks that are high in sugar and preservatives and low on taste. This chapter can change that forever. It is full of ideas for making bright, fruity drinks that will please and delight your nondrinking guests at a dinner party and some that will even bulk up to serve a crowd. High in nutrients, luscious on the taste buds and a visual treat, these drinks are showstoppers and, best of all, but don't shout about it, they are made with very little effort.

752 Gingered Melon Spritzer

This is a refreshing drink to have with a summer meal — the ginger helps with digestion, too.

INGREDIENTS

2 cantaloupe, honeydew, or
  galia melons, chopped
½ orange, chopped
7.5-cm (3-inch) piece ginger,
  peeled
Sparkling water

Process the melon, orange and ginger through the juice extractor. Pour into glasses and top off with sparkling water.

Makes 4 to 6 glasses

HANDY TIP

It is worth chopping the melon into chunks, as these are handled more efficiently by the juice extractor.

Variations

753   GINGERED MELON JUICE

Prepare the Gingered Melon Spritzer, omitting the sparkling water and serving over crushed ice.
Serving tip: This is a lovely juice to serve with pretzels as a starter.

754   GINGERED MELON AND APPLE SPRITZER

Make the Gingered Melon Spritzer, adding 2 large quartered apples with the melon.
Handy tip: You can omit the ginger and this will still be a delicious spritzer.

755   GINGERED MELON AND CUCUMBER SPRITZER

Add 1 large cucumber and 2 peeled limes to the juice extractor when making the Gingered Melon Spritzer.
Serving tip: Serve with a Chinese-style stir fry.

756   MELON MEDLEY MINTED SPRITZER

Use 1 honeydew and 1 cantaloupe melon and process with 8 sprigs of mint.
Handy tip: Cut leftover melon flesh into cubes and freeze. The cubes can be used from frozen.

757   BLENDED MELON SPRITZER

Make any of the melon spritzer variations, but process in batches in a blender instead of through a juice extractor. This will make a thicker, but still lovely, spritzer once topped off with sparkling water.

758 Pineapple, Lemongrass and cardamom crush

Cardamom is most familiar in Western kitchens as a spice used in curries and Asian-style dishes. Yet in southern Asia and the Middle East, it is commonly used in sweet preparations too – and it works wonderfully as a warm aromatic in Asian-flavoured juices like this one.

INGREDIENTS

2 pineapples, peeled
2 limes, peeled
4 lemongrass stalks, trimmed
Seeds from 8 cardamom pods

Put the pineapples, limes and lemongrass stalks through a juice extractor. Stir in the cardamom seeds. Pour into glasses and serve immediately.

Makes 4 to 6 glasses

Shopping Tip

Fresh lemongrass should feel heavy and firm and look rather like a pale, fat green onion. If it feels light or is at all wrinkly, it has probably dried out on the shelf.

variations

759 PINEAPPLE, LEMONGRASS AND CHILI CRUSH

Make the Pineapple, Lemongrass and Cardamom Crush, replacing the cardamom with 1 to 3 seeded red chilies. The chilies must be put through the juicer instead of being stirred in at the end.
Handy tip: As always, juice the chili last and add slowly.

760 PINEAPPLE, LEMONGRASS AND MINT CRUSH

Make the Pineapple, Lemongrass and Cardamom Crush, replacing the cardamom with 8 sprigs of fresh mint.
Handy tip: This would also work with 8 sage leaves.

761 PINEAPPLE, LEMONGRASS AND GINGER CRUSH

Make the Pineapple, Lemongrass and Cardamom Crush, replacing the cardamom with a 10-cm (4-inch) piece of peeled ginger. The ginger must be put through the juicer instead of being stirred in at the end.
Serving tip: Serve with Southeast Asian noodle dishes.

762 PINEAPPLE, GINGER AND CHILI CRUSH

Make the Pineapple, Lemongrass and Cardamom Crush, omitting the cardamom and replacing the lemongrass with a 10-cm (4-inch) piece of peeled ginger and 2 to 4 seeded red chilies.

763 Watermelon and Mint Granita

Granita is an Italian, semi-frozen dessert made from sugar, water and flavourings, most often fruit or coffee. The texture of the finished granita varies from district to district. It is a light and fragrant combination that both looks and tastes exotic, refreshing and luxurious.

INGREDIENTS

2 kg (4 ½ lb) watermelon, cut
  into chunks
Ice cubes
Bunch of fresh mint

Put the watermelon through a juice extractor. Working in batches, put 10 ice cubes in the blender, pour the juice batches over the ice cubes and add leaves from 3 mint sprigs. Blend until smooth and icy. Pour into glasses and serve immediately.

Makes 6 to 8 glasses

HANDY TIP

This is a slushy-style granita. It is faster to prepare than the traditional granita, which takes several hours to freeze.

Variations

764 WATERMELON AND CITRUS GRANITA

Juice 1 peeled and chopped orange and 1 ½ peeled and chopped limes and add to the watermelon juice when making the Watermelon and Mint Granita.
Handy tip: There should be sufficient sweetness in the watermelon juice, but add a little icing sugar to balance the lime, if required.

765 WATERMELON, GINGER AND CITRUS GRANITA

Make the Watermelon and Citrus Granita variation, processing a 7.5-cm (3-inch) piece of peeled ginger through the juice extractor with the other ingredients.
Serving tip: Garnish the glass with an additional mint sprig if desired.

766 WATERMELON, ROSE AND LAVENDER GRANITA

Juice 1 peeled and chopped lime and add to the watermelon juice. Replace the mint with 2 teaspoons dried culinary lavender, 2 to 3 teaspoons rose water, to taste and a pinch of salt.
Handy tip: Substitute lavender syrup (see page 253).

767 STRAWBERRY AND MINT GRANITA

Make the Watermelon and Mint Granita, replacing the watermelon with 1 kg (2 ¼ lb) strawberries.
Serving tip: You can serve this as a low-calorie dessert garnished with fresh strawberries and raspberries.

granitas make a perfect low-calorie dessert

768 MANGO AND MINT GRANITA

Prepare the Watermelon and Mint Granita, replacing the watermelon with 1 kg (2 ¼ lb) of peeled and chopped mango.
Handy tip: Make any of these granitas in advance and keep in the freezer until 30 minutes before required.

769 APPLE AND MINT GRANITA

Make the Watermelon and Mint Granita, replacing the watermelon with 12 apples.
Serving tip: Prepare the juice before the guests arrive and make the granita fresh on demand.

770 APPLE AND TARRAGON GRANITA

Make the Apple and Mint Granita variation, replacing the mint with fresh tarragon.
Serving tip: This complements a chicken meal perfectly.

771 APPLE AND BASIL GRANITA

Prepare the Apple and Mint Granita variation, replacing the mint with fresh basil.

772 Moroccan Mint Iced Tea

Moroccans, like many other people from North Africa, drink tea all through the day and give it to family, friends and passing strangers as a symbol of hospitality and goodwill.

INGREDIENTS

1 tbsp green tea or 3 green tea bags
10 sprigs fresh mint, plus extra
   for garnish
1 L (1 ¾ pt) boiling water
Approximately 3 tbsp sugar
Crushed ice

Put the tea leaves or bags in a teapot or heatproof jug, add the mint and pour over the water. Steep for 3 minutes. Drain, sweeten to taste with sugar and leave to cool.

Pour over crushed ice, which has been studded with mint leaves and serve immediately.

Makes 4 glasses

SERVING TIP

Moroccans serve tea in pretty coloured glasses, which makes a beautiful way of presenting this tea.

Variations

773 TRADITIONAL MOROCCAN TEA

Make the Moroccan Mint Iced Tea, but pour the tea immediately after sweetening; serve hot to warm.
Handy tip: Moroccans like foam on their tea, so make this drink in a teapot and ceremoniously pour it into heatproof glasses from a great height.

774 MOROCCAN LEMON AND MINT ICED TEA

Thinly slice ½ a lemon and add to the teapot with the mint when preparing the Moroccan Mint Iced Tea. Serve with a slice of lemon.
Serving tip: This is delicious served with orange honey cake or a slice of baklava.

775 MOROCCAN PEACH AND MINT ICED TEA

Slice ½ a peach into four and add to the teapot with the mint when preparing the Moroccan Mint Iced Tea. Return the peach to the liquid when strained, to infuse, then remove again before serving. Serve with a slice of fresh peach.
Serving tip: For a milder hint of peach, do not return the peach slices to the teapot to infuse. Serve them instead for dessert with ice cream.

776 MOROCCAN POMEGRANATE AND LIME ICED TEA

Make the Moroccan Mint Iced Tea, replacing the mint with a thinly sliced lime. Add 500 ml (17 fl oz) pomegranate juice to the cold tea.
Interesting fact: In North Africa, the women do the cooking but the men, most often the head of the family or the most respected man in the group, make the tea.

777 MOROCCAN CLEMENTINE ICED TEA

Make the Moroccan Mint Iced Tea, replacing the mint with a thinly sliced clementine. Add 125 ml (4 ¼ fl oz) clementine juice to the cold tea.
Handy tip: Sweeten the tea after adding the clementine juice.

778 MOROCCAN FLORAL ICED TEA

Make the Moroccan Mint Iced Tea, adding 15 g (½ oz) edible flower petals such as orange blossom, marigold, or hibiscus.
Serving tip: Float a few edible flowers on the surface of the tea as garnish.

779 Mango and Grape Frappé

This delicious drink makes a perfect aperitif by combining the rich-scented taste of the mango with sparkling grape notes.

INGREDIENTS

1 large ripe mango, peeled, stoned and sliced

5 ice cubes

600 ml (1 pt) sparkling grape juice

Maraschino cherries

Reserve a few small slices of mango for decoration, then put the remaining mango flesh in a blender with the ice cubes and process until smooth. Drain into a serving jug, pour in the sparkling grape juice and serve immediately with the reserved mango slices and maraschino cherries.

Makes 3 to 4 glasses

HANDY TIP

If your blender isn't up to processing ice cubes, put the ice cubes into a resealable freezer bag and crush with a mallet before putting in the blender.

Variations

781 PEACH AND GRAPE FRAPPÉ

Prepare the Mango and Grape Frappé, replacing the mango with 2 small peeled, stoned and chopped peaches.
Handy tip: Make sure the peaches are ripe by checking to see that they are bright yellow or red in colour with no green patches; there should be some give in the flesh when lightly pressed.

782 MANGO AND ORANGE FRAPPÉ

Prepare the Mango and Grape Frappé, replacing the sparkling grape juice with a good-quality sparkling orange soda.
Shopping tip: Always read the labels – some orange sodas are made from oranges while others are orange-flavoured and contain synthetic flavourings.

783 GRAPE AND PASSION FRUIT FRAPPÉ

Prepare the Mango and Grape Frappé, replacing the mango with the sieved flesh of 2 passion fruit.
Handy tip: Don't be tempted to leave the seeds in the passion fruit for this drink as it would spoil the sophistication.

780 CANTALOUPE AND GRAPE FRAPPÉ

Prepare the Mango and Grape Frappé, replacing the mango with ½ a peeled, stoned and chopped cantaloupe.
Handy tip: Cantaloupe seeds are edible. Dry roast them, sprinkle with salt and paprika and serve with the aperitif.

784 MANGO AND APPLE FRAPPÉ

Make the Mango and Grape Frappé, replacing the soda with sparkling apple juice.
Serving tip: This drink looks wonderful served in a cocktail glass that has been pre-chilled in the fridge.

785 Lemonade

Fresh-squeezed lemonade is surely the drink that lemons were made for. This is the still version of this drink, as made by our grandmothers and their grandmothers before them.

INGREDIENTS

4 to 5 lemons
225 g (8 oz) sugar
About 1.25 L (2 ¼ pt) filtered
    or mineral water, divided,
    plus extra to dilute
Lemon slices, to garnish

Cut the zest from 2 lemons into strips. Combine the sugar, 240 ml (8 fl oz) of the water and the lemon zest strips in a saucepan and cook over a low heat, stirring until the sugar has dissolved. Simmer without boiling for 5 minutes. Leave to cool.

Meanwhile, juice the lemons using a citrus press or cut off the peel and juice in a juice extractor; you need to juice sufficient lemons to make 240 ml (8 fl oz) juice. Drain the sugar syrup to remove the lemon zest, pour into a large jug and combine with the lemon juice. Add the remaining water. The juice may be made several hours before required and left in the fridge to chill. Serve garnished with lemon slices.

Makes 6 to 8 glasses

HANDY TIP

If you are not using the lemonade immediately, do not fill the jug with slices of lemon as the rind will make the lemonade taste bitter over time.

Variations

786 SICILIAN LEMONADE

Prepare the Lemonade and add 10 sprigs of mint with the lemon zest.
Handy tip: Make lemonade ice cubes so that the ice in the glass won't dilute the lemonade.

787 STRAWBERRY LIMEADE

Make the Lemonade, replacing the lemons with 7 to 8 limes. Purée 225 g (8 oz) strawberries in the blender. Sieve through a fine-mesh nonmetallic sieve to remove the seeds. Pour into the jug with the lime juice.
Handy tip: This is a good use for slightly over-ripe strawberries but discard mouldy or bruised strawberries.

788 MEXICAN STRAWBERRY LIMEADE

When making the Strawberry Limeade variation, use a sharp knife to poke 6 holes in 1 jalapeño chili. Add the jalapeño with the lime zest.
Handy tip: Poking holes in the chili allows a subtle spiciness to be infused.

789 PINK LEMONADE

Purée 225 g (8 oz) raspberries in the blender. Sieve through a fine-mesh nonmetallic sieve to remove the seeds. Pour into the jug with the lemon juice when making the lemonade.

790 ROSEMARY WATERMELON LEMONADE

Make the Lemonade, adding the leaves from 2 sprigs of rosemary with the lemon zest. Remove the skin and seeds from 1.5 kg (3 ¼ lb) watermelon. Purée the flesh in batches in the blender. Drain through a fine nonmetallic sieve. Pour into the jug with the lemon juice instead of water.

791 VANILLA CHERRYADE

Prepare the Lemonade, adding a split vanilla bean with the lemon zest. Purée 225 g (8 oz) stoned, halved cherries in the blender and pass through a fine mesh nonmetallic sieve to remove the seeds. Pour into the jug with the lemon juice.

792 THAI LEMONADE

Make the Lemonade, adding ¼ stick lemongrass, 6 basil leaves, 6 coriander leaves and 6 mint leaves with the lemon zest. Purée a small cucumber in the blender and pass through a fine-mesh nonmetallic sieve. Pour into the jug with the lemon juice.
Handy tip: Try to find Thai basil for authenticity.

793 BRAZILIAN CREAMY LIMEADE

Make the Lemonade recipe, replacing the lemons with 7 to 8 limes. Add 75 ml (2 ½ fl oz) sweetened condensed milk into the jug and stir into the lime juice.
Serving tip: Top off with sparkling water.

794 PINK GRAPEFRUIT LEMONADE

Prepare the Lemonade, replacing the water with the freshly squeezed pink grapefruit juice.
Handy tip: If this drink is too acidic for your taste, dilute with a little water.

795 Instant Limonada

This is what you get when you ask for 'limonada' in a café in Mexico, Brazil and stations in between. It takes just moments to make, so it can be made to order at a lunchtime party.

INGREDIENTS

4 limes, peeled and roughly chopped

150 g (5 ¼ oz) sugar

240 ml (8 fl oz) filtered or mineral water

750 ml to 1.25 L (1 pt 6 fl oz to 2 pt) filtered or mineral water or soda water

Put the limes, sugar and the 240 ml (8 fl oz) water into a blender and process until the limes are pulverised and the resulting liquid is creamy and foamy.

Pour the mixture into a fine-mesh nonmetallic sieve over a tumbler, pressing through as much juice as possible. Top off with water or soda water to taste and serve immediately.

Makes about 6 glasses

HANDY TIP

Never squeeze a lime directly from the fridge. Limes yield more juice when squeezed at room temperature or after 10 seconds in a microwave.

Variations

797 HIBISCUS LIMONADA

Make a strong hibiscus fruit tea infusion from 4 hibiscus tea bags and 8 sprigs mint. Leave to cool. In a jug, combine with the Instant Limonada recipe or Instant Lemonade variation.
Handy tip: For an alternative version, make the Instant Limonada but top off with Hibiscus Cooler, page 158.

798 QUICK GINGER FIZZ

Add a 5-cm (2-inch) piece peeled ginger to the blender with the limes when making the Instant Limonada. Top off with soda water.
Shopping tip: Key limes are smaller than regular limes and have a thinner skin. They are more astringent than common limes and have a tangy sour flavour.

799 QUICK MANGO LIMONADA

Make the Instant Limonada, adding 170 g (6 oz) chopped mango with the limes.
Serving tip: Serve with a complementary syrup such as rosemary, raspberry or vanilla syrup. Guests can use these syrups to sweeten the limonada further if it is too sharp for their liking.

796 INSTANT LEMONADE

Make the Instant Limonada, replacing the limes with 3 lemons.
Interesting fact: In South and Central America, limes are called 'limones', which confuses English speakers.

800 QUICK PASSION FRUIT LIMONADA

Make the Instant Limonada, adding the pulp of 3 passion fruit with the limes.
Handy tip: Buy unwaxed organic limes and wash extremely well.

801 Yuletide Cranberry Punch

This punch is made from fresh cranberries cooked down with sugar and spices to bring out the flavour of Christmas.

INGREDIENTS

300 g (10 ½ oz) fresh cranberries

250 g (8 ¾ oz) granulated or brown sugar

4 strips orange zest

6 cloves

6 allspice berries

2 (7.5-cm/3-inch) sticks cinnamon

1 star anise

175 ml (6 fl oz) water

300 ml (10 fl oz) orange juice, preferably freshly squeezed

75 ml (2 ½ fl oz) lime juice, preferably freshly squeezed

Approximately 1.5 L (2 ½ pt) soda water, chilled

Put the cranberries, sugar, orange zest, cloves, allspice, cinnamon, anise and water in a saucepan. Cook over medium heat, stirring occasionally for 8 to 10 minutes or until cranberries begin to pop. Cool slightly, then pour the mixture through a nonmetallic fine-mesh strainer into a large punch bowl or jug, pressing down to extract as much of the fruit pulp as possible. Leave to cool.

Stir the orange and lime juice into the punch bowl or jug and, when ready to serve, add the soda water, to taste.

Makes about 20 glasses

HANDY TIP

Prepare the punch the day before the party, adding the club soda when about to serve.

Variations

802 GINGERED YULETIDE PUNCH

Prepare the Yuletide Cranberry Punch, omitting the allspice berries and star anise and adding 2 tablespoons grated ginger. Replace the soda water with ginger beer.
Handy tip: If you don't have a punch bowl, use a large salad bowl and a kitchen ladle. You can always stand it in a holly wreath or decorate the outside of the bowl.

803 QUICK YULETIDE PUNCH

Replace the home-cooked cranberry sauce with two 450-g (1-lb) tins whole berry cranberry sauce and process in a food processor until smooth before continuing as directed with the Yuletide Cranberry Punch recipe.

804 YULETIDE CREOLE PUNCH

Add 300 ml (10 fl oz) pineapple juice, preferably freshly squeezed, to the Yuletide Cranberry Punch with the other juices.
Handy tip: Make this variation with club soda, ginger beer or sparkling lemonade.

805 YULETIDE SHERBET PUNCH

Make the Yuletide Cranberry Punch, adding 1 L (1 ¾ pt) of orange, cranberry, or raspberry sherbet with the soda water.
Handy tip: Add half the sherbet straight from the freezer at the very last moment, then the rest as it starts to melt.

806 RHUBARB PUNCH

Make the Yuletide Cranberry Punch, replacing the cranberries with 900 g (2 lb) chopped rhubarb. Replace the orange juice with pineapple juice, if desired.

807 GINGERED RHUBARB PUNCH

Make the Rhubarb Punch variation, omitting the allspice berries and star anise and adding 2 tablespoons grated ginger. Cook for 10 to 15 minutes until the rhubarb is soft. Replace the club soda with ginger beer.

808 Green Appetiser Juice

This thirst-quencher is light, refreshing and easy to drink and makes a good starter before a formal or buffet meal. You can make it in advance and keep it chilled in the fridge until ready to serve.

INGREDIENTS

1 cucumber
1 honeydew or Ogen melon, peeled and chopped
2 celery stalks
6 sprigs fresh mint

Put all the ingredients through a juice extractor. Pour into glasses and serve immediately.

Makes 4 glasses

HANDY TIP

An Ogen melon would be a delicious choice, but any green-fleshed melon will do.

Variations

809 MELON AND CUCUMBER JUICE

Prepare the Green Appetiser Juice, omitting the mint and celery and increasing the quantity of cucumber to 1 ½ cucumbers.
Shopping tip: If buying English cucumber, you need only ⅔ cucumber for the Green Appetiser Juice and a whole cucumber for this variation.

810 MINTED GINGER GREEN APPETISER JUICE

Make the Green Appetiser Juice, adding a 4-cm (1 ½-inch) piece peeled ginger with the other ingredients.
Handy tip: Use a ginger syrup (see page 252) if you do not have fresh ginger.

811 CUCUMBER, APPLE AND MINT JUICE

Make the Green Appetiser Juice, omitting the melon and celery and adding 2 quartered apples.
Serving tip: This drink would be the perfect accompaniment to a plate of cold meat antipasto.

812 CUCUMBER AND CELERY JUICE

Make the Green Appetiser Juice, omitting the melon and mint and increasing the quantity of celery to 4 stalks and the cucumber to 1 ½ cucumbers.

813 TABASCO GREEN APPETISER JUICE

Prepare the Green Appetiser Juice, adding a few drops of Tabasco sauce and a few drops of lime juice to each glass.
Serving tip: Serve the Tabasco and lime wedges at the table so that everyone can season their juice to their liking.

814 ORANGE AND GREEN APPETISER JUICE

Make the Green Appetiser Juice, adding 1 large peeled and chopped orange with the other ingredients.
Serving tip: Serve over melon juice ice cubes in small cocktail glasses.

815 CUCUMBER AND STRAWBERRY JUICE

Make the Green Appetiser Juice, replacing the melon with 450 g (1 lb) strawberries.
Handy tip: It is best to use fully ripe strawberries for juicing since under-ripe strawberries have less juice and are not as sweet and flavoursome.

816 GREEN APPETISER SMOOTHIE

Peel the cucumber and strip the leaves from the mint sprigs. Working in two or three batches, depending on your blender's capacity, process in a blender until smooth.

817 Virgin Sangria

This wonderful drink will transport you to the sunlit bars of southern Spain. It is a delicious melding of grape juice and fruit. Choose a good-quality red grape juice that is full of flavour, given that it is replacing the bold taste of Spanish red wine.

INGREDIENTS

4 purple plums, stoned and sliced

3 oranges, peeled and chopped

2 lemons, peeled and chopped

1 lime, peeled and chopped

6 sprigs mint

700 ml (1 pt 4 fl oz) red grape juice, chilled

240 ml (8 fl oz) pomegranate juice, chilled

1 small red apple, cored and sliced

4 kumquats, sliced

1 star fruit, sliced

2 sprigs rosemary

2 (7.5-cm/3-inch) cinnamon sticks

Ice

Process the plums, oranges, lemons, lime and mint in a juice extractor. In a jug, combine the juice with the red grape juice and pomegranate juice. Add the apples, kumquats, star fruit, rosemary and cinnamon. Leave to infuse for 1 hour. Serve over ice.

Makes 6 to 8 glasses

HANDY TIP

To make giant citrus ice cubes, which look fantastic in a large jug, put a thin slice of lemon or lime in each cup of a muffin tin (the silicone ones are best) and two-thirds fill with water. Freeze until required.

Variations

818 VIRGIN GOJI SANGRIA

Prepare the Virgin Sangria, replacing the pomegranate juice with goji berry juice.
Handy tip: Don't forget to eat all the lovely infused fruit – or, it can also be enjoyed later with yoghurt.

819 VIRGIN WHITE SANGRIA

Make the Virgin Sangria, replacing the red grape juice with white grape juice, the purple plums with yellow plums and the pomegranate juice with the juice from 3 sharp apples.

820 VIRGIN PEACH SANGRIA

Make the Virgin Sangria, replacing the plums with 2 peeled and stoned peaches.
Handy tip: Kumquats are small citrus fruits with sweet skins and can be eaten whole.

821 SPARKLING VIRGIN SANGRIA

Make the Virgin Sangria, replacing the grape juice with sparkling grape juice. Three-quarters fill the glasses and top off with soda water, lemon-lime soda, or orange soda. Serve immediately.

822 MULLED WINE WITHOUT

Make Virgin Sangria, replacing the apple, kumquat, and star fruit with a sliced orange. Pour into a saucepan. Add 1 teaspoon allspice berries, ½ teaspoon peppercorns and a 4-cm (1 ½-inch) piece ginger. Simmer for 10 minutes. Serve warm.

823 Halloween Juice

The spooky green makes this juice perfect for Halloween – but kids will love it any time of year.

INGREDIENTS

4 kiwi fruit, peeled
600 g (1 ¼ lb) seedless green grapes
1 small honeydew melon, peeled and chopped
6 green apples

Put all the ingredients through a juice extractor. Pour into a glass and serve immediately.

Makes about 6 glasses

SERVING TIP

For the full effect, look out for plastic tumblers decorated with spiders' webs or spooky faces, garnish with an orange sugar rim and serve with a black straw.

824 HALLOWEEN JUICE WITH WORMS

Prepare the Halloween Juice, adding some jelly worms to the glass for an extra scare.
Handy tip: Red or black shoestring liquorice would also be fun additions.

825 RED MONSTER JUICE

Make the Halloween Juice, replacing the kiwi fruits, green grapes and melon with 4 purple plums, red seedless grapes and chopped watermelon.

826 GRAPE AND KIWI FRUIT JUICE

Prepare the Halloween Juice, omitting the honeydew melon and apples. Instead add 2 extra kiwi fruits and double the quantity of grapes.
Nutritional tip: Kiwi fruit is good for pregnant women.

827 MELON AND GRAPE JUICE

Make the Halloween Juice, omitting the kiwi fruit and apples. Increase the quantity of grapes to 800 g (1 ¾ lb) and use 1 large honeydew melon.
Nutritional tip: Both the melon and grapes are low-calorie.

828 Cherry Fruit Spritzer

The sour flavour of cranberries is very refreshing and it makes this juice a real thirst-quencher.

INGREDIENTS

150 g (5 ¼ oz) stoned cherries
2 apples
2 oranges, peeled and
   chopped
500 ml (17 fl oz) soda water

Put the fruit through a juice extractor. Pour into glasses and top off with soda water. Serve immediately.

Makes about 4 glasses

SERVING TIP

Serve with a maraschino cherry on a toothpick bridged across the rim of the glass.

Variations

829 CHERRY AND APPLE SPRITZER

Prepare the Cherry Fruit Spritzer, replacing the oranges with 2 more apples.
Handy tip: Select sweet apples to balance out the sourness of the cranberries.

830 CHERRY AND PEACH SPRITZER

Make the Cherry Fruit Spritzer, replacing the apples with 1 peeled and stoned peach.
Shopping tip: Buy cherries in summer when they are abundant, then stone and freeze them for later use.

831 CHERRY AND STRAWBERRY SPRITZER

Prepare the Cherry Fruit Spritzer, omitting 50 g (1 ¾ oz) fresh cherries and replacing them with 50 g (1 ¾ oz) strawberries.
Handy tip: Defrost frozen strawberries and cherries before juicing.

832 BERRY FRUIT SPRITZER

Make the Cherry Fruit Spritzer, replacing 50 g (1 ¾ oz) fresh cherries with 50 g (1 ¾ oz) raspberries.
Serving tip: Replace the soda water with half the quantity of still water and pack in a thermos for lunch.

Serve topped with a few stoned cherries for a sophisticated summer refresher

 ### MINTY CHERRY FRUIT SPRITZER

Make the Cherry Fruit Spritzer, adding 8 fresh mint leaves to the other ingredients and serve garnished with fresh mint.

 ### CHERRY AND PEAR SPRITZER

Make the Cherry Fruit Spritzer, replacing the apples with pears.
Handy tip: Very soft pears will clog up the juicer, so choose firm but ripe pears and chop before juicing.

835 Tomato Frappé

A refreshing accompaniment to brunch. Juice fresh tomatoes when they are in season; nothing in a bottle tastes half as good.

INGREDIENTS

1 tbsp olive oil	¼ tsp Worcestershire sauce
1 small red onion, finely chopped	Dash sea salt
¼ red pepper, finely chopped	1 L (1 ¾ pt) tomato juice, preferably freshly juiced
¼ celery stalk, finely chopped	
1 tsp sugar	
1 tbsp lime juice	

Heat the olive oil in a small skillet, add the onion and sauté for 2 minutes, then add the pepper and celery; continue to cook until the vegetables are very soft.

Put the cooked vegetables, sugar, lime juice, Worcestershire sauce and salt in a blender with 240 ml (8 fl oz) tomato juice. Blend until smooth. Combine with the remaining tomato juice, pour into a roasting tin or freezer container and freeze.

About 30 minutes before serving, remove from the freezer and let sit. Break the mixture into chunks, put in the blender in batches and process on a low speed until smooth. Serve with a wedge of lime.

Makes 4 to 6 glasses

HANDY TIP

325 g (11 ½ oz) tomatoes yield about 240 ml (8 fl oz) juice.

Variations

836 TOMATO AND WATERCRESS FRAPPÉ

Make the Tomato Frappé, adding a small bunch of watercress to the blender with the other ingredients.
Handy tip: If watercress is not available, you can substitute rocket.

837 CURRIED TOMATO FRAPPÉ

Make the Tomato Frappé, adding ½ teaspoon medium curry powder with the pepper.
Handy tip: Curry powder is a blend of up to 20 ground spices, herbs and seeds and can vary in flavour depending on the brand and country of origin. Avoid Madras or very hot curry powder, unless you and your guests are seasoned fans.

838 PEPPERED TOMATO FRAPPÉ

Make the Tomato Frappé, adding a generous dash each of hot pepper sauce, cayenne pepper and ground black pepper with the Worcestershire sauce.
Handy tip: Serve with additional Worcestershire sauce and Tabasco sauce on the table for those who like things really spicy.

839 TOMATO AND CUCUMBER FRAPPÉ

Make the Tomato Frappé, adding ½ peeled and seeded cucumber to the blender with the tomato and reducing the tomato juice down to 750 ml (1 pt 6 fl oz).
Handy tip: You can juice the cucumber without peeling and seeding, if preferred.

840 MEXICAN-STYLE TOMATO FRAPPÉ

Make the Tomato Frappé, adding a peeled and stoned avocado and 6 coriander stalks to the blender with the tomato juice. Replace the Worcestershire sauce with Tabasco.
Handy tip: Replace the Tabasco with a seeded jalapeño chili, if preferred.

841 ITALIAN-STYLE TOMATO FRAPPÉ

Make the Tomato Frappé, but replace the cooked vegetables with the juice of 1 courgette, 1 large carrot, 8 sprigs basil and 1 garlic clove. Combine this fresh juice with the tomato juice. Replace the lime juice with lemon juice.

842 Fresh Peach Iced Tea

Iced tea is a popular summer party drink and the addition of freshly juiced peaches makes this all the more enticing.

INGREDIENTS

2 tbsp loose-leaf black tea or 6 tea bags

750 ml (1 pt 6 fl oz) boiling filtered or mineral water

60 to 115 g (2 to 4 oz) sugar, to taste

4 large peaches, peeled and stoned

1 lemon, peeled and chopped

750 ml (1 pt 6 fl oz) chilled filtered or mineral water

Peach slices, lemon slices and mint leaves, to garnish

Put the tea leaves or bag in a teapot or heatproof jug and pour over the boiling water. Steep for 10 minutes. Drain, if using tea leaves, or remove tea bags. Stir in the sugar until dissolved. Leave to cool.

Process the peaches and lemon in the juice extractor and pour the juice into a jug with the cooled tea. Top off with the chilled water. Add the peach and lemon slices and the mint and serve over ice.

Makes 10 to 12 glasses

HANDY TIP

English breakfast tea is perfect for this recipe.

Variations

843 FRESH PEACH EARL GREY ICED TEA

Make the Fresh Peach Iced Tea using Earl Grey tea.
Handy tip: Sweeten the tea with calorie-reduced or no-calorie sugar substitute, to taste.

844 FRESH PEACH ICED CHAI

Make the Fresh Peach Iced Tea using chai tea.
Handy tip: Chai is full of the flavours of exotic spices. For another tropical touch, substitute coconut water for up to half of the chilled water.

845 ORANGE AND LEMON ICED TEA

Make the Fresh Peach Iced Tea, replacing the peaches with the juice squeezed from 2 small oranges and 1 additional lemon.
Serving tip: Reserve some orange and lemon zest for garnishing.

846 CITRUS TARRAGON ICED TEA

Make the Orange and Lemon Iced Tea variation, adding 5 sprigs of tarragon with the tea bags.
Serving tip: For a tarragon sugar-rimmed glass, sprinkle sugar and finely chopped tarragon on a saucer, moisten the glass and dip in the sugar to coat.

HAWAIIAN ICED TEA

847

Make the Fresh Peach Iced Tea, replacing the peach with ½ a small peeled and chopped pineapple and 3 sprigs of mint.
Handy tip: Use 3 sprigs of pineapple sage instead of the mint.

MANGO AND PINEAPPLE ICED TEA

848

Make the Fresh Peach Iced Tea, replacing the peach with 1 peeled and stoned mango and ¼ peeled and chopped pineapple.
Handy tip: Orange Pekoe tea complements this variation well.

LEMON ICED TEA

849

Make the Fresh Peach Iced Tea, replacing the peach with the juice squeezed from 3 additional lemons.
Handy tip: If the tea is cooled too quickly, the tannins in it will cause the tea to become cloudy. Should this happen, simply add a little boiling water and it will become clear.

MANGO ICED TEA

850

Make the Fresh Peach Iced Tea, replacing the peach with 2 peeled and stoned mangoes or 375 ml (12 ½ fl oz) mango nectar.
Handy tip: Organic Alphonso mangoes are best.

PEACH AND RASPBERRY ICED TEA

851

Make the Fresh Peach Iced Tea, replacing one of the peaches with 150 g (5 ¼ oz) raspberries.
Handy tip: Do not be tempted to add the fruit until the tea is completely cold.

852 Cantaloupe Refresco

Refrescos are blended fruit drinks that are popular in Mexico and other Central American countries, where they are sold by street vendors. They make a great way to try out new and exotic fruits.

INGREDIENTS

320 g (11 oz) peeled, seeded and chopped cantaloupe

2 to 4 tsp chopped piloncillo (unrefined cane sugar) or granulated sugar

2 to 4 tbsp lime juice

500 ml (17 fl oz) chilled filtered or mineral water

Put the cantaloupe in a blender and process until smooth. Add the piloncillo or sugar and lime juice, to taste – the juice should be just sweet enough and very tangy. Pour into a jug and top off with the chilled water.

Makes 4 glasses

INTERESTING FACT

Piloncillo is a form of raw cane sugar, which has a golden brown colour and a delicious, rich, treacle-like flavour. Traditionally it is sold pressed into a hard cone shape, although some shops sell it in ordinary packages.

Variations

853 SOURSOP REFRESCO

Prepare the Cantaloupe Refresco, replacing the cantaloupe with 500 ml (17 fl oz) soursop (guanábana) pulp. Serve garnished with a little ground nutmeg. You could also add 1 to 2 tablespoons sweetened condensed milk instead of the sugar.
Shopping tip: The soursop is an almost heart-shaped fruit with small spikey protrusions.

854 TAMARIND REFRESCO

Prepare the Cantaloupe Refresco, replacing the melon with one 200-g (7-oz) package of tamarind pulp. Drain the tamarind mixture through a sieve into the jug before adding the water.
Handy tip: Tamarind pulp consists of the podlike tamarind fruit already prepared for cooking.

855 REFRESCO ROSADO

Prepare the Cantaloupe Refresco, replacing the melon with 2 medium-sized carrots and ¼ pineapple, peeled, cored and chopped.
Serving tip: Serve topped with finely chopped walnuts and a small pineapple wedge.

856 MANGO REFRESCO

Prepare the Cantaloupe Refresco, replacing the cantaloupe with 330 g (11 ½ oz) peeled, stoned, chopped mango.
Interesting fact: These drinks are sometimes served from barrel-shaped glass flasks called 'vitroleros'.

858 TANGERINE AND SAPOTE REFRESCO

Prepare the Cantaloupe Refresco, replacing the cantaloupe with 375 ml (12 ½ fl oz) sapote pulp and 240 ml (8 fl oz) tangerine juice, preferably freshly squeezed.

Interesting fact: The term 'sapote' refers to a number of unrelated soft fruits found in Central and South America.

859 DRAGONFRUIT REFRESCO

Prepare the Cantaloupe Refresco, replacing the cantaloupe with the flesh of 2 dragonfruits. Scoop the flesh into the blender and process until smooth. Drain the resulting purée through a fine-mesh nonmetallic strainer into the jug and proceed as directed.

Interesting fact: Another name for dragonfruit is pitaya.

860 PASSION FRUIT REFRESCO

Prepare the Cantaloupe Refresco, replacing the cantaloupe with the flesh of 3 passion fruits. Pass the flesh through a fine-mesh nonmetallic strainer into the jug and proceed as directed.

Serving tip: Garnish with a couple of slices of star fruit.

857 STRAWBERRY REFRESCO

Make the Cantaloupe Refresco, replacing the cantaloupe with 300 g (10 ½ oz) strawberries.

Handy tip: If you don't like seeds in the drink, sieve through a fine-mesh nonmetallic strainer.

861 APRICOT REFRESCO

Prepare the Cantaloupe Refresco, replacing the cantaloupe with 10 skinned and stoned apricots.

Handy tip: For a short cut, use 500 ml (17 fl oz) good-quality apricot nectar.

862 Red Grape Fizz

This is a dazzling combination of sweet grapes and sour apples. It makes an excellent drink to serve with a meal or is equally useful as a nonalcoholic drink at a party where others are drinking wine.

INGREDIENTS

900 g (2 lb) red seedless grapes
8 sour apples, quartered
1 lemon, peeled and chopped
Icing sugar, to taste
Crushed ice
500 ml (17 fl oz) sparkling water

Put the grapes, apples and lemon through a juice extractor. Pour into a jug and sweeten to taste with icing sugar. Pour into glasses over crushed ice and top off with sparkling water.

Makes 4 glasses

SERVING TIP

The apple makes this a particularly good drink to serve with pork dishes.

Variations

863 RASPBERRY AND RED GRAPE FIZZ

Make the Red Grape Fizz, adding 100 g (3 ½ oz) of raspberries with the grapes.
Serving tip: Reserve a few whole raspberries to use as a garnish.

864 WHITE GRAPE FIZZ

Make the Red Grape Fizz, replacing the red grapes with green grapes and 4 of the apples with ½ a honeydew or Ogen melon.
Interesting fact: Grapes are classed as berries because the fruit is derived from one ovary and the fruit wall is fleshy all the way around.

865 GREEN GRAPE FIZZ

Make the Red Grape Fizz, replacing the red grapes with green grapes and 4 of the apples with 3 peeled kiwi fruit.
Serving tip: Serve with thin slices of kiwi fruit.

866 FLUFFY RED GRAPE FIZZ

Take ¼ of the blended, sweetened fruit, put it in a cocktail shaker with 1 fresh egg white and shake vigorously for 30 seconds. Add 3 ice cubes and continue to shake for 1 minute. Drain into a glass and top off with sparkling or soda water. Serve with a twist of lemon.
Health warning: Pregnant women should avoid raw eggs.

867 caribbean Punch

When it comes to a party, what could be better than a big bowl of punch? You can use good-quality purchased juices because juicing this quantity of fruit would be quite a task and would make refilling the bowl quite a chore.

INGREDIENTS

1 L (1 ¾ pt) bottled pomegranate juice, chilled

1 L (1 ¾ pt) bottled or tinned unsweetened pineapple juice, chilled

60 ml (2 fl oz) lime juice

500 ml (17 fl oz) ginger beer, chilled

500 ml (17 fl oz) soda water, chilled

Pomegranate seeds, mint leaves and small pineapple wedges, to garnish

Combine all the ingredients in a punch bowl and float the pomegranate seeds and mint sprigs on top. Garnish each glass with a wedge of pineapple.

Makes about 12 glasses

HANDY TIP

Make pomegranate ice cubes from pomegranate juice the day before the party. That way the ice doesn't dilute the punch.

Variations

868 POMEGRANATE AND GRAPEFRUIT PUNCH

Make the Caribbean Punch, replacing the pineapple juice with pink grapefruit juice and omitting the lime juice.
Handy tip: If the punch is not sweet enough, stir in agave syrup, to taste.

869 BLUEPOM PUNCH

Make the Caribbean Punch, replacing the pomegranate juice with pomegranate-blueberry juice.
Handy tip: To reduce the calories, replace the ginger beer with additional soda water.

870 GEORGIAN PEACH PUNCH

Make the Caribbean Punch, replacing the pomegranate and pineapple juices with 500 ml (17 fl oz) apricot nectar and 1.5 L (2 ½ pt) orange juice.
Handy tip: For a more complex flavour, add a pinch of cinnamon and a few drops of almond extract to this punch.

CARIBBEAN
SLUSHY PUNCH

When making the Caribbean Punch, combine the juices and freeze overnight. Remove from the freezer 2 hours before required. Just before serving, add the ginger beer and soda water and serve slushy.

Serving tip: Just before serving, purée 300 g (10 ½ oz) strawberries and drizzle through the slushy.

LUAU PUNCH

Make the Caribbean Punch, replacing the pomegranate juice with orange juice.

Serving tip: A luau is a Hawaiian word for a party or feast where chicken cooked in coconut milk or kalua, and barbecue pig are signature dishes. Don't forget the lei – the necklace of colourful flowers.

LUAU COCONUT
PUNCH

Make the Luau Punch variation, adding one 410-g (15-oz) tin of coconut milk.

Handy tip: You can replace the ginger beer with lemon-lime soda, if preferred.

CARIBBEAN
SHERBET PUNCH

Make the Caribbean Punch, reducing the pomegranate juice to 240 ml (8 fl oz) and adding 300 g (10 ½ oz) of lime, orange, or raspberry sherbet to the punch.

Handy tip: Pour the ginger beer into the punch bowl first to minimise the fizzing of the ginger beer.

Mocktails

Mocktails are all about fun and this is a chapter full of taste sensations and wonderful tongue teasers. The difference between a mocktail and a fruit drink is something edgy, a depth of flavour that makes it a distinctly adult drink with a cunning balance of sweet and sour. This chapter has a range of short and long drinks, fruity and spicy drinks, old favourites and new contenders. The basic syrups early on in this chapter can be infused with spices and herbs to form the basis of many of the later recipes. Don't be tempted to skip this process, they take minutes to prepare but will hugely impress your guests.

875 Virgin Strawberry Daiquiri Fizz

Perfect for a barbecue, this sweet and sharp sparkling drink sets off the heat of summer. If you want to get closer to the flavour of a true daiquiri, add a few drops of rum flavouring. The bitter lemon soda gives the drink an edgy adult flavour, but for a sweeter option use lemon-lime soda. Serve in a tumbler or highball glass over ice cubes.

INGREDIENTS

4 medium to large strawberries
2 tsp caster sugar
2 tbsp fresh lime juice
350 ml (11 ½ fl oz) good quality bitter lemon or lemon-lime soda, chilled
4 ice cubes
Slices of strawberry and lime, to garnish

Put the strawberries, sugar, lime juice and a dash of bitter lemon or lemon-lime soda in the jug of a blender. Process on low until puréed. Add the ice and blend until smooth. If your blender cannot handle ice, add crushed or shaved ice instead.

Divide between two glasses and top off with bitter lemon or lemon-lime soda. Garnish with slices of strawberry and lime.

Makes 2 glasses

HANDY TIP

For a smooth mocktail, drain the mixture through a fine nonmetallic sieve after blending and discard the seeds before mixing with the soda.

Variations

876 VIRGIN STRAWBERRY DAIQUIRI

Make the strawberry base as instructed in the Virgin Strawberry Daiquiri Fizz recipe, but use 6 strawberries and add 3 tablespoons of pomegranate juice and 1 tablespoon of milk. Do not top off with soda. Serve in cocktail glasses.
Shopping tip: Try to avoid well-travelled, mass-produced, out-of-season strawberries that are low on flavour.

877 VIRGIN STRAWBERRY DAIQUIRI SLUSH

Make the strawberry base as instructed in the Virgin Strawberry Daiquiri Fizz recipe, but use 6 strawberries and 6 mint leaves; omit sugar. Add 2 scoops of orange sorbet. Process until smooth.
Serving tip: Try serving this in a small glass bowl as a frozen dessert, garnished with slices of strawberries and oranges.

878 MELON GINGER FIZZ

Make the Virgin Strawberry Daiquiri Fizz, replacing the strawberries with 160 g (5 ½ oz) chopped, seeded cantaloupe flesh and use ginger beer instead of bitter lemon.
Serving tip: The hint of ginger is the perfect foil for the fruit. To accentuate the flavour, serve with thin slices of stem ginger or crystallised ginger.

879 VIRGIN WATERMELON DAIQUIRI FIZZ

Make the Virgin Strawberry Daiquiri Fizz, replacing the strawberries with 210 g (7 ½ oz) chopped, seeded watermelon flesh. Omit the sugar.
Handy tip: The other variations can be made from this watermelon purée base.

880 VIRGIN MANGO DAIQUIRI

Make the Virgin Strawberry Daiquiri Fizz, replacing the strawberries with 210 g (7 ½ oz) chopped mango flesh.
Handy tip: The taste of mango is always enhanced with a little squeeze of lime.

881 VIRGIN PEACH DAIQUIRI

Make the Virgin Strawberry Daiquiri Fizz, replacing the strawberries with one small ripe stoned and skinned peach and adding 2 tablespoons peach juice or nectar and 1 tablespoon milk. Replace the lime juice with lemon juice and omit the lemon-lime soda.
Handy tip: This drink works well with tinned peaches in natural juice. Use the juice from the tin instead of peach juice.

882 Ginger beer

This is a vital ingredient in many mocktails, combining as it does fizz, spiciness and, that all-important ingredient, panache. You should buy good-quality ginger beer; after all, even the most expensive still only costs a fraction of champagne, which it often replaces. Better still, try making your own based on your own ginger syrup.

INGREDIENTS

240 ml (8 fl oz) Fiery Ginger
  Syrup (see page 252)
1 L (1 ¾ pt) soda water, chilled

Pour the ginger syrup into a jug and pour over the soda water. Stir to mix. Adjust the syrup to water ratio to taste.

Makes 4 to 6 glasses

HANDY TIP

The exact amount of ginger syrup to soda water is a matter of taste. Also consider what the drink will be used for. For a subtle-tasting bellini, you might use a 1:5 ratio of syrup to soda water, but might prefer the stronger 1:4 ratio when paired with a strong-flavoured juice, like pineapple.

883 Fiery Ginger Syrup

Adding an herb or spice syrup to a drink can turn something ordinary into something quite unexpected. It is worth experimenting and finding the flavour combinations that you love. Add about 1 tablespoon per 240 ml (8 fl oz) juice.

INGREDIENTS

240 ml (8 fl oz) water
60 g (2 oz) sugar
115 g (4 oz) ginger, peeled and
    thinly sliced

Put the sugar and water in a saucepan and dissolve over a low heat, stirring. Increase the heat to medium-high, bring to the boil, then boil for 1 minute. Add the ginger; leave to cool. Infuse for 30 minutes before straining the mixture. Pour into a small bottle or jar; the syrup will thicken on cooling. Will keep in the fridge for several months.

Makes about 240 ml (8 fl oz)

HANDY TIP

As well as forming the base for ginger beer (see page 251), ginger syrup is great added to any orange- or pineapple-based juice or smoothie. It is also good drizzled on your breakfast yoghurt with chopped, fresh banana and chopped Brazil nuts.

Variations

884 VANILLA SYRUP

Make the Fiery Ginger Syrup, replacing the ginger with 1 split vanilla bean.
Serving suggestion: Use in combination with berry juices, smoothies and shakes.

885 MINT SYRUP

Make the Fiery Ginger Syrup, omitting the ginger. Once off the heat add 60 g (2 oz) torn mint leaves. Infuse and continue as directed.
Handy tip: Other herbs to try include lemon verbena, lemon balm, tarragon and basil.

886 ROSEMARY SYRUP

Make the Fiery Ginger Syrup, omitting the ginger. Once off the heat add 4 sprigs of roughly chopped rosemary, very lightly bashed with a mallet or the end of a rolling pin. Infuse and continue as directed.
Handy tip: Other herbs to try include sage, thyme and bay leaves. The latter make a lovely, smoky syrup.

887 SIMPLE SYRUP

Make the Fiery Ginger Syrup, omitting the ginger and the infusing time.
Handy tip: This syrup is used to sweeten mocktails because it doesn't add any competing flavour.

888 STAR ANISE AND ORANGE SYRUP

Make the Fiery Ginger Syrup, replacing the ginger with 8 star anise, 2 whole cardamom pods and the zest of ½ an orange, cut into strips. Infuse and continue as directed.
Serving tip: Try adding this to watermelon or pineapple juice.

889 LAVENDER SYRUP

Make the Fiery Ginger Syrup, replacing the ginger with 1 tablespoon lavender flowers. Infuse and continue as directed.
Serving tip: Lavender works well in combination with lemon juices and with strawberry-based drinks.

890 CINNAMON SYRUP

Make the Fiery Ginger Syrup, replacing the ginger with three 7.5-cm (3-inch) sticks cinnamon. Infuse and continue as directed.
Handy tip: Add ¼ of a vanilla pod or two large slices of orange zest for another flavour dimension. You could also use brown sugar.

891 LEMONGRASS SYRUP

Make the Fiery Ginger Syrup, replacing the ginger with 2 stalks of fresh lemongrass, chopped into small pieces. Infuse and continue as directed.

892 JUNIPER SYRUP

Make the Fiery Ginger Syrup, replacing the ginger with 1 tablespoon juniper berries. Infuse and continue as directed.

893 Raspberry and Mint Bellini

Served in an elegant champagne glass, this sophisticated sparkling fruit mocktail makes the perfect welcome drink. The fruit very subtly infuses the drink with a hint of raspberries and mint, so use the very best you can find.

INGREDIENTS

1 raspberry

2 drops vanilla extract

2 small mint leaves, slightly crushed

Generous 75 ml (2 ½ fl oz) white grape juice

Generous 75 ml (2 ½ fl oz) ginger beer

Press the raspberry through a nonmetallic sieve into a champagne glass and add the vanilla and mint leaves. Half fill with white grape juice, then top off with ginger beer. Serve immediately.

Makes 1 glass

HANDY TIP

The grape juice and ginger beer should be icy cold. Keep the bottles in an ice bucket as you serve them.

Variations

894 STRAWBERRY AND MINT BELLINI

Make the Raspberry and Mint Bellini, replacing the raspberry with 1 strawberry.
Handy tip: For a slightly more infused flavour, let fruit sit in the white grape juice for an hour before serving.

895 STRAWBERRY AND BALSAMIC BELLINI

Make the Strawberry and Mint Bellini variation, replacing the vanilla with ¼ teaspoon balsamic vinegar.
Handy tip: Strawberry and balsamic vinegar is a classic combination.

896 SOFT PEACH BELLINI

Make the Raspberry and Mint Bellini, omitting the raspberry, vanilla and mint. Purée 1 peeled and stoned peach in the blender. One-third fill the glass with the peach purée, top off with the grape juice and ginger beer.

897 LYCHEE AND BASIL BELLINI

Make the Raspberry and Mint Bellini, replacing the raspberry and mint with 1 lychee and a small basil leaf.
Handy tip: Use Thai basil, if possible, since its common origin with lychees make them great bedfellows.

898 VANILLA AND CHERRY BELLINI

Prepare the Raspberry and Mint Bellini, replacing the raspberry and mint with 2 ripe stoned cherries and using 4 drops of vanilla.

899 TANGERINE AND MINT BELLINI

Make the Raspberry and Mint Bellini, replacing the raspberry with 1 tablespoon freshly squeezed tangerine juice.
Serving tip: Garnish with two quarters of tangerine.

900 PEAR AND FENNEL BELLINI

Make the Raspberry and Mint Bellini, replacing the raspberry with the juice of ⅛ of a pear. Garnish with a pinch of fennel frond.
Handy tip: Gently roll the fennel to release its flavour.

901 PEAR AND GINGER BELLINI

Make the Raspberry and Mint Bellini, replacing the raspberry with the juice of ⅛ of a pear. Garnish with a very thin slice of ginger.

902 ROSE WATER AND JUNIPER BELLINI

Make the Raspberry and Mint Bellini, replacing the raspberry, vanilla and mint with 6 drops of rose water and 3 drops of Juniper Syrup (see page 253).
Handy tip: The use of botanicals adds depth.

903 BAY AND GINGER BELLINI

Make the Raspberry and Mint Bellini, replacing the raspberry, vanilla and mint with ½ teaspoon bay leaf syrup (see Rosemary Syrup recipe on page 252). Garnish with a very thin slice of ginger.

904 Clementine, Lavender and Sage Delight

Fresh fruit juice is given another dimension with the addition of flavoured syrups. There are an abundance of syrups on the market, or you can use one of the syrup recipes on pages 252–3.

INGREDIENTS

240 ml (8 fl oz) clementine juice, preferably freshly squeezed
Crushed ice

Sage leaf
1 to 2 tsp lavender syrup (see page 252), or to taste

Pour the clementine juice into a large glass with plenty of crushed ice and a sage leaf. Stir in the lavender syrup to taste. Serve immediately.

Makes 1 glass

HANDY TIP

Some people find freshly squeezed fruit juice too intense; if so, water it down with 60 ml (2 fl oz) filtered or mineral water.

906 CLEMENTINE AND MINT DELIGHT

Make the Clementine, Lavender and Sage Delight, replacing the lavender syrup with mint syrup (see page 252) and serving with a sprig of coriander or lemon balm. **Handy tip:** This works well with grapefruit juice, too.

905 CLEMENTINE, GRAPE AND LAVENDER DELIGHT

Make the Clementine, Lavender and Sage Delight using only 125 ml (4 ¼ fl oz) clementine juice and adding 125 ml (4 ¼ fl oz) sparkling grape juice.

907 CLEMENTINE AND GINGER DELIGHT

Make the Clementine, Lavender and Sage Delight, replacing the lavender syrup with ginger syrup (see page 252).
Serving tip: Make this drink at the first hint of a cold.

908 Watermelon and Juniper Delight

Fresh watermelon juice on a hot day is a wonderful thing. Make it more sophisticated with the simple addition of a flavoured syrup.

INGREDIENTS

240 ml (8 fl oz) watermelon
   juice
1 tbsp lime juice

Crushed ice
1 small bay leaf
1 to 2 tsp juniper syrup
   (see page 253)

Pour the watermelon juice and lime juice into a large glass with plenty of crushed ice and a bay leaf. Stir in the juniper syrup, to taste. Serve immediately.

Makes 1 glass

HANDY TIP

You need about 225 g (8 oz) of watermelon to make 240 ml (8 fl oz) of juice.

variations

909 WATERMELON AND STAR ANISE DELIGHT

Prepare the Watermelon and Juniper Delight, replacing the juniper syrup with star anise and orange syrup (see page 253). Garnish with a small bay leaf or sprig of mint.

Nutritional tip: Much of the nutritional content of watermelon is in the rind, so consider not peeling it before juicing, although this slightly alters the flavour.

910 WATERMELON AND ROSEMARY DELIGHT

Prepare the Watermelon and Juniper Delight, replacing the juniper syrup with rosemary syrup (see page 252).

Serving tip: This refreshing drink goes well with lamb or pork dishes.

911 WATERMELON, POMEGRANATE AND JUNIPER DELIGHT

Prepare the Watermelon and Juniper Delight using only 125 ml (4 ¼ fl oz) watermelon juice and adding 125 ml (4 ¼ fl oz) pomegranate juice.

Nutritional tip: The watermelon and pomegranate combination has been referred to as a natural Viagra. Both fruits have properties that improve blood vessel structure and so can help with erectile dysfunction.

912 Cupid's Thin Arrow

This drink is based on cherries, apple and lemon juice, but if fresh cherries are not available, raspberries will work equally well. This mocktail should be served in a small tumbler, which is sometimes called an 'old-fashioned' glass, with lots of ice.

INGREDIENTS

Ice

2 tbsp apple juice

1 tbsp lemon juice

1 drop almond extract

3 drops Angostura bitters

4 fresh cherries, stoned

Approximately 125 ml (4 ¼ fl oz) sparkling white grape juice, chilled

Put the ice into a small tumbler. Pour over the apple and lemon juices and add the almond extract and Angostura bitters. Stir well to mix. Add the cherries, then top off with the sparkling grape juice.

Makes 1 glass

HANDY TIP

Angostura bitters contains alcohol, but given that it is used in such tiny quantities its inclusion in a nonalcoholic drink is generally permissible. If you are serving those who follow the very strictest of rules, omit the bitters. You could substitute with the juniper syrup (see page 253) instead.

variations

913 CUPID'S PEAR OF ARROWS

Prepare Cupid's Thin Arrow, replacing the apple juice with fresh pear juice or pear nectar.

Handy tip: As pear juice turns brown rapidly, juice it with a piece of peeled and chopped lemon and adjust the lemon juice to taste in the finished mocktail.

914 CUPID'S PASSION

Prepare Cupid's Thin Arrow, replacing the apple juice with the juice of ½ a passion fruit, strained through a nonmetallic sieve.

Handy tip: It is always best to taste a drink before serving for the first time. Both apple juice and sparkling grape juice vary in sweetness.

915 CUPID'S FLAME

Prepare Cupid's Thin Arrow, replacing the apple juice with freshly squeezed apricot juice or apricot nectar.

Handy tip: Peach juice or nectar could replace the apricot in this drink.

916 CUPID'S RED ARROW

Prepare Cupid's Thin Arrow, replacing the apple juice with freshly squeezed pomegranate juice and the lemon juice with a 1 teaspoon lime juice.

Handy tip: If you are buying pomegranate juice, buy organic and very good quality.

917 Slim and Tonic

This is a simple drink based on tonic water. There are a number of brands available and it is worth trying them out and buying the best for this drink, where it is so exposed. It is worth spending the time making a fancy ice cube for this drink, for the sheer novelty of it.

INGREDIENTS

3 generous dashes Angostura bitters (see note under recipe 912)

Approximately 150 ml (5 fl oz) tonic water

Small lemon wedge

Pomegranate seed ice cube

Direct 3 generous dashes of Angostura bitters into a champagne flute and swirl around the glass. Pour over the tonic water and drop in the lemon wedge and pomegranate ice cube.

Makes 1 glass

SERVING TIP

To make pomegranate seed ice cubes, drop a few pomegranate seeds into each of the cubes in an ice-cube tray, then top off with filtered or mineral water. For even more flair, you can add the thinnest sliver of lemon zest, too.

919 MANDARIN AND TONIC

Make the Slim and Tonic, replacing the Angostura bitters with 2 teaspoons mandarin syrup. Replace the lemon wedge with a wedge of lime.
Interesting fact: Mandarin and other fruit syrups are popular in European countries such as France, where they are often served mixed with sparkling wine.

918 GRENADINE AND TONIC

Make the Slim and Tonic, replacing the Angostura bitters with 2 teaspoons grenadine and a squeeze of lime juice. Replace the lemon wedge with a wedge of lime.
Handy tip: Grenadine, like Angostura bitters, contains small amounts of alcohol.

920 BLACK AND TONIC

Make the Slim and Tonic, replacing the Angostura bitters with 2 teaspoons blackcurrant syrup or cordial and a squeeze of lemon.
Handy tip: For a spicy touch, add ½ to 1 teaspoon ginger syrup (see page 252).

921 Orange, Mango and Lime Cup

This is a drink overflowing with flavour. The trick with mocktails is to create a complex drink with just enough sharpness or bitterness to balance out the sweetness without it becoming cloying.

INGREDIENTS

3 oranges, peeled
1 large mango, peeled, stoned
  and cut into chunks
Pinch sea salt
Juice of ½ lime

Put the oranges and mango through a juice extractor. Pour through a nonmetallic strainer into a glass and top with a pinch of sea salt and the lime juice. Serve immediately.

Makes 2 glasses

HANDY TIP

Don't think you can get away with bottled juices; for mocktails to be worthy of presentation to friends, they must be made with freshly juiced fruit.

Variations

922 MANGO, PASSION FRUIT AND LIME SHAKER

Make the Orange, Mango and Lime Cup, replacing the oranges with another mango and adding the strained pulp of 2 passion fruits along with the lime juice. Put in a shaker with 4 ice cubes and 1 tablespoon egg white.
Health tip: Pregnant women are advised to avoid raw egg white.

923 MANGO AND PINEAPPLE CUP

Make the Orange, Mango and Lime Cup, replacing the oranges with 250 g (8 ¾ oz) fresh pineapple chunks. Put crushed ice in the base of the glass and drizzle with grenadine or pomegranate syrup. Pour over the prepared fruit juice.
Serving tip: This drink is best served with a swizzle stick for mixing.

924 ORANGE AND MANGO HIGHBALL

Juice the oranges and mango as instructed in the Orange, Mango and Lime Cup recipe. Put crushed ice in the base of the glass and drizzle with grenadine or pomegranate syrup. Pour over the prepared juice to half fill the glass and top off with club soda or tonic water.
Handy tip: You could replace the sea salt with a pinch of the Mexican spice Tajín, *salsa en polvo*, which is made from ground chili peppers, dehydrated lime and salt.

925 Grape Maccha Mocktail

Not only is green tea reputed to have considerable health benefits, it also blends perfectly with fresh fruit and provides the drink with the sophisticated flavour undertones that we expect from a cocktail. This mocktail seems to have it all.

INGREDIENTS

1 pinch maccha (green tea) powder

125 ml (4 ¼ fl oz) boiling water

1 apple

180 g (6 ½ oz) seedless green grapes

Ice, to serve

Mix the maccha powder with the boiling water; leave to cool, then leave in the fridge to chill. Put the apple and grapes through a juice extractor. Mix the juice with the chilled green tea and serve over ice.

Makes 1 glass

HANDY TIP

It is best to make the maccha tea well ahead of time so you are not worried about it cooling as the guests arrive.

927 PEACH MACCHA MOCKTAIL

Prepare the Grape Maccha Mocktail, replacing the grapes and apples with 3 stoned peaches.
Handy tip: If you prefer the flavour, you could use a green tea with jasmine tea bag instead of the maccha.

928 MANGO MACCHA MOCKTAIL

Make the Grape Maccha Mocktail, replacing the grapes and apples with 250 g (8 ¾ oz) peeled and chopped mango.
Handy tip: As these are small quantities of fruit, let the juice extractor run for 20 seconds before adding fruit.

926 APPLE MACCHA MOCKTAIL

Prepare the Grape Maccha Mocktail, omitting the grapes and increasing the quantity of apples to 2.
Shopping tip: Be on the lookout for unusual cocktail paraphernalia and buy them when you see them.

929 PINEAPPLE MACCHA MOCKTAIL

Prepare the Grape Maccha Mocktail, replacing the grapes and apples with 250 g (8 ¾ oz) peeled, chopped pineapple.
Shopping tip: Buy your tea from a respected store so it is fresh and hasn't been going stale on a shelf for ages.

930 Mockito

This drink takes you right to the dance floors of the Havana bars where the drink was first created. Laced with the bright taste of fresh lime mixed with the refreshing flavours of fresh mint, it is a drink that will enliven the body and satisfy the senses.

INGREDIENTS

10 fresh mint leaves, slightly bashed
1 tsp caster sugar
3 small lime wedges, about ⅓ lime
¼ tsp ginger juice
Ice
2 cucumber slices
Soda water

Put the mint leaves, sugar and lime wedges in a tumbler and muddle them together to combine. Don't skip this pounding stage as it releases and combines the flavours. Pour in the ginger juice, followed by the ice and cucumber slices, then fill the glass with soda water.

Makes 1 glass

HANDY TIP

To 'muddle' is to pound the ingredients together, usually in the bottom of a mixing glass, by pressing them with a muddler, a pestlelike implement. If you haven't got one, use the handle of a big wooden spoon.

Variations

931 LIME AND ORANGE MOCKITO

Make the Mockito using just 2 wedges of lime and adding 1 wedge of orange.
Handy tip: To squeeze tiny amounts of fresh ginger, peel and push through a garlic press.

932 BLOOD ORANGE AND MANGO MOCKITO

Make the Mockito, replacing the lime with 2 thin wedges of blood orange. Half fill the glass with freshly squeezed mango juice or mango nectar before topping off with soda water.
Interesting fact: Traditionally, muddlers were made of wood, but steel and plastic ones are now finding favour; however, they all do the job.

933 PINK GRAPEFRUIT MOCKITO

Make the Mockito, replacing the lime wedges with 1 wedge of pink grapefruit cut into 3 or 4 pieces.
Nutritional tip: Red and pink grapefruit contain more nutrients than white grapefruit.

934 PINK GINGER VIRGIN COSMO

Make this in a small jug. Make the Mockito using only 1 lime wedge and adding 1 wedge of pink grapefruit cut into three or four pieces. Replace the soda water with 3 tablespoons cranberry juice. Put in a shaker, shake well, drain into a cocktail glass, then add 1 slice of cucumber.

Handy tip: For a short cut, put into the shaker: 3 tablespoons pink grapefruit juice, 2 tablespoons cranberry juice, 1 ½ teaspoons lime juice and ¼ teaspoon ginger juice.

935 PRICKLY PEAR MOCKITO

Make the lime-ginger base as in the Mockito recipe. Half fill the glass with prickly pear juice before topping off with soda water.

Handy tip: If you cannot find prickly pears, then buy the juice from an international food shop. It is sometimes simply called cactus juice.

936 MOCKITO JUG

In a jug combine 50 g (1 ¾ oz) mint leaves, 60 g (2 oz) sugar, 3 large limes sliced into quarters and 2 ½ tsp fresh ginger juice. Muddle as instructed. Add plenty of ice and cucumber slices and fill with soda water. Serves 10.

Handy tip: Old ginger is much drier and more fibrous than young ginger and will not juice successfully.

937 Primm's Jug

Nothing says summer more than a fruit-filled jug of Pimm's! Here we make a mock version of this English classic. Don't be put off by the long ingredients list; you are making a simple infused syrup base, which looks more daunting than it is!

INGREDIENTS

For the syrup

75 g (2 ½ oz) granulated sugar
75 g (2 ½ oz) brown sugar
150 ml (5 fl oz) water
2 tbsp juniper berries
1 tsp coriander seeds
½ tsp star anise
Zest of ½ orange
2 strips lemon rind

1.25 cm (1 inch) sliced ginger
2 jasmine tea bags

For the jug

60 ml (2 fl oz) orange juice
60 ml (2 fl oz) lemon juice
Sliced cucumber, orange, lemon, strawberries and mint sprigs or lemon balm, to garnish
Ginger beer

Put the sugars and water in a saucepan and dissolve over a low heat, stirring. Increase the heat to medium-high and bring to the boil. Add all the remaining syrup ingredients, then boil for 1 minute; leave to cool. Infuse for at least 30 minutes before straining the mixture. Pour the syrup into a jug with the orange and lemon juice and the sliced cucumber, fruit and mint. Top off with ginger beer.

Makes 10 servings

HANDY TIP

If making by the glass, add 1 ½ to 2 tablespoons of the syrup mixture per glass, depending on the size of the glass. Add the same quantity of orange and lemon juice and top up with ginger beer. Add plenty of cucumber slices, fruit and herbs; they are not optional!

Variations

938 PRIMM'S JUG WITH BITTER LEMON

Make the Primm's Jug, replacing the ginger beer with bitter lemon soda.
Handy tip: Bitter lemon is used in preference to lemonade, which is too sweet in this drink.

939 PRIMM'S JUG WITH CUCUMBER

Make the Primm's Jug, adding the juice of ½ a cucumber with the orange juice.
Serving tip: For a real sense of summer, add borage or other edible flowers to the fruit in the jug.

940 PRIMM'S ORANGE CUP

Use 1 ½ to 2 tablespoons of the Primm's Jug syrup with 75 ml (2 ½ fl oz) each of orange juice and ginger beer. Serve with mint leaves and cucumber slices.
Handy tip: If you do not use all the syrup in one sitting, keep the remainder in a sealed bottle in the fridge. It will last for about one month.

941 PRIMM'S PINEAPPLE MOCKTAIL

Use 1 ½ to 2 tablespoons of the Primm's Jug syrup
with 60 ml (2 fl oz) each of pineapple juice and
ginger beer. Serve with pineapple sage leaves or a
sprig of rosemary and cucumber slices.
Serving tip: Serve this in a cocktail glass and enjoy
in small sips.

942 HOT PRIMM'S AND APPLE CUP

Put 1 ½ to 2 tablespoons of the Primm's Jug syrup
mixture in a heatproof glass, top off with apple juice
and stir well. Heat in the microwave for 1 to 1 ½
minutes, or until hot enough to drink.
Serving tip: Make this to welcome guests on a cold
winter's day. Prepare the glasses of juice in advance
and heat a glass on each guest's arrival.

943 Shirley Temple

This cocktail was famously created for the young Shirley Temple when she was a child star – or was it? Other claims have been made as to its origin. Either way, all these years later, kids still love it!

INGREDIENTS

5 ice cubes
Generous dash grenadine syrup
Approximately 125 to 175 ml (4 ¼ to
  6 fl oz) ginger beer
3 maraschino cherries

Half fill a highball or other tumbler with ice and add a dash of grenadine syrup. Pour over the ginger beer and mix to taste. Garnish with the cherries and serve with a straw.

Makes 1 glass

HANDY TIP

The amount of grenadine syrup added to the drink very much depends on how sweet you wish to make the drink. For children, use as little as you can get away with.

Variations

944 YOUNG TEMPLE

Make the Shirley Temple, replacing the ginger beer with lemon-lime soda and garnish with a slice of orange.
Handy tip: For a healthier fresh option, make with the Instant Lemonade (see page 228).

945 ROY ROGERS

Make the Shirley Temple, replacing the ginger beer with coca cola. Serve with a wedge of lemon.
Interesting fact: This drink was named after the much-loved Roy Rogers, the clean-living 'King of the Cowboys'.

946 PINEAPPLE SHIRLEY TEMPLE

When making the Shirley Temple, half fill the glass with pineapple juice before topping off with ginger beer.
Interesting fact: Grenadine is made from pomegranates and derives its name from the French word *grenade*, meaning pomegranate. Other fruits, such as blackcurrants or redcurrants, may also be used in the production of this syrup.

947 POMEGRANATE SHIRLEY TEMPLE

Fill the glass one-third full of freshly squeezed orange juice, then add one-third pomegranate juice and one-third ginger beer. Do not stir, but serve with a straw or swizzle stick.

Serving tip: This goes well with hot dogs.

948 SWEET SUNRISE

Half fill a highball or other tumbler with ice, then fill up with freshly squeezed orange juice and 1 tablespoon lime juice. Stir to mix. Slowly pour in 1 tablespoon grenadine syrup and let it sink to the bottom.

Handy tip: Drink this one without stirring; the grenadine syrup will gradually rise to the surface as you drink.

949 GLORIOUS SUNRISE

In a highball glass combine 60 ml (2 fl oz) each of freshly squeezed orange juice, pineapple juice and cranberry juice. Add ice and top off with soda water. Slowly pour in 1 tablespoon grenadine syrup and let it sink to the bottom.

Serving tip: This is one of the prettiest drinks, so why not reflect its colours by threading a maraschino cherry, an orange slice and a tiny piece of pineapple on a cocktail stick to garnish the glass?

950 Island Spice

A heady mix of tropical fruit, coconut and spices transports you to white beaches and the gentle lapping of turquoise waters. You can make your own cinnamon syrup (see page 253) or use a coffee syrup for this drink.

INGREDIENTS

60 ml (2 fl oz) soursop (guanábana) juice	2 tsp cinnamon syrup
60 ml (2 fl oz) pineapple juice	½ tsp lime juice
60 ml (2 fl oz) coconut water	¼ tsp ginger juice
	Cinnamon stick, to garnish

Combine all the ingredients in a shaker and shake to mix well. Pour over ice into a glass and serve garnished with a small cinnamon stick.

Makes 1 glass

INTERESTING FACT

Cinnamon was used as an embalming agent in ancient Egypt; this is probably due to the same chemical properties that enable it to slow down the rate at which food spoils.

Variations

951 SPICE GIRL

Make the Island Spice, replacing the soursop juice with the pulp from a passion fruit.
Handy tip: It is important to drain this juice into the glass to remove the seeds from the passion fruit.

952 CHINA SPICE

Make the Island Spice, replacing the soursop with lychee juice.
Serving tip: Serve with a single star anise instead of a cinnamon stick.

953 SPORTY SPICE

Make the Island Spice, replacing the soursop with watermelon juice.
Serving tip: Serve with a small wedge of watermelon instead of a cinnamon stick.

954 POSH SPICE

Prepare the Island Spice, replacing the soursop with papaya juice.
Handy tip: Cinnamon sticks will keep for two years if kept in a cool, dark place, while powdered cinnamon loses its flavour after about six months.

955 Safe Sex on the Beach

There are hundreds of variations of this cocktail, which is hardly surprising given its provocative name. It seems that every bartender has his special blend and here is one that captures the magical flavours in its own way. Your guests will never guess the two special ingredients.

INGREDIENTS

60 ml (2 fl oz) orange juice, preferably freshly squeezed
60 ml (2 fl oz) cranberry juice
½ tsp pomegranate molasses

Generous pinch fine ground white pepper
Pomegranate seeds, to garnish

Combine all the ingredients in a cocktail shaker. Shake well to mix, then pour over ice in a glass. Garnish with a few pomegranate seeds.

Makes 1 glass

INTERESTING FACT

Pomegranate molasses is a Middle Eastern specialty made by boiling pomegranate juice into thick syrup. It has a rich, dark flavour and a dense fragrance. It enhances the fruit flavours in this cocktail but can be used like balsamic vinegar in meat and vegetable dishes, too.

Variations

956 SAFE SEX ON THE POMMY BEACH

Make the Safe Sex on the Beach, replacing the cranberry juice with pomegranate juice.
Health tip: There are many claims for the health benefits of pomegranates – one of the more interesting is the suggestion that, taken for at least two weeks, it increases the testosterone levels in both men and women.

957 SAFE SEX ON A NORTHERN BEACH

Make the Safe Sex on the Beach, replacing the orange juice with apple juice and adding ½ teaspoon lime juice.
Handy tip: You can substitute equal quantities of liquid honey and balsamic vinegar for pomegranate molasses in most recipes.

958 SAFE SEX ON THE BEET

Make the Safe Sex on the Beach, replacing the cranberry juice with 3 tablespoons beetroot juice and increasing the amount of orange juice to 75 ml (2 ½ fl oz).
Serving tip: The beetroot juice gives this drink a surprising edge. It's still sweet but with a mellowness that makes it a good pre-dinner aperitif.

959 SAFE SEX ON THE SAND

Make the Safe Sex on the Beach, replacing the cranberry juice with 3 tablespoons fresh apricot juice or nectar and increase the orange juice to 75 ml (2 ½ fl oz).
Handy tip: Use dried apricots to make an intense apricot juice for this cocktail (see page 198).

960 Rosemary's Lemon Botanical

Unashamedly sharp and loaded with botanicals, this is a very adult glass with an air of sophistication about it.

INGREDIENTS

Juice of ½ lemon

1 tsp rosemary syrup
  (see page 252)

Dash of Angostura bitters

2 tsp sugar syrup

1 ice cube

Soda water

Maraschino cherry

Combine the lemon juice, rosemary syrup, Angostura bitters, sugar syrup and ice cube in a cocktail shaker. Shake to mix. Pour into a chilled cocktail glass and top off with soda water. Serve garnished with a maraschino cherry.

Makes 1 glass

HANDY TIP

Always adjust the sweetness to taste, adding a little more sugar syrup, if required.

Variations

961 ROSEMARY'S LEMON GRENADINE BOTANICAL

Make the Rosemary's Lemon Botanical, adding ½ teaspoon grenadine.
Serving tip: Serve with a little wedge of lemon or a sprig of rosemary instead of the maraschino cherry.

962 ROSEMARY'S LIME BOTANICAL

Make the Rosemary's Lemon Botanical, replacing the lemon with juice from ½ a lime. Adjust the sweetness with an additional ½ to 1 teaspoon sugar syrup, if required.
Handy tip: A traditional metal lime press makes short work of pressing limes. They come in a variety of sizes designed for the different citrus fruits.

963 ROSEMARY'S LIME AND BLACKCURRANT BOTANICAL

Make the Rosemary's Lime Botanical variation, adding ½ teaspoon blackcurrant cordial or syrup.
Handy tip: When making mocktails, a tiny hint of a contrasting flavour can completely alter the flavour of a drink. Do not be tempted to be heavy-handed when a small amount of an ingredient is suggested in the recipe.

964 ROSEMARY'S CLEMENTINE BOTANICAL

Make the Rosemary's Lemon Botanical, replacing the lemon with juice from ½ a clementine and adding 2 teaspoons lemon juice. Adjust the sweetness with an additional ½ to 1 teaspoon sugar syrup, if required.
Handy tip: Rosemary is an evergreen herb, so it is useful when making drinks in winter when other herbs are unavailable.

965 ROSEMARY'S PINK GRAPEFRUIT BOTANICAL

Make the Rosemary's Lemon Botanical, replacing the lemon with 3 tablespoons of freshly squeezed pink grapefruit juice.
Handy tip: Although the redder, the sweeter, there is little difference between the flavour of red and pink grapefruit; the real difference lies with the more sour white grapefruit.

966 ROSEMARY'S PINK GRAPEFRUIT AND RASPBERRY BOTANICAL

Make the Rosemary's Pink Grapefruit Botanical variation, adding ½ teaspoon raspberry syrup.
Handy tip: Use a raspberry syrup that you have made yourself (see page 177) or one designed for drinks. A fruit syrup made for topping ice cream is too thick to work in the drink.

967 Piña colada

Although this classic cocktail has been the subject of lighthearted songs, its intense Caribbean flavours deserve to be taken seriously. Because of the strong flavours in this delicious drink, the alcohol-free version is still full of taste.

INGREDIENTS

250 g (8 ¾ oz) peeled pineapple chunks
60 ml (2 fl oz) coconut milk
4 ice cubes
Sparkling water
Slice of pineapple, to serve
Maraschino cherries, to serve

Put the pineapple through a juice extractor. Pour into a blender along with the coconut milk and ice. Blend for 1 minute. Pour into a tall glass or goblet. Top off with a splash of sparkling water. Serve with a slice of pineapple and a couple of maraschino cherries.

Makes 1 glass

HANDY TIP

The rum in the original version has a caramel-like flavour, so if you want to have a hint of this, or want a sweeter drink, add up to 1 tablespoon dark brown sugar.

Variations

968 QUICK PIÑA COLADA SMOOTHIE

In a blender combine 240 ml (8 fl oz) pineapple juice, 60 g (2 oz) coconut cream and 240 ml (8 fl oz) crushed ice and process until smooth.
Serving tip: Of all the cocktails, this is one that really does lend itself to excessive decoration. Try dipping the rim of the glass in slightly beaten egg white and then dipping the glass in coloured sugar.

969 QUICK PIÑA COLADA AND PEACH SMOOTHIE

Make the Quick Piña Colada Smoothie variation, adding 1 peeled and stoned small peach to the blender.
Serving tip: If serving in a small glass, cut straws down to size so that they don't topple over.

970 MANGO COLADA

Prepare the Piña Colada, replacing the pineapple with 250 g (8 ¾ oz) peeled and chopped mango.
Handy tip: Leftover coconut milk will store for up to one week in the fridge. Alternatively, freeze leftovers for up to two months. It will separate when defrosted but recombines with stirring.

971 BANANA COLADA

Prepare the Piña Colada, replacing the pineapple with 1 ½ peeled and chopped bananas.
Serving tip: This makes an excellent partner with a spicy Mexican dish such as fajitas.

972 PAPAYA COLADA

Prepare the Piña Colada, replacing the pineapple with 300 g (10 ½ oz) peeled and chopped papaya.
Nutritional tip: Many people take papaya enzyme as a supplement for digestion, but the real thing is always better.

973 STRAWBERRY COLADA

Prepare the Piña Colada, replacing the pineapple with 150 g (5 ¼ oz) strawberries.
Handy tip: Alcohol-free rum-flavoured syrups and extracts are available if you miss the rum flavour.

974 Frozen Innocent Margarita

This Mexican classic, much-beloved in Tex-Mex cafés the world over, is traditionally served in a glass with a salted rim. This alcohol-free version includes a little orange zest for extra colour and flavour.

INGREDIENTS

¼ tsp grated orange zest	3 tbsp lime juice
1 tbsp salt	2 tbsp orange juice
Lime wedge	2 tbsp lemon juice
60 ml (2 fl oz) Simple Syrup (see page 252)	175 ml (6 fl oz) crushed ice

Mix the orange zest with salt. Rub the rim of the glass with lime juice, then dip into the salt mixture.

Combine all the remaining ingredients in a blender and process until smooth. Pour into the prepared glass and serve immediately.

Makes 1 glass

SERVING TIP

Try winding lime zest around the stem of the cocktail glass as well as using as a garnish.

variations

975 INNOCENT MARGARITA

Make the Frozen Innocent Margarita, replacing the crushed ice with 1 ice cube. Combine all the ingredients in a cocktail shaker. Shake to mix. Pour into the prepared glass and serve garnished with a twist of lime zest.
Serving tip: Margaritas are best served with a plate of hot nachos topped with cheese and chilies.

976 FROZEN INNOCENT STRAWBERRY MARGARITA

Make the Frozen Innocent Margarita, adding 4 frozen or fresh medium strawberries to the blender.
Handy tip: Frozen strawberries are marginally better than fresh in this recipe as they keep the mixture well chilled when blending.

977 FROZEN INNOCENT PINEAPPLE MARGARITA

Make the Frozen Innocent Margarita, replacing the lemon juice with pineapple juice.
Serving tip: Pineapple pairs well with pork, so this is excellent with good sausage or grilled pork kebabs.

978 FROZEN INNOCENT CUCUMBER MARGARITA

Make the Frozen Innocent Margarita, adding a 7.5-cm (3-inch) piece of peeled and seeded cucumber to the blender.

Serving tip: This variation is good for anyone who finds lime juice too sour. The cucumber adds a mellowness and makes it an excellent drink to serve with spicy fajitas.

979 FROZEN INNOCENT BLACKBERRY MARGARITA

Purée 8 blackberries through a nonmetallic sieve to remove the seeds. Add to the blender with the other ingredients when making the Frozen Innocent Margarita.

Handy tip: The strawberry, pineapple, cucumber and blackberry frozen margaritas can all be adapted to make a flavoured Innocent Margarita variation, following the instructions above.

980 FROZEN INNOCENT LAVENDER MARGARITA

Prepare the Frozen Innocent Margarita, replacing the simple syrup with lavender syrup (see page 253).

Serving tip: Lay a sprig of lavender on the rim of the glass or replace the orange zest with a few dried lavender flowers.

981 FROZEN INNOCENT CHILI MARGARITA

When salting the glass for the Frozen Innocent Margarita, omit the orange zest and use a generous pinch of chili powder instead.

Handy tip: For a smoky flavour, use a chipotle chili powder.

982 Iceberg

This is a fun addition to the mocktail repertoire and would be a great introductory drink at a costume party to get folks in the mood for letting their hair down. You can fill up the glasses with sparkling white wine, if some guests prefer an alcoholic drink.

INGREDIENTS

240 ml (8 fl oz) each lemon and
    peach sorbet
1 bottle chilled sparkling white
    grape juice

Chill 6 cocktail glasses. Add a mini scoop of sorbet to each glass then top off with the sparkling grape juice.

Makes 6 drinks

HANDY TIP

Either allow your guests to choose which sorbet flavour they fancy and make these drinks to order, or make up the drinks using both flavours, then place on a tray which can be circulated among the guests.

984 GRAPE CRUSH

Put 240 ml (8 fl oz) peach sorbet in the blender with 125 ml (4 ¼ fl oz) white grape juice and process until smooth. Fill the glasses halfway with sorbet mixture and top off with the sparkling white grape juice.
Handy tip: This works better with the stronger-flavoured peach sorbet than it does with the lemon sorbet.

983 RED ICEBERG

Make the Iceberg, replacing the white sparkling grape juice with red sparkling grape juice and the lemon sorbet with raspberry sorbet.
Handy tip: If making to order, keep the sorbet in an ice bucket while preparing these drinks.

985 NORMAN ICEBERG

Make the Iceberg, replacing the sparkling grape juice with sparkling apple juice and the peach sorbet with raspberry sorbet.
Serving tip: If preparing for children, they love the visual appeal of the multicoloured, multiflavoured sorbets.

986 Kumquat Verbena Mocktail

Lemon verbena is a common herb to find growing in gardens. Use it to make this elegant drink with a unique, delicate floral taste and a slightly provocative tang.

INGREDIENTS

500 ml (17 fl oz) boiling water

50 g (1 ¾ oz) lemon verbena leaves, about 40 leaves, plus extra to garnish

2 tsp agave or sugar syrup, or more to taste

2 kumquats, seeded and sliced

Ice

Bring the water to a boil and pour over the lemon verbena leaves. Leave to cool, then sweeten to taste. Refrigerate for at least 1 hour or, better, overnight. Muddle 1 sliced kumquat and 1 teaspoon of syrup in each of 2 tumblers. Add ice cubes, then drain over the lemon verbena tea. Serve garnished with fresh lemon verbena leaves.

Makes 2 glasses

HANDY TIP

Do not boil the lemon verbena leaves in the water. This destroys the delicate flavour and the leaves turn slimy.

Variations

987 LEMON VERBENA ICED TEA

Make the Kumquat Verbena Mocktail, replacing the kumquat with ½ a sliced lemon. Do not muddle; simply pour the tea over the lemon slices.
Serving tip: This is a great cocktail to serve with canapés because a sip clears the palate, priming it for the next taste sensation. Lemon verbena tea is a home remedy for indigestion, often induced by cocktail parties.

988 BLUEBERRY VERBENA MOCKTAIL

Make the Kumquat Verbena Mocktail, replacing the kumquat with 20 blueberries.
Handy tip: If you don't have access to fresh lemon verbena, you can use 2 lemon verbena tea bags instead.

989 MINT VERBENA MOCKTAIL

Make the Kumquat Verbena Mocktail using ⅔ of the quantity of lemon verbena leaves and ⅓ of the mint leaves.
Interesting fact: Lemon verbena is believed to reduce stress – great for some cocktail parties!

990 Romanov Fizz

Perfect for summer days when strawberries are full of scent and flavour. Serve in tall glasses and garnish with strawberries and mint leaves.

INGREDIENTS

10 medium strawberries
125 ml (4 ¼ fl oz) orange juice,
    preferably freshly squeezed
Ice cubes
125 ml (4 ¼ fl oz) soda water

Combine the strawberries and orange juice in the blender and process until smooth. Put ice cubes in each of two glasses and pour over the strawberry-orange juice. Pour the soda water into the blender and pulse, then use the faintly coloured soda to top off the glasses. Stir, then serve immediately.

Makes 2 glasses

SERVING TIP

Romanov Fizz is such a splendid colour, it deserves the full cocktail treatment – garnish with strawberries, mint leaves and a fancy straw.

Variations

991 ROMANOV PINK FIZZ

Make the Romanov Fizz, replacing the orange juice with freshly squeezed pink grapefruit juice.
Serving tip: Take a zester and pull over the section of the grapefruit that displays the most blush, then twirl it around a spoon handle. The zest will keep the twist once it is removed.

992 ROMANOV BLACK BELT FIZZ

Pour 1 tablespoon blackcurrant syrup into the base of each glass before adding the ice when making the Romanov Fizz. Do not stir but serve with a swizzle stick.
Handy tip: If blackcurrant syrup is not on hand, grenadine would work, too.

993 PINOV FIZZ

Make the Romanov Fizz, replacing the orange juice with freshly pressed pineapple juice.
Serving tip: Kids are guaranteed to love this sparkling pineapple and strawberry drink.

994 RASMANOV FIZZ

Make the Romanov Fizz, replacing the strawberries with 20 raspberries. Pour the resulting purée through a nonmetallic sieve into the glasses to remove the seeds.
Serving tip: For each drink, dip two raspberries in orange juice, roll them in caster sugar, then pop on a stick with small mint leaves, to serve.

995 POMANOV FIZZ

Make the Romanov Fizz, replacing the orange juice with pomegranate juice.
Serving tip: Serve with a tagine or other Middle Eastern or Arabic stew; it works perfectly with the spices.

996 ROMANOV SLUSH

Make the Romanov Fizz but omit the soda water. Put the strawberry-orange liquid in a plastic container and transfer to the freezer for 1 hour. Take the frozen fruit purée and put it in the blender; add 60 ml (2 fl oz) chilled mixed berry tea and process until slushy. Pour into cocktail glasses and serve immediately.

997 shampagne cocktail

variations

998 PINK SHAMPAGNE COCKTAIL

Make the Shampagne Cocktail, adding 2 tablespoons pomegranate juice before adding the sparkling grape juice. Garnish with a single raspberry.
Serving tip: This is the perfect drink to serve to toast a special occasion such as an anniversary or to celebrate an engagement.

INGREDIENTS

1 sugar cube
Dash blood orange bitters
Sparkling white grape juice,
   chilled
Orange zest, to garnish

Drop the sugar cube into a champagne flute and add a generous dash of bitters, sufficient to saturate the sugar cube. Slowly pour in the sparkling grape juice and serve, garnished with a twist of orange zest.

Makes 1 glass

999 SHAMPAGNE HULA

Make the Shampagne Cocktail, adding 2 tablespoons pineapple juice and 1 tablespoon orange juice to the glass before adding the sugar cube. Add a dash each of bitters and grenadine syrup. Top off with sparkling grape juice.
Serving tip: Garnish with a small wedge of pineapple and a maraschino cherry.

INTERESTING FACT

Bitters were originally marketed as a cure for seasickness. Today they are mainly used to add body to cocktails. Blood orange bitters are a blend of blood oranges and mellow spices and give this drink an unexpected and intriguing flavour.

1,000 SHUCKS FIZZ

Prepare the Shampagne Cocktail but omit the sugar cube. Two-thirds fill a tall champagne glass with freshly squeezed orange juice. Add a dash of bitters and top off the glass with sparkling white grape juice.
Serving tip: Bucks Fizz is traditionally served on Christmas morning; this version keeps to the no-alcohol-before-noon rule.

INDEX

ACKNOWLEDGEMENTS

The publishers would like to thank Andrew James UK Ltd. for supplying the equipment used for the preparation of the recipes in this book.

PICTURE CREDITS

All photographs by Simon Pask with the exception of: pages 7, 10, 13, 15, 18, 21, 45, 59, 133, 141, 187, 195, 233, 239, 243, © Shutterstock and 16, 43, 75, 165, 181, © iStockphoto. Illustrations: pages 10 and 17 © iStockphoto.